MW00805411

AN OLDER AND MORE BEAUTIFUL
BELGRADE
A VISUAL CHRONICLE OF THE MILOŠEVIĆ ERA

AN OLDER AND MORE BEAUTIFUL
BELGRADE
A VISUAL CHRONICLE OF THE MILOŠEVIĆ ERA

Mileta Prodanović

Translated by **Maria Milojković**
Edited by **Robert Horvitz**
Foreword by **Milena Dragićević Šešić**

CEU PRESS

Central European University Press
Budapest—Vienna—New York

Published in 2023 by
Central European University Press

Nádor utca 9, H-1051 Budapest, Hungary
Tel: +36-1-327-3138 or 327-3000
E-mail: ceupress@press.ceu.edu
Website: www.ceupress.com

Originally published as *Stariji i lepši Beograd* (Belgrade: Stubovi Kulture), 2002.

An electronic version of this book is freely available thanks to the libraries supporting CEU Press's Opening the Future initiative. More information and links to the Open Access version can be found at *ceup.openingthefuture.net.*

Cover photo: Emil Vaš, 23 April 1999. Ivan Meštrović's monument "Vesnik pobede" [Herald of victory] in the foreground. Behind that is Belgrade's Museum of Contemporary Art. Behind that is the just-bombed skyscraper where the Socialist Party of Serbia had its headquarters, and behind that is New Belgrade.

ISBN 978-963-386-630-6 (hardback)
ISBN 978-963-386-632-0 (paperback)
ISBN 978-963-386-631-3 (ebook)

A catalogue record for this book is available from the Library of Congress.

Contents

Editor's Note

I first heard about this book in 2001, while it was being written, because I knew both the author, Mileta Prodanović, and the book's designer, Dušan Šević. They were excited about the project and eagerly described its scope and ambition. But I didn't actually see a printed copy until a few years later. It proved quite disappointing. Financial constraints imposed by Serbia's grim economic situation had forced the publisher to minimize production costs. The pages were small, the photographs blurry, and many images were deleted to reduce the page count. Surely the book deserved better.

In 2021 I suggested that we try to get an English translation published with better visuals. Finding the right translator would be crucial, of course, and fortunately, that happened quickly. I had been reading Maria Milojković's reports about her life in Belgrade on the *Medium.com* website, so I wrote to her asking if she did translations. She replied that that was how she earned a living. Although she knew Mileta's other books (he'd published over a dozen), she did not know about *An Older and More Beautiful Belgrade*. So I sent her a copy and asked her to translate the "Author's Note" as a test. Her translation left no doubt that: a) Mileta had produced a unique work that merited a much wider audience, and b) Maria was an excellent translator.

When the Central European University (CEU) Press expressed interest in the project, copies of the Serbian edition were sent to outside peer reviewers, who unanimously recommended it for translation and re-publication, though not as a simple reissue. Having been written for a Serbian audience, many references to people, places and events were not explained by the author because they were already known to the readers. Foreigners, however, would need explanations, which Maria and I agreed to provide as footnotes.

As the book had been written 20 years earlier, we thought an addendum would be useful to elucidate changes—and non-changes—in Belgrade after 2001. We asked

Milena Dragićević Šešić to supply it because she knew Mileta's work well and wrote often and insightfully about Belgrade's cultural environment. Meanwhile, since electronic publishing supports color imagery at no extra cost, I began looking for pictures to replace some of the Serbian editions' monochrome images.

Even though the elements of this project came together smoothly, we were concerned that some readers might not understand why a book about a small atypical country in the 1990s is relevant today. In fact, the relevance is all too clear. Many aspects of Donald Trump's American presidency seem foreshadowed in Milosevic's populist makeover of Serbia (fortunately, without reaching the same level of criminal violence). Both men were demagogues who undermined the rule of law, exploited their supporters' real and imagined grievances, attacked professional journalism and violated public trust in election results. Both used tribalism to sabotage democracy.

Figure 0.1. Interview with Donald Trump featured on the cover of *Nedeljnik*, a Serbian magazine (13 October 2016). The headline says: "I apologize to Serbia." The bottom text says: "The bombing of the Serbs, our Allies in both World Wars, was a big mistake. I will do everything to fix the chaos that the Clintons created in the Balkans." When the US news media reported this, the Trump campaign said the interview never happened.

On the other hand, NATO's bombing of Serbia in 1999 and the border changes that gave Kosovo independence are now cited by Russia as precedents justifying its bombing of Ukraine and border changes to "protect" Crimea and Donbass. The Russian and Serbian governments' unwavering support for each other on these issues keeps this analogy alive, and the situations are similar in a structural sense. But the analogy obscures the fact that the reasons for military action in the two situations are quite different, as are the tactics and scale.[1] More importantly, NATO did not invade, occupy or annex Serbian territory, as Russia has done in Ukraine.

----

1   The scale of destruction and number of civilian deaths that Russia are responsible for in Ukraine is orders of magnitude greater than what NATO did in Serbia, even according to the Serbian Ministry of Foreign Affairs, *White Book: NATO Crimes in Yugoslavia* (1999), http://www.slobodan-milosevic.org/wb1/index.htm. "Human Rights Watch found the two-volume compilation of the FRY Ministry of Foreign Affairs entitled *NATO Crimes in Yugoslavia* generally reliable... If one accepts

A more enduring relevance (which actually motivated this translation project) is that the insights gained from a book like *An Older and More Beautiful Belgrade* support George Kubler's argument for expanding the history of art to include all man-made things:

> Let us suppose that the idea of art can be expanded to embrace the whole range of man-made things, including all tools and writing in addition to the useless, beautiful and poetic things of the world. By this view the universe of man-made things simply coincides with the history of art. It then becomes an urgent requirement to devise better ways of considering everything man has made.[2]

Focusing only on collectible masterpieces ignores the possibilities of learning from daily life, which leads to an incomplete understanding of context. Understanding the context is a prerequisite for unlocking the meanings and values embodied in any visual expression, regardless of whether it is an icon or a beer label—or both.

Robert Horvitz

---

the figures in this compilation of approximately 495 civilians killed and 820 civilians wounded in documented instances, there is simply no evidence of the necessary crime base for charges of genocide or crimes against humanity." –United Nations International Criminal Tribunal for the Former Yugoslavia, *Final Report to the Prosecutor by the Committee Established to Review the NATO Bombing Campaign Against the Federal Republic of Yugoslavia* (The Hague, Netherlands, 2000), https://www.icty.org/x/file/Press/nato061300.pdf.

2   George Kubler, *The Shape of Time: Remarks on the History of Things* (New Haven: Yale University Press, 1962), 1.

Interrupted Memories, Transitory Identities: Urban Culture in Belgrade

Milena Dragićević Šešić

> The city is always a space already constituted
> and structured by symbolic mechanisms.
>
> (James Donald, *Imagining the Modern City*, 8.)

M ileta Prodanović's book is an absolutely original contribution to the social sci-ences and humanities, in its methodology as well as its interpretations and re-sults. An artist-researcher even before practice-based research and artistic PhDs en-tered contemporary art discourse, he was frequently invited to give lectures in the field of art theory and the interpretation of cultural phenomena, which were hard for social scientists to perceive and analyze because they lacked his breadth of knowledge and sensitivity—to comprehend, for example, the experience of modern city life in all its in-teracting dimensions. In his already very interdisciplinary explorations, Prodanović in-tegrated scientific methods and art historical insights. Thus, it is not by chance that he was the first artist awarded the Doctorate of Arts degree in Serbia (many of his ear-lier projects could have won him this honor if it had been available earlier).

The fact that his research was commissioned by such different agencies, from cru-cial innovators in the field of art theory such as the Center for Contemporary Arts, to the experimental Alternative Academic Network (where he taught a course on "Visual Forms and Everyday Life"), to the Interdisciplinary postgraduate study department of Belgrade's University of the Arts, indicates his mastery of a wide range of disciplines. In fact, it would be difficult to find another author capable of making such broadly trans-disciplinary integrations. His knowledge of the histories of art and architecture, banknotes and numismatics, archaeology and contemporary pop culture, heraldry and political campaign strategy, and so on, enable him to write in an equally informed man-ner about the social values expressed through religious icons, shop windows, grave-stones, student protests, and the diaries of Mira Marković (Slobodan Milošević's wife).

Although written at different times and for different purposes, the three blocks of text that comprise this book offer a unique and comprehensive approach to the changes Belgrade went through in the 1990s. The three parts are: 1) New forms of

1

sacrilege; 2) Pathopolis; and 3) Necropolis. All of them investigate phenomena that were signs of an even deeper crisis linked to the extensive nationalism, war, and social anomy that, unlike most countries in Central and Eastern Europe, predominated in Serbia. The city of Belgrade is not only the subject of Prodanović's research and the object of transformations caused by social anomy, it is also the agent of a distorted society's culture. However, Prodanović always puts things in a wider context, noting similar phenomena at different moments in history elsewhere in the world. Even the title of the book—*An Older and More Beautiful Belgrade*—uses the far-fetched phrasing which sought to justify military action against Dubrovnik.

Mileta Prodanović's book claims that our cities talk to us through urban structures, through new and mostly unregulated initiatives, but most of all through the ways people use places and spaces. He explores *genius loci* and ways that the uses and meanings of certain places are defined or changed in official and collective memories. The book brings a new narrative to cultural and urban studies. In official histories, urban culture is usually presented as a set of top-down visions. In Belgrade's case, all those efforts made throughout history were to conceptualize and realize the city as the national (Serbian) capital, as the regional capital (capital of the Kingdom of Yugoslavia), but also as the city becoming a modern cosmopolitan capital of socialist non-aligned Yugoslavia. However, the focus of this book is on "pathopolis," the stage in which neither leaders nor society have a clear vision or a consistent value system. Belgrade is a city of multiple interrupted identities,[1] but also a city of parallel cultures with paral-

---

1   In spite of the fact that on the territory of Belgrade the remains of an important Neolithic culture (Vinca) were found, the history of Belgrade as an urban settlement starts with the Celts who lived in a city that had only a Roman name—Singidunum. (Allegedly, *Singi* is the name of an ancient Celtic tribe, while *dunum* meant city or settlement.) The Slavic population came later and built Belgrade without integrating any of the remnants of the Roman city. Medieval Slavic Belgrade, Serbia's capital in the fifteenth century, burned completely, leaving no traces for its foreign inheritors—the Ottomans and the Austrians—who often alternated with each other in ruling the city. From those periods, only nine buildings built before 1804 survived when Belgrade was conquered by the Serbian revival movement. But Belgrade only became a Serbian city again after 1830, and Serbia's capital in 1841. Most of the buildings in the city center were created by Serbs who came from and were educated in the Austro-Hungarian Empire. Even the main Orthodox church was built in the style imposed by Austria-Hungary. The suburbs were developed around a central street with private houses, a church, green market, and several shops in the middle, like small towns elsewhere in Serbia. The end of the nineteenth century brought Europeanization of the city center with different influences, mostly Hungarian art deco and French apartment buildings with mansard roofs. In World War I, much of Belgrade was destroyed, but emigrants from Russia, among whom were many architects, brought their academic style to the Serbian capital (the buildings of the Government of Serbia and the Ministry of Foreign Affairs, for example). This sent to oblivion all pre-war efforts to create a modern Serbo-Byzantine architectural style. World War II brought new destruction by the Germans (1941) and then by the Allies (1944). After the war, Yugoslavia's socialist government wanted to create a completely new city across the river Sava from older Belgrade, which would symbolize both cosmopolitanism and social equity (values highlighted in Mo-

lel memories that ignore one another. Once a cosmopolitan city, it was separated from its multiple legacies during the 1990s and turned into a large small town—or, to be more precise, an agglomeration of small towns (*palanka*).[2]

But the dreams of the Belgrade that once was—the dreams of a great metropolis from the time of the Nonaligned Movement (utopian dreams about a future community of equals), the dreams that built New Belgrade using Le Corbusier's ideas, ambitions to position the city on the world's cultural map with international theatre festivals, underground film programs, etc., dreams of Belgrade as a future south Slavic regional cultural center and a place of intercultural dialogue—all these dreams were suppressed but never killed, in spite of Milosevic's war politics, the emigration of young people, the trade embargo, and most of the population's misery. Belgrade remained an exciting multicultural city in which different generations and diverse cultural models co-exist, albeit with different memories and experiences.

Belgrade's evolution went through several phases in the last thirty years. In the 1990s, most of the republics that had constituted Yugoslavia sought independence and created new identity politics, while Serbia and Montenegro publicly defended the idea of Yugoslavia, retaining the name of Yugoslavia, just deleting the word "socialist." But for many, Yugoslavia as such became an unwanted past. Thus, Serbia's national cultural canon was revisited and a new politics of memory became a tool of nation-state building. Policies regarding monuments diversified: socialist monuments were displaced, removed, or ignored, while new ones reflected a need to reconstruct an ethnocentric narrative. Many artists felt a responsibility to react—to raise awareness of the importance of safeguarding the antifascist past, or clarifying and re-contextualizing socialism.[3] These processes were extremely important in Belgrade, which became an urban battlefield between two identities: Serbian and Yugoslavian.

During the 1990s, Belgrade lost the aura of a cosmopolitan city, but on its margins and in the underground, remnants of its previous values and openness remained. The "cultural counterpublic," led by the Belgrade Circle—an association of intellectuals that included Mileta Prodanović—used new places for alternative thinking and

---

MA's 2018 exhibition "Toward a Concrete Utopia: Architecture in Yugoslavia, 1948–1980"). But the crush of socialism brought new demands: on the one hand, a new class of small entrepreneurs (including numerous *Gastarbeiters*, but later on, refugees from other parts of Yugoslavia), and on the other, big investors, companies that treated urban space as a profitable resource, building confectionary architecture indistinguishable from elsewhere in the world.

2   As a result, the postmodern kitsch of Požeška street became the official culture of the 1990s (Dragićević Šešić, *Neofolk kultura*, 108). Or, as Mileta Prodanović claims in this book, it became "a manifesto of 'anti-bureaucratic' architecture" which wanted to aestheticize and spectacularize (according to new commercial values) suburbs that used to have the ambience of a small town.

3   Dragićević Šešić, "Counter-Monument: Artivism against Official Memory Practices."

creation, such as the Centre for Cultural Decontamination and the Cultural Center Rex, as well as public spaces that had lost their original meaning through official recuperation. In this sense, the Kalemegdan Fortress is a paradigm of an open urban space full of memories that had been turned into a huge park without any meaning during this period. Remaking it as an entertainment district (with gondolas connecting Kalemegdan and the Ušće shopping mall) began to dominate public discourse and the cutting down of trees started. It was only through the efforts of various artistic collectives—such as Group FIA, the Dah Theatre, the Mimart Theatre, Group Škart, as well the BELEF festival—that the destruction of this important urban landmark was prevented.

"Cultural counterpublics" must constantly reappraise the local (historic) and the global (modern and worldly) with ironic distance and innovative approaches. The goal is not a culture of consumerism or media representation, but a transcultural platform that demands high-value social and cultural capital[4] to be accepted. Still on the social margins, it is open to the new and different, and is therefore capable of developing new forms of cultural capital, even though kitsch patriotism based on the Serbian ethnic cultural canon still dominates the mass media and political thinking.[5]

Thus, Belgrade's counterpublics became "learning networks" that provided spaces for an abundance of adventures and experiences outside the dominant cultural models and matrices. At the same time, the artists believed that the dream of multiculturalism could not be restored in a time of destruction without speaking openly about genocide, massacres, ethnic cleansing, and criminal war actions in Bosnia and Kosovo. The politics of oblivion, of forgetting, of "not-knowing," as the official policy of the Serbian State, is challenged by the cultural counterpublic. Instead, we propose a new self-generated memory policy—the policy of remembering the city's past, including not only past ideals but also the unpleasant recent real past—a past that is controversial from all standpoints, dividing not only people belonging to different ethnic groups but also those who interpret Balkan history in different ways. Creativity and cultural variety through small, innovative cultural productions based on an ethics of responsibility is gaining a new sense of purpose, with multiplicative effects across the cultural landscape.[6] By engulfing its own heritage through contemporary practice in dialogue with other cultures, routes of future development are discovered and a new, more complex image of the city is created, which is not yet visible in the urban structures controlled by the political and financial elites.

------

4   Bourdieu, "The Forms of Capital."
5   Dragićević Šešić, *Neofolk kultura*, 183–207.
6   Grginčević, *Led Art—dokumenti vremena 1993–2003.*

Building multiparty democracy in Serbia and the Balkans generally, after Milošević, is a long and complex process. Citizens' expectations and their enthusiasm for a change quickly met disappointment and cynicism. The communist nomenklatura, with information, contacts, and funding possibilities both in the country and abroad, privatized enterprises that were previously operated as social and self-governing, often closing them, leaving the workers unemployed. The UN embargo on Serbia and the armed conflicts in Croatia and Bosnia-Hercegovina contributed to the collapse of local industries and the creation of a new generation of businessmen: war profiteers. Mass unemployment turned people toward the "black market" and the "grey economy," where those with negotiating skills survived while the majority became "losers of the transition." This led to rampant social injustice, private occupation of public spaces, and illegal constructions. The number of inhabitants in the capital cities increased but the economy was not generating jobs and employment. Thus, kiosks became the symbol of the transitional city. They appeared everywhere, on the banks of rivers, along sidewalks, in parks and public squares, offering mostly goods coming from illegal trade, from cigarettes to drinks and gadgets.

After the period described by Prodanović, "kioskization" was replaced by "investor urbanism," with new housing and business spaces being developed without adequate infrastructure for traffic, parking spaces, etc. Politicians saw in "new towers" the opportunity to claim success for their policies, while municipalities enlarged their budgets by issuing construction permits, often neglecting their own rules. Investors rarely engage the best architects or make public competitions for architectural projects, even for mega-projects in city centers. The impoverished middle class sold their private homes to investors who planned to replace them with big apartment blocks, offering the previous occupants two apartments while building twenty at the same address. Thus, urban investors started reshaping Belgrade and other capital cities in the region, making them look more and more alike.

Nationalist movements developed in the 1980s when a modest increase in media freedom enabled people to speak about subjects that the socialists in power had made taboo, such as rethinking national cultural history to include books and personalities banned because they were anti-communist or accused of collaborating with foreign occupiers. This new-found freedom was also used to launch private economic initiatives suppressed under socialism: micro-enterprises, from crafts through services to marketing agencies, fashion houses, design studios, etc. Private architectural studios existed under socialism, but only if they had less than six employees.

Micro-entrepreneurialism started changing the face of the city, and a new kind of "micro-urbanism" appeared, in which everyone thought they could build anywhere, on any empty spot in the city, or reconstruct even historical landmark buildings without any respect for the architectural or cultural values that they represented. In other words, the modest expansion of freedom in the 1980s grew into the "wild urbanism" of the 1990s, which Kulić called the period of "spectacular destructions"[7]—due not just to NATO bombing, but mainly due to the self-motivated efforts of the local population.

Thus, the beginning of the new millennium which brought democratic political change was also characterized by a revival of urban development. The process of urban evolution restarted with new vigor and all remaining public enterprises (including those that belonged to cultural industries, such as cinemas) were offered for privatization. Most of the buyers did not intend to continue any kind of productions or services that had previously been offered in them. They merely saw the huge profit potential in repurposed spaces.

The latest phase in Belgrade's urban development is dominated by the project known as the Belgrade Waterfront. It is not the first of such projects, but it is definitely the most ambitious and the most controversial, due to the way it was approved and the aggressive way it has been implemented. The deconstruction of existing buildings that were still being used occurred overnight, without any legal basis or in such cases necessary permits, and with the complete silence of the authorities. Police did not intervene when private security services expelled people from their premises. The most significant urban object in this area is the former Belgrade Cooperative building (also known by the name of its later occupant, the Geodetic Institute, *Geozavod*). The Cooperative was established in 1882 to promote savings and support small enterprises, craftspeople, and the poor of Belgrade, and was one of the first projects of the architects Nikola Nestorović and Andra Stevanović. Since 1966, the building has had the status of a cultural monument, and in 1979 it was denoted a monument of extreme importance. It was frequently used as a film location due to its unique interior, preserved intact since 1906. This building and the area around it were given to investors who destroyed this exceptional interior. They also illegally destroyed and transformed the area around the building to create new edifaces for the new political and financial elite.

The process of rethinking the city had started on the margins of social and cultural activism, involving numerous collaborations, individual artists, and cultural workers. They had to confront this wild urbanism that was destroying the plural identities that Belgrade had developed through history. The fate of "CK" (former headquarters of the Central Committee of the League of Communists in New Belgrade) is paradigmatic:

---

7   Kulić, "Refashioning the CK," 289.

The old seat of the League of Communists shed its obsolete skin and is changing into a new post-communist cloak, happily erasing its previous identity and taking on a new one, more appropriate for the coming times. This may suggest a rather cynical attitude towards memory, one that denies any meaning intrinsic to material traces of history, thus implying that architecture may be as much about forgetting as about remembering.[8]

Consequently, four Belgrades—the Balkan hub, the cosmopolitan-bourgeois city, the dream of cosmopolitan socialism, and the latest Belgrade of hybrid consumerist entertainment—coexist and lean on one another, intermingling and fighting each other to define the future.

Belgrade's urban identity combines old and new content to create new meanings of space. But it also enhances or erases community memories of now-lost institutions, activities, people, and places. We sometimes call it nostalgia, especially when it comes to Turkish toponyms or remnants of tradition, such as the Question Mark restaurant. Sometimes it even embraces nostalgia for socialism or a futile effort like the Non-Aligned Movement's Friendship Park. But these memories are more and more suppressed by the new urban markers of globalization: shopping malls, fast-food chains, casinos, and night clubs.

Many of the places and neighborhoods that Mileta Prodanović explores in this book have been forgotten by or are still unknown to most of Belgrade's current residents, who simply commute between their home and workplace and always shop in the same stores. That is why Belgrade's countercultural projects—some of them long established, like the Belgrade International Theatre Festival (BITEF)—as examples of anti-capitalist bottom-up culture[9] seek out unfamiliar and marginal locations in order to separate themselves from the official favoring of spaces which symbolize the success of rising capitalism in Serbia, like Ušće or the Belgrade Waterfront. Art which wants to enter into dialogue with the city, to develop *in situ* as site-specific projects, chooses street corners, vivid or forgotten neighborhoods, endangered urban structures, post-industrial and post-communist sites, and known and unknown courtyards (socially valuable hidden spaces). It chooses places of memory, of meaning, avoiding *non-lieux* (Augé)—that is to say, non-places like shopping malls, despite their glamorous appearance and attractiveness to the public. Non-places are the same everywhere in the world: spaces for anonymous individuals and common consumption needs. Belgrade's identity could be rebuilt through those non-places, but it would be a fake, non-

---

8 Kulić, "Refashioning the CK," 301.
9 Kisić, Tomka, and Dragićević Šešić, "Imagining Postcapitalist Cultural Policy Futures."

interiorized identity, an identity without a past. That is why artists always prefer spaces that embed diverse meanings and carry great signifying potential.

Mileta Prodanović has spent his whole life combining artistic and social research. He has succeeded in translating his research findings into many different domains—the visual arts, literature, theater, and teaching—crossing all boundaries. His lectures about the images on bank notes or about the Balkan identities embodied in everyday artifacts are still remembered by his former students in the Alternative Academic Network. The exhibition devoted to the use and misuse of the Mileševa monastery's "White Angel" fresco raised for the first time important questions of national self-representation. He recognized in its earliest stages the path towards development of the populist policy of medievalization[10] which would culminate in the violent conquest of public spaces.[11]

All of his results have been enriched by diverse methodologies coming from neighboring but quite different disciplines. Thus, this text is an interwoven fabric of facts, reflections, insights, and photographs as complex as urban culture itself. In this respect, even though it was first published in Serbian twenty years ago, *An Older and More Beautiful Belgrade* is still an urgent contribution to the increasingly interdisciplinary scholarship in cultural studies, visual anthropology, and urban history.

This book deserves a wide readership among both scholars and the general public who are interested in social and cultural policy, the history of nationalism, architecture and urbanism, and artistic disciplines based on research. Other books offer interdisciplinary views of popular culture and architectural history, such as *Learning from Las Vegas* (Venturi, Izenour, and Scott Brown, 1972), *America* (Baudrillard, 2010), and *Eventful Cities* (Richards and Palmer, 2010). But it is hard to find such studies about the post-communist transition in Central and Eastern Europe. There are, of course, academic books, such as *Culture and Sustainability in European Cities: Imagining Europolis* (Hristova, Dragićević Šešić, and Duxbury, 2015), *The Creative City* (Landry, 2000), *Cities and the Creative Class* (Florida, 2004), and *Art World City: Dakar* (Grabski, 2017). But all of these books are either one-sidedly critical or promotional. Prodanović's book is unique in passing beyond the limits of academic research to resonate with much broader public interests.

---

10 It is interesting to note that in most of the Balkan countries the new memory politics relate to a specific historical period: antiquisation in Macedonia, iliryzation in Albania and Kosovo, and medievalisation in Croatia and among the Bosniac population in Bosnia and Herzegovina.
11 Dragićević Šešić, "Memory Policies and Monument Building in Southeastern Europe."

References

Ando, Tadao. "I want to create an architecture that touches people with its beauty." Interview for the Bourse de Commerce/Pinault Collection. Paris: 2021. https://www.pinaultcollection.com/en/boursedecommerce/tadao-ando-i-want-create-architecture-touches-people-its-beauty.

Augé, Marc. *Non-Places: An Introduction to Supermodernity*. New York: Verso, 1995.

Baudrillard, Jean. *America*. New York: Verso, 2010.

Bourdieu, Pierre, "The Forms of Capital," Chapter 1. In *Handbook of Theory and Research for the Sociology of Education*, edited by John Richardson. Westport: Greenwood, 1986, 241–58.

Donald, James. *Imagining the Modern City*. Minneapolis: University of Minnesota Press, 1999.

Dragićević Šešić, Milena. *Neofolk kultura* [Neofolk culture]. Novi Sad: Izdavačka knjižarnica Zorana Stojanovića, 1994.

Dragićević Šešić, Milena. "Politika programiranja—kulturni diverzitet i zabava na RT Vojvodina" [Programming policy—cultural diversity and entertainment on Radio-Television Vojvodina]. *Kultura,* nos. 120-121 (2008): 214–240.

Dragićević Šešić, Milena. "Memory Policies and Monument Building in Southeastern Europe." In *Memory of the City*, edited by Dušica Dražić, Slavica Radišić, and Marijana Simu. Belgrade: Kulturklammer, Centar za kulturne interakcije, 2012.

Dragićević Šešić, Milena. "Counter-Monument: Artivism against Official Memory Practices." *Kultura* 6, no. 13 (2016): 7–19.

Dragićević Šešić, Milena. *Umetnost i kultura otpora* [Arts and the culture of dissent]. Belgrade: Institute for Theatre, Film, Radio and Television, Faculty of Dramatic Arts, *Clio,* 2018.

Đukić-Dojčinović, Vesna. *Tranzicione kulturne politike: konfuzije i dileme* [Transitional cultural policies: Confusions and dilemmas]. Belgrade: Zadužbina Andrejević, 2003.

Florida, Richard. *Cities and the Creative Class*. Oxfordshire, UK: Routledge, 2004.

Grabski, Joanna. *Art World City: The Creative Economy of Artists and Urban Life in Dakar*. Bloomington: Indiana University Press, 2017.

Grginčević, Vesna, ed. *Led Art—dokumenti vremena 1993–2003,* [Led Art—Documents of time 1993–2003]. Novi Sad: Multimedijalni centar/LED ART, 2004.

Hristova, Svetlana, Milena Dragićević Šešić, and Nancy Duxbury, eds. *Culture and Sustainability in European Cities: Imagining Europolis*. Oxfordshire, UK: Routledge Studies in Culture and Sustainable Development, 2015.

Kisić, Višnja, Goran Tomka, and Milena Dragićević Šešić. "Imagining Postcapitalist Cultural Policy Futures." *Cultural Trends* 31, no. 3 (2021): 273–286.

Kulić, Vladimir. "Refashioning the CK: Transitory Meanings of Belgrade's Tallest Building." In *Theatre—Politics—City—Case study Belgrade*, edited by Radivoje Dinulović and Aleksandar Brkić. Belgrade: YUSTAT centre for performing arts and technology, 2007, 288–301.

Landry, Charles. *The Creative City: A Toolkit for Urban Innovators*. Oxfordshire, UK: Earthscan Publications/Routledge, 2000.

Foreword

Merenik, Lidija. *Mileta Prodanović: moya sesstra* [Mileta Prodanović: My sister]. Novi Sad: The Pavle Beljanski Memorial Collection, 2012.

Prodanović, Mileta. *Brandopolis*, exhibition catalogue. Skopje, North Macedonia: Museum of Contemporary Art, 2005.

Prodanović, Mileta. *Godina lava* [Year of the lion], exhibition catalogue. Belgrade: Museum of Contemporary Art, 2008.

Prodanović, Mileta. *Ekfraze: razumeti konačne stvari i posetiti tajna mesta* [Expressions: Understand final things and visit secret places], exhibition catalogue. Smederevo, Serbia: Museum in Smederevo, 2016.

Prodanović, Mileta. *Genus—porodične priče* [Genus—Family stories], exhibition catalogue. Čačak, Serbia: Art Gallery "Nadežda Petrović," 2017.

Richards, Greg, and Robert Palmer. *Eventful Cities*. Oxfordshire, UK: Routledge, 2010.

Venturi, Robert, Steven Izenour, and Denise Scott Brown. *Learning from Las Vegas*. Cambridge, USA: MIT Press, 1972.

Author's Summary

The title of this book—*An Older and More Beautiful Belgrade*—is an ironic paraphrase of an equally ironic promise given at the end of 1991: "If we need to, we'll build a more beautiful and older Dubrovnik." Different versions of that sentence could be heard everywhere in Yugoslavia in the first half of the 1990s. As the press reported at the time, it was first uttered by Božidar Vučurević, a former road hauler, folk poet, and warlord of the municipality of Trebinje.

Behind the various warriors clearing the ground for future "more beautiful and older" reconstructions in the neighboring republics, there was a moral, material, mental, and every other kind of decline in Belgrade. Some aspects of this decline are portrayed in this book through the selection of cases in which social changes have had visual manifestations.

Since images punctuate the texts, this is more of a picture book than a sustained polemic or a series of essays. The essays hardly fit today's popular but demanding category of theory. Although they use certain theoretical notions, they are only commentaries on what was visible in the urban tissue as shown in the photographs.

The three parts of this book were created at different moments. The first text in the book is an expanded version of the paper "New Forms of Sacrilege" originally published in the collection *New Readings of the Icon* prepared by Dejan Sretenović (Belgrade Center for Contemporary Art) and published by Geopoetika in 1999. It describes the place of the icon, a Byzantine cult painting, in the social ambiance of Serbia at the end of the twentieth century. The growing presence of icons came as a consequence of the "return to tradition" that started in the late 1980s. Following Soviet examples, many visual manifestations of Yugoslav socialist society used toposes taken from the Orthodox religion: pictures of company managers in public displays often had the form of an iconostasis. And the grave of President Tito in Belgrade became a place of pilgrimage.

Figure 0.2. January 1997—Students protesting the falsification of local election results attempt to shame the policemen blocking Kolarčeva Street using a mirror to show them what they look like. Photo credit: Dragoljub Zamurović.

Changes in Eastern Europe after the fall of the Berlin Wall allowed a "demarginalization" of religious practices and symbols. A theology of the icon had been defined in the Byzantine Empire after the Iconoclastic Controversy (from the eight to ninth century). Although it had the form of a theological argument, Byzantine iconoclasm was essentially a battle for control over the power and authority of representation. However, in Serbia at the end of the twentieth century, the icon became a symbol of tradition. Therefore, we find it in places that could be described as appropriate, but also in completely inappropriate contexts. Such occurrences, despite the intentions of the people who placed them there, comprise a new form of sacrilege.

The second essay in the book is titled "Pathopolis." The title is a paraphrase from Lewis Mumford's periodization of ancient Rome. According to him, Rome was first *Parasitopolis*, then it turned into *Pathopolis*, under Nero it became *Psychopatholopolis*, and finally *Necropolis*.[1] In this essay, you can follow the influence of politics on changes visible in Belgrade's urban landscape at the end of the twentieth century.

---

1   "The city of the dead."

Since one of the most familiar faces of the state is money, the essay starts with an analysis of the iconography of Yugoslav banknotes from the socialist and post-socialist eras.

"Pathopolis" was the result of two lectures I gave at the Small Winter School organized by the Center for Contemporary Art in Belgrade in March 2000. I would like to thank Branislav Dimitrijević who was the *spiritus movens* of this cycle of lectures. If it had not been for his encouragement (at least as much as for the hesitation to speak by those who knew much more about the subject than me), this handbook of Belgrade in the 1990s would not exist. An initial, much shorter version was published in the June 2000 issue of the magazine *Reč* [The Word]. I returned to this subject when Zoran Milutinović persuaded me to become a lecturer in an elective course titled "Visual Forms and Everyday Life" in the Studies of Culture and Gender program of the Alternative Academic Educational Network. Since the course encompassed a wider field, I had to collect additional material, which led me to reach new conclusions. But the form of the text appearing in this book was also influenced by stimulating conversations I had with the students. I do not like to say "the final form" of the text because production, just like destruction of the city, is an ongoing process. When you decide to cut that flow, new elements always arise and throw new light on what has already been stated. Still, one must stop at some point. The regime change in Serbia on 5 October 2000 very quickly became the source of new myths. Regardless of the level of mystification of that date, I believe I can say that political change is the line between the new (transitional) brutality emerging in Belgrade and the Belgrade of the Miloševićs' era, marked by the erosion of urban and mental norms.

A city doesn't only consist of its currently visible constructions, but also of the memory of lost buildings that contributed to the *genius loci*. Using written and visual records, I analyze a range of buildings missing today that still influence the spirit of Belgrade. The reasons why they were built, and demolished, reveal much about the forces of political and cultural change. Even before the corruption associated with the last decade of the twentieth century, Belgrade was a kind of "patchwork" city, consisting of patches created by the urban tissue being tattered by bombing, carelessness, greed, and many other forces. The quarter around the Cathedral of St. Michael, the Orthodox Patriarchate, and the National Bank building, is analyzed as an example of the coagulation of different architectural languages.

After this pre-history and overview of the current state of Belgrade's architecture, we explore the influence of ideology on Belgrade's urbanism between the end of the 1980s and the end of the twentieth century. Historically speaking, modernist architecture was hard to achieve and radically disputed. Still, between the two world wars and especially after World War II, it managed to dominate traditionalism and pseudo-historical styles. However, social migrations in the last decade of the twentieth century threatened to destroy the legacy of modernism. Therefore, one of the most common visual aspects of "de-Titoization"[2] was the mutilation of modernist buildings. The examples analyzed range from the jarring addition of new floors and diverse façade changes to the physical destruction of some of the best examples of modernist architecture by the 1999 NATO bombing.

The phenomenon of "anti-bureaucratic architecture" is most notable in the quasi-postmodern redesign of Požeška Street, as well as in a multitude of improvised grey economy premises. The grey-zone trade (that is, the resale of smuggled goods, which became a big business during the economic sanctions against Serbia in the 1990s) found its way into spatial forms. Thus, the kiosk became a paradigmatic form during Slobodan Milošević's rule.

The urban environment also consists of signage, graffiti, and advertisements. In Belgrade at the end of the twentieth century, there are hand-painted, often very naïve-looking ads, as well as the most modern professional billboard designs. This chapter focuses on the increased presence of the quasi-traditional "Miroslav" alphabet (designed in the second decade of the twentieth century but resembling a twelfth century manuscript) in public and commercial signage in Serbia.

The arrival of multi-party politics brought polarization to the visual identity of certain political parties. We analyze their urban presentation strategies in the 1990s. The "war via posters" provides new examples of iconoclasm and the defacement of pictures as remnants of ancient beliefs connected to sympathetic magic, such that the destruction of an image is believed to somehow damage the person depicted.

There is a special focus on two separate constructions in Belgrade in the second half of the 1990s: "The International Art Center Šećerana"[3] founded by former stage director Ljubiša Ristić as the fruit of a personal obsession to build as a leader of the neo-communist party JUL [Jugoslovenska Levica]. The second construction, analyzed in the final part of the essay "Pathopolis," is the "Obelisk of the Eternal Flame." Constructed in less than two weeks and unveiled at the time of the first anniversary of the end of the NATO bombing, it presents (at least in concept) a memorial of victory. After the arrival of the international military forces in Kosovo, the Milošević regime's propaganda strove to present capitulation as victory. The 27-meter-tall concrete structure topped by a bronze sculpture of a flame, with a real flame inside it, can be considered a pinnacle of dishonest representation. Its real meaning can be seen in the fact that, because of problems with the gas supply, the fire of the "Eternal Flame"

---

2   The effort to destroy the legacy of Yugoslav president Josip Broz Tito.
3   Also known as the Sugar Refinery because of its earlier function.

went out even before Serbian society changed with the overthrow of Slobodan Milošević on 5 October 2000.

We conclude that, unlike the former communist times, Milošević's Serbia did not develop a consistent visual language, and its ideology was similarly a hodge-podge. This can be seen in numerous examples of eclectic visual practices.

The final text "Necropolis" also originated from my course at the Alternative Academic Educational Network. To create this book, I edited, shortened, and revised the text after the end of the course, then published it in the first Serbian edition [*Stariji i lepši Beograd*, Stubovi Kulture, 2002].

Like "Pathopolis," "Necropolis" owes its title to Mumford. It starts with a letter from the self-proclaimed Anjou Prince Alexei II Romanov-Dolgoruki-Nemanjić, Bourbon-Condé, the Volodar of Ruthenian Ukraine, and Grand Duke of Kyiv and Duke of Durrës and Bourbon. He was one of numerous international crooks who, in the post-socialist period, tried to present themselves as the successors of long-gone dynasties and pretenders to the throne. In a letter from late 1991, the fake prince addresses the then-President of Turkey Halil Turgut Özal, asking him to give back the decapitated head of Prince Lazar of Serbia. Lazar was killed in the legendary Battle of Kosovo in the fourteenth century. However, Lazar's relics, including his head, were not in fact in Turkey. Throughout history, in wars and major migrations, Serbs kept carrying them around like some kind of Ark of the Covenant. After nearly three centuries they were returned to a mausoleum that Prince Lazar himself erected in central Serbia. A procession to deliver the head lasted almost a year (1988–89) and in several places, belligerent actions started soon after the procession passed through. Apart from the religious dimension, the transport of relics had the effect of "time compression." In this way events from the ancient past became a part of the present. This was just one of the ways the topics of death and relics re-entered Serbian political discourse in the late 1980s and 1990s. After a verbal and symbolic phase, it turned into real gun talk.

After a short overview of royal burials (the Habsburgs, popes, Lenin, and Tito), the essay presents norms and innovations in Serbian sepulchral sculpture from the Middle Ages to modern times. In the final part of the essay, I analyze the newest gravestones of paramilitary fighters and members of Belgrade's underworld. Among the most bizarre examples is the startlingly contemporary monument which, apart from a bronze figure of the murdered, also includes an arrangement of artifacts reproduced in stone including a Coca-Cola bottle, a pack of cigarettes, and an ashtray—some of the most cherished elements which, in the shadow of war and the total impoverishment of society, defined everyday life in Belgrade in the 1990s. This life was summarized in the lyrics of a then-popular turbofolk song:

Author's Summary

> Coca-Cola, Marlboro, Suzuki,
> Discos, guitars, bouzouki.
> That's life. It isn't a commercial.
> No one has a better time than us.

While I was preparing lectures and processing this material for publication, many friends alerted me to texts or photographs in my areas of interest. I would especially like to thank Aleksandar Palavestra, who put invaluable material at my disposal, as well as Ivan Čolović who found time in impossible conditions to read the manuscript of the book's third section. His observations and suggestions made the chapter richer with many important details and references. Dubravka Vujošević and Branka Savić from the Media Center library were ready to dig into the archives and find incredible data at any moment. Thanks to Branka Bulatović from the National Library of Serbia, this book includes better quality versions of photographs initially published in periodicals.

A small part of the visual material was taken from publications listed in the annotations, from either daily newspapers or periodicals. Thanks to Jelena Mrđa and Goranka Matić, I obtained certain photographs, mostly those from protests and election campaigns published in the magazine *Vreme*. During final preparations for publishing the first edition of this book, we received news about the tragic death of the author of those photographs, Draško Gagović. May this book, at least in part, preserve the memory of that wonderful man, who was one of the most important visual chroniclers of Serbia in the 1990s.

Imre Sabo gave us his photos from the transfer of Prince Lazar's relics. Colleagues Goran Delić and Branimir Karanović each contributed photos of the overthrow of Slobodan Milošević in Belgrade on 5 October 2000. Most of the other photographs were taken by the author with an instant camera he received thanks to a respectable Belgrade lawyer, Dragoš Jovović.

I believe that Belgrade's cultural crisis in the last decade of the twentieth century deserves to be a subject of larger studies. Therefore, this book can only be a pointer or preparatory sketch of material to be revised many times. But then again, many sights recorded in these photos are already gone. Time will decrease the monstrosity of the scars in the urban tissue from the 1990s. Still, some interventions will remain as permanent markers of that decade. I do not doubt that some future readers will claim they do not recognize some aspects of the Belgrade presented in this book. It is already hard to find people who remember their elation in the late 1980s or the beginning of the 1990s.

I would especially like to thank those who worked on the last stage of the book's creation. Among them, Dušan Šević and Nenad Baćanović deserve special recognition for their patience and effort, and for their belief that it made sense to publish such an investigation.

Addendum for the English edition

I owe a great deal of gratitude to Robert Horvitz, who recognized the continuing value and topicality of this book and who put great effort into making it available in English. *An Older and More Beautiful Belgrade* was created in a specific historical period for my city and my country. Unfortunately, the world's physical and moral devolution continues, so this book is not just history but an ongoing narrative. I would be happy if it makes at least one reader think about the world we are leaving for the generations that come after us.

I owe special thanks, too, to Maria Milojković, who translated my often baroquely digressive text with great care and dedication and who, with Robert, added a series of necessary footnotes to facilitate readers' understanding of certain local historical, social and political contexts.

I believe that the detailed introduction written by Prof. Dragićević-Šešić will make the text more meaningful for readers. I thank her for this, and for her long-term friendly support.

Finally, I am grateful to the CEU Press and its editors—especially Frances Pinter, Emily Poznanski, and Linda Kunos—who generously supported and made possible this book's publication.

Mileta Prodanović

1

New Forms Of Sacrilege

The Icon: Between The World And God

The icon, a cult image of the Eastern Orthodox Church, has been studied from many different perspectives, all of which fail to grasp the phenomenon as a whole. Can we all agree that it is not simply a picture—a mere portrait of a saint or an event presented according to principles stated more or less precisely in the *hermeneiai* (icon painters' manuals)?[1]

Theologians stress that an icon is much more than an ordinary object. The shortest definition could be that an icon is some kind of a membrane, maybe even a window between the worlds of heaven and earth. It enables two-way communication: on the one hand, the person standing in front of the icon can communicate with the depicted saint. As Saint Basil the Great stated in a letter to his protégé Amphilochius of Iconium (which iconophiles often quote), "the honor given to the icon passes to its prototype." On the other hand, through that window, saints can influence the earthly world where those who pray live.[2] Ideally, characters appearing on icons are some kind of miraculous and always two-dimensional projections of archetypal characters—heavenly prototypes.

After the period of iconoclasm, when the supporters of icons were victorious, the Byzantine concept of an image was clearly defined.[3] The discussions were mostly intended to distinguish between an icon and indisputably prohibited idols: icons must be respected, but they must not be objects of *adoration*. Although we certainly do not

----

1   See Emmanuel Moutafov, "Post-Byzantine hermeneiai zographikes in the eighteenth century and their dissemination in the Balkans during the nineteenth century," *Byzantine and Modern Greek Studies* 30, no. 1 (2006), 69–79.
2   Ernst Benz, *The Eastern Orthodox Church: Its Thought and Life* (New York: Anchor Books, 1963).
3   For English translations of the most relevant texts, see St. Theodore the Studite, *On the Holy Icons* (Crestwood, NY: SVS Press, 1981) and St. John of Damascus, *Three Treatises on the Divine Images* (Crestwood, NY: SVS Press, 2003).

see an icon as the place where a saint or deity resides (in contrast to an idol), popular religiosity has often given certain icons such treatment. Icons were often claimed to act like living beings: if hurt, they bled. In some cases, they cried or even acted as guarantors in court proceedings. In one instance, an icon took over the function of the Mother Superior of a monastery on Mount Athos. Endangered by iconoclasts, the famous icon of Madonna from Constantinople went on its own to Ostia, like a ship or, even better, by emulating Christ's walk across the surface of water. It found itself in Rome, with only its lower edge being soaked and marked with sea salt after the transfer. Secretly scraped matter from the surface of the icon served as a natural health product, which made it quite like a relic.

In his introduction to the study of the history of painting before codification of the fine arts, Hans Belting summarizes the social position of the icon: "[the icon] not only represented a person but also was treated like a person, being worshipped, despised, or carried from place to place in ritual processions: in short, it served in the symbolic exchange of power and, finally, embodied the public claims of the community."[4]

In Luis Buñuel's autobiography, there is a much later example of personalization of a cult figure from the western end of the Mediterranean cultural zone. During one extremely dry year in ever-dry Aragonia, when dark clouds gathered over Bunuel's native village, the villagers organized a huge procession to beg the sky for a downpour. But when the clouds dispersed before the procession ended, the participants "got hold of Madonna's statue at the front of the procession and, while crossing the bridge, they threw it into the Guadalupe River."[5]

Apart from the status of an icon as an object, its liturgical purpose, or the complexity of questions about the social role of holy images, there is also the issue of style, which is important to art historians. In the last thirty years, the icon has become a favorite of collectors. They point out its unusual appearance and, thanks to a certain kind of stylization, an educated person in the West will not confuse an icon with other old pictures. For Romans or Byzantine Greeks[6] (or Byzantines, as some call them by mistake), the images on the iconostases and church walls were not unusual or rustic: they were the only possible way to decorate churches. When in 1438 the delegation of the Patriarchate of Constantinople attended the Council of Ferrara-Florence,[7] Patriarch Gregory objected to the reunification of the Catholic and Eastern Orthodox

---

4 Hans Belting, *Likeness and Presence: A History of the Image before the Era of Art* (Chicago: University of Chicago Press, 1994), xxi.
5 Luis Buñuel, *My Last Breath* (London: Virgin, 1983).
6 Greek-speaking descendants from the eastern part of the Roman Empire.
7 The ecumenical council at which the Roman Catholic and Greek church hierarchies tried to overcome their doctrinal differences and end their schism.

churches. Among other arguments, he gave the cult of images as an example: "When I enter a Latin church, I cannot pray to any saint because I recognize none of them. Although I recognize Christ, I cannot pray to him either because I do not recognize the way he is presented."[8]

It is important to acknowledge the origin of icons in the ancient art of portraiture. Even the root of the word, *eiko*, is Greek for "I am like." Therefore, an icon can be described most simply and without mystification as a portrait. Even so, pictures of the saints gradually moved toward idealization and a generalization of iconographic types. However, common people still believed these were accurate

Figure 1.1. A 12th century Mandylion, in the form of a Novgorod icon of "Christ Acheiropoietos," from the Assumption Cathedral in the Kremlin. Photo credit: Tretiakov Gallery, Moscow (via Wikimedia).

representations. The Third Council of Constantinople (869–870) declared that those who reject icons would not be able to recognize Christ on the day of the Second Coming.[9] Therefore, they defined a system of archetypes and templates in the creation of cult images and icons. No deviations were allowed. Originality was considered a sacrilege. Christ's face had to be rendered as on the Mandylion.[10] For the Madonna, the portrait painted by Saint Luke was the model. And so on.

Apart from the canonical obligation to copy good prototypes, icon painting in Byzantium was preserved under Turkish rule. Still, it was not immune from global trends in art. The traditional model of the icon was gradually infected with elements of the Baroque and illusionism, so that at one moment sacral art completely stepped out of

---

8   Belting, *Likeness and Presence*, 1.

9   George Ostrogorsky, *Odluke Stoglava o slikanju ikona i principi vizantijske ikonografije* [The decisions of the Church Council on painting icons and principles of Byzantine iconography] (Belgrade: Sabrana dela V, 1970). A thorough study of appearance, recognition, and the place of saints in the Eastern Roman Empire is in Henry Maguire, *The Icons of Their Bodies: Saints and Their Images in Byzantium* (Princeton: Princeton University Press, 1998).

10 The Mandylion—an icon of Christ's face not painted by hand—comes from a medieval legend that Christ once wiped his face with a napkin and the napkin retained an imprint of his face more accurate than any painter could make. The name of this icon type comes from the Byzantine Greek word μανδύλιον (mandúlion), meaning napkin. See Svetlana Pejić, "Mandilion u poslevizantijskoj umetnosti" [The mandylion in post-Byzantine art] in *Zbornik Matice srpske za likovne umetnosti* [Collection of Matica Srpska for the Fine Arts], nos. 34–35 (Belgrade, 2003).

traditional parameters. The last traditional zographs[11] seen by contemporary experts were made by masters from a few Macedonian families that had been producing icons for generations. They explained the end of their craft as the process of "ruining" those standards which today's public finds incomprehensible due to the entropy of good templates.[12]

Only in an epoch sufficiently distant from initial and then canonically frozen principles could new discussions about the style of the Orthodox Church's cult images occur. Most interesting was the debate about the "Orthodoxy" of iconography during the transition from Romanticism to Realism in Serbian art.[13] The period after World War I in Serbia was marked by an upswing in the fine arts which broke from pre-war tendencies. Among the many contrasting movements and phenomena in architecture and painting, one group of artists stood out: they advocated a return to the old forms of art, or at least they looked there for inspiration.[14] Stratification in the artistic scene finally separated art created for religious needs into a separate field. There the return to Byzantine norms was completely clear.

One must add that after a multitude of Russian painters skilled in the traditional Byzantine manner arrived in Yugoslavia, wall paintings of better or worse quality appeared in a large number of churches, all conforming to canon law. These painters confronted difficult challenges when they had to fit contemporary elements into images that were supposed to be timeless. A quite bizarre case can be found on the walls of a village church in the area of Mount Rudnik in central Serbia: next to a saint painted in the Byzantine manner, there is the donor, a rich twentieth-century industrialist living in the capital but born in that area. He is dressed in a tailcoat with a top hat and shoes with spats, accompanied by his wife and daughters in ball gowns. A similar and even better known case of clashing codes of representation is in the mosaics of the Karadjordjević royal dynasty's endowment on Oplenac.[15] Among the mosaic copies of medieval frescoes, there is a composition with the donor, King Peter I Karadjordjević. The effect of this anachronism is lessened by the fact that the king is also dressed in a non-contemporary way: he wears an ermine fur coat, atypical for his time.

---

11 Traditional Orthodox painters of icons. The word comes from the Greek ζωγραφοσ (painter).
12 Svetozar Radojčić, "Zografi, O teoriji slike i slikarskog stvaranja u našoj staroj umetnosti" [Zographs: On the theory of image and painting in Serbian Old Art], *Zograf*, no. 1 (Belgrade 1966), 4.
13 The texts of the discussion are found in Lazar Trifunović, *Srpska likovna kritika* [Serbian art criticism] (Belgrade: Srpska likovna kritika, 1967), 87–140.
14 Lazar Trifunović, "Stara i nova umetnost, Ideja prošlosti u modernoj umetnosti" [Old and new art, the idea of the past in modern art], *Zograf*, no. 3 (Belgrade, 1969), 39.
15 Oplenac is a hill in the town of Topola where the royal family's mausoleum was built.

Differentiating Icon from Idol

Representation was not the main issue in the period that historians define as Byzantine Iconoclasm. The main issue was the proliferation of cults.

Icons were intermediaries between people and God. In the Eastern Roman Empire, church and country were fully interconnected: In the Byzantine Empire, political and religious orders were mixed, and that mix was created through ceremony and ritual. A ritual that consisted of a set of symbolic forms proved that the world as it was (sociopolitical) and the world as it was imagined to be (religious) were in fact one.[16] Therefore, the ruler's role was important because he was God's representative on earth—that is, an intermediary between God and the people, as well as between the sociopolitical and religious worlds. In other words, he was quite like an icon himself. This was shown in the way visual representations of both saints and rulers functioned in their cults and consequently in society.

Often there was an inversion: the living emperor had to take on some aspects of a picture. He had to sit motionless in the reception hall. During an audience, a curtain was opened and closed in front of him. Some travel writers also state that on certain occasions, the platform in which the throne stood was raised and lowered with special mechanisms, to display the ruler more impressively.[17]

Of course, the rise of radically iconoclastic Islam near Byzantium cannot be ignored. Symbolic presentations of Christ were forbidden by the Council convened by Justinian II in 692—which, paradoxically, made figurative art and icon veneration thrive, provoking a crisis of imperial authority. It went so far that the defense of Constantinople from the Arabian siege in 717 was unanimously attributed to an icon of Madonna, not to Leo III the Isaurian, the emperor who would introduce iconoclasm nine years later.[18]

The year 726 is considered the formal beginning of the iconoclastic period. Leo III ordered the removal of an image of Christ (probably an icon on wood or a mosaic panel) from its prominent place above the main entrance into the Great Palace. Then

----

16 John Elsner, "Image and Iconoclasm in Byzantium," *Art History* 11, no. 4 (December 1988), 473.
17 Elias Canetti, *Mass and Power* (Zagreb: Grafički Zavod Hrvatske, 1984), 333–34. Canetti discusses this unusual court ritual and quotes parts of the travelogue written by Liutprand of Cremona, Otto I's diplomat, who was granted an audience at the Byzantine court in Constantinople. Also mentioned in the reference notes of *Audience* and *Automata* in Alexander Kazhdan, ed., *The Oxford Dictionary of Byzantium* (New York, Oxford: Oxford University Press, 1991).
18 Anthony Bryer and Judith Herrin, eds., *ICONOCLASM—Papers given at the 9th Spring Symposium of Byzantine Studies* (Birmingham: University of Birmingham, Centre for Byzantine Studies, 1975). This is the most complete collection of studies in chronological order and an anthology of original texts which became one of the most stimulating in the whole history of Byzantium.

he had it destroyed and replaced by a crucifix.[19] It was no coincidence that the first manifestations of iconoclasm happened at this place. Belting says:

> In an image, a person is made visible. It is completely different with a symbol. One can register one's presence with a symbol but without the help of an image which offers both appearance and presence. Where God is present, the emperor cannot represent Him.[20]

Replacing Christ's picture with a crucifix can only be understood in the context of other social developments at the time—namely, other efforts to remove figurative representations from the Christian cult. These, however, did not produce major social disorders, nor did they create a movement, let alone cause a wave of icon

Figure 1.2. Long-handled brushes used by iconoclasts to obliterate images of Christ were equated with the spears used to stab Christ on the cross in this page from the Chludov Psalter (mid-9th century), now in the collection of Moscow's State Historical Museum.

destruction. It seems a combination of historical circumstances brought success and a relatively long duration to the iconoclastic movement.

A few monuments have retained traces of the deliberate destruction of old figurative pictures until the present day (or at least until contemporary historians could study them), such as the Church of Hagia Sophia in Constantinople and one in Salonica, as well as the Church of Assumption in Nicaea, now gone. Nevertheless, we cannot fully determine the true level of destruction due to iconoclasm. Based on written testimonies, we know that portable icons were burned, chalices melted, miniatures from illustrated books were cut out, and mosaics scraped off the walls or simply covered with plaster. Still, those actions did not seem to have a comprehensive character since some representations from the patriarchate—the very center of the iconoclastic movement—were only removed forty years after they were banned.[21]

----

19 There are no precise data about this incident, but based on an analogy with the documented action after a short iconophile period in December 814, a crucifix probably replaced Christ's image in both incidents.

20 Belting, *Likeness and Presence,* 9.

21 Cyril Mango, *Byzantium: The Empire of New Rome,* 2nd edition (London: Phoenix, 1994), 264.

Subsequent iconophile texts portray the whole iconoclastic movement as heretical, and the destruction or removal of icons as sacrilege. Visual evidence of this attitude can be found in the drawings which illustrate the Chludov Psalter (made around 830). One illustration that stands out shows iconoclasm as comparable to the crucifixion of Christ.[22]

As already mentioned, debates about the use of images in cults produced a precise theory of icons. The church gave so much significance to the triumph of figurative representation that the date of victory over iconoclasm was declared an Orthodox holiday and is still celebrated in local churches. This victory resulted in a range of legends about the miraculous powers of holy images and the virtues of those who resisted their destruction or died defending them. And thus the names of new saints were added to the church calendar.

The attributes and principles of Byzantine art remained long after the empire disappeared. However, the specific symbiosis of empire and church also disappeared. Perhaps most surprisingly, some cult aspects of holy images migrated to social formations that were intent on abolishing religion.

Profane Icons: A Socialist Innovation

After the October Revolution in Russia and the emergence of the first resolutely atheist state in 1917, many hundreds of monasteries and churches were closed all over the newly founded Soviet Union. Many of them had workshops or small manufactories for icon creation. In the new social environment, their products became not only unnecessary but unwanted. Iconographers who neither managed to get to the West nor died in the revolutionary turmoil found a new outlet for their skills: Palekh. The style (named for the village in which it first developed in the 1920s) applies mainly to wooden objects covered with paper maché and lacquer, painted in intricate and colorful detail—something like a souvenir insecurely rooted in folk traditions.[23] The themes illustrated in Palekh are mostly from old Russian fairy tales, but one could also find scenes celebrating the triumphs of socialist construction. With their composition, colors, and even ornamentation, Palekh repurposed the motifs of "hagiographic" icons. Palekh workshops even created monumental wall paintings for public buildings similar to what had previously decorated churches.

----

22 Maria V. Shchepkina, ed., *Miniatyury Khludovskoy psaltyri* [Miniatures of the Chludov Psalter] (Moscow, 1977) in Russian.
23 N. M. Zinoviev, Искусство Палеха [The Art of Palekh], 2nd edition (Leningrad: Khudozhnik RSFSR, 1975).

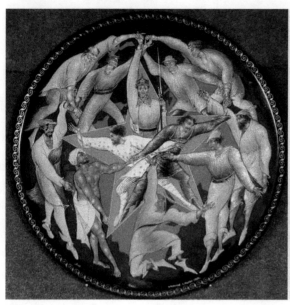

Figure 1.3. An early example of the Palekh style, in which characteristic features of icons are repurposed to illustrate milestones in the development of socialism, Russian fairytales, folk themes, etc. Lacquered plate by Ivan Golikov, "The Third International", (1927).

In Soviet Russia, the whole body of religious motifs went through a broad transformation. They not only appeared to be, but substantively were, creations from Palekh workshops. Of course, traditional icons were an essential source of imagery but not the only ones. New potentates were well aware of how deeply rooted religion was in the Russian people and it was natural to use some of the existing frameworks for political purposes. The first who wrote about this was Nikolai Berdyaev, a Russian philosopher of religion between the two world wars.[24] Later an extensive literature appeared, more or less based on his premises. It expanded after the fall of real socialism in the Soviet Union and the countries of Eastern Europe.

The exploitation or misuse of religious references was not without precedent. Even the last Romanovs and many pretenders to the Russian throne before them commissioned portraits in the style of icons to appeal to the Russian people. In his famous history of Russian culture, James Billington claims that during the rule of the former theologian Stalin, icons did not continue to live as inspiration for creative art. Instead they became a model for mass indoctrination. Lenin's pictures in factory "red corners" and public places replaced icons of Christ and the Virgin Mary. Photographs of Lenin's successors were placed in a well-regulated order, both left and right from Stalin,

---

24 Nicholas Berdyaev, *The Russian Revolution: Two Essays on its Implications in Religion and Psychology* (London: Sheed & Ward, 1932).

Figure 1.4. 16th century Deisis from Russia (anonymous) in the collection of the Walters Art Museum, Baltimore, Maryland USA.

replacing the Deisis where saints were put in a well-established order on both sides of Christ on the throne.[25]

Based on the system of transferring idols, this practice spread to the countries that introduced socialism after World War II. One of those states was the Socialist Federal Republic of Yugoslavia.

Possibly the best sublimation of para-religious motifs into the figure of a Soviet leader can be seen in Nikita Mikhalkov's film *Burnt by the Sun*. In the film's final scene, a gigantic face of Stalin painted on a canvas resembling a sail or the Mandylion is raised by a balloon and flown over the Russian landscape. Flying over sunny fields

Figure 1.5. Pictures of party leaders were set up at congresses and along parade routes in a deliberately ordered way resembling the order of icons in a Deisis. Photo source unknown.

----

25 James Billington, *The Icon and the Axe: An Interpretative History of Russian Culture* (New York: Vintage, 1970), translated by B. Vučićević into Serbian as *Ikona i sekira, istorija ruske culture* (Belgrade 1988), 57.

with its frontality and mysterious smile, Stalin's representation here approaches a type of Pantocrator.[26]

In portraits of the new communist potentates, one of the first things that can be seen is a source filtered through the concept of an icon: the ancient imperial portrait. Just like icons of later periods, imperial portraits were the subject of special and very precise legislation. Sent to provinces, they literally replaced the figure of the tsar. People were supposed to show them the same respect they would show the actual person.

As already noted, icons developed as a tradition in the Eastern Roman Empire, which was a highly ritualized society. The socialist countries were also highly ritualized, but of course, they differed from societies whose spiritual backbone was

Figure 1.6. "Almighty" Stalin–the final scene of Nikita Mikhalkov's film *Burnt by the Sun* (1994).

Christianity. After a short interruption, the ideologists of socialism realized how deeply rooted icons and rituals were in public consciousness. The new socialist governments knew it was pointless to reject the possibilities these cult manifestations offered for shaping public opinion. So they adapted and used some of the familiar patterns: they created secular versions of almost all the rituals that had marked life in the pre-socialist period. The ceremony of "giving a name" in Soviet society was a kind of profane baptism. Acceptance into the Young Pioneers replaced the first Communion. Civil marriage ceremonies took many elements from former church weddings.

Countries in the former socialist bloc tried to emulate Soviet practices in many fields, sometimes producing strange caricatures. For example, at the end of the 1960s, Bulgaria founded a state commission for rituals. According to reports in the Serbian newspaper *Politika*, they established the first concrete measures to realize the idea of rituals and symbols as important emotional elements in patriotic communist upbringing. The Council of Ministers decided that the executive committees of national

---

26 The Pantocrator is a depiction of Christ as ruler of the universe, one of the earliest and most common concepts in the decoration of Byzantine churches. "Pantocrator" might be translated as "almighty" or "all powerful."

councils, along with labor unions and the committees of the Fatherland Front and Komsomol[27] should adopt measures to expand, strengthen, and popularize new civic rituals connected to the important moments in people's lives—birth, marriage, death, etc. They directed national boards to provide suitable rooms and professional staff for organizing ceremonies such as civil marriages, the naming of new-borns, etc. Architects were told to create special facilities for these rituals in administrative buildings, cultural centers, study halls, and elsewhere. The Ministry of Finance and the People's District Committee would provide funding for these activities in their annual budgets. Also, orders were given to open special shops where people could get the supplies needed for these rituals. The government committee for art and culture was obliged to enable the creation of works of art, music, and literature to give form and meaning to these new civil rituals.

In the Yugoslav practice, there were no explicit examples of standardization. Still, over time, not only the calendar but certain categories of civic ritual iconography emerged. Apart from those already mentioned, there was a ritual of vital importance in Yugoslavia: sending one's son to the army. In rural areas, this rite would last a few days, as if it were a wedding. Celebrations of national holidays in socialist Yugoslavia (which affirmed the legitimacy of the state, as in any other country) incorporated some practices from abandoned traditions.[28]

The cult of relics (very closely related to the cult of icons) also gained profane analogues. The remains of the father of "real socialism," Vladimir Ilyich Lenin, were mummified. First, a makeshift temple was constructed, then the permanent mausoleum on Red Square.[29] Lenin died in his home in Gorky Park on 21 January 1924. More than a year before this event, Lenin's health started to deteriorate. The right side of his body was paralyzed, he lost the power of speech, and he had terrifying hallucinations. Therefore, as early as October 1923, amid political intrigues and the fight between Stalin and Trotsky over who should succeed Lenin, there were already discussions about where to inter the leader of the world proletariat. Stalin was the first to come up with the idea of embalming him. In a speech to top party leaders, he noted that "comrades from the provinces" would not understand if Lenin were cremated because that was not a Russian custom. Some party leaders suggested that modern science should be able to preserve his body for a while, "at least as long as we need to get

----

27 The youth organization for spreading the teachings of communism.

28 Dunja Rihtman-Auguštin, *Ulice moga grada* [The streets of my town] (Belgrade: Biblioteka XX vek, 2000). See especially "Metamorfoze socijalističkih praznika" [The metamorphoses of socialist holidays], "Kako je umro Osmi mart" [How 8 March died], and "Djed Mraz u tranziciji" [Santa Claus in transition]. All texts in Serbian.

29 A. N. Kotirev, *Mavzoley Lenina: Proyektirovaniye i stroitel'stvo* [Mausoleum of Lenin: Design and construction] (Moscow: Sovetskiy khudozhnik, 1971).

used to the idea that he is no longer with us." Trotsky criticized this as "the replacement of Sergiy Radonezhsky's and Saint Seraphim of Sarov's relics with Vladimir Ilyich's." Bukharin agreed with that criticism, saying it would be an insult to Lenin to turn his body into a relic (he had asked to be buried). Kamenev believed there were better ways to preserve Lenin's memory. He suggested that St. Petersburg should be renamed Leningrad. Stalin was in the minority in this argument but in the end, things turned his way. (The same happened in his fight for power.) There is no doubt that Stalin saw embalming as a good way to hold the interest of the primitive masses and portray the regime as Lenin's caretaker. And of course, the para-religious cult of the founder of the state was a way to strengthen his own power.[30]

The cult of relics and the establishment of a link to older mythic histories take an even more grotesque form in societies like North Korea. As the daily press reported,[31] for the permanent resting place of Kim Il-Sung, the recently discovered tomb of Tan-Gun, the mythical founder of the Korean nation, was chosen. As Korean children learn at school, Tan-Gun was born from the mating of a tiger with a she-bear who lived in a cave filled with garlic cloves. Among sculptures and glass cases with the remains of Tan-Gun and his wife, there would also be a specially-created glass case with the body of "The Great Leader." A new spiritual/technological experience would be offered: the Korean leader's body would be positioned to give visitors the impression it was floating in the air. Vapors of a special liquid hidden in the lower part of the display case would make annual repairs of the mummy unnecessary.

Figure 1.7. Stalin and Lenin together again (1953–1961). Photo from the KGB archive.

---

30 This discussion, as well as many other details about Lenin's embalmment, were reported by the son of one of the experts who preserved the body. His father and colleagues apparently turned their connections and experience into a business, preserving the bodies of leaders of other Communist countries, and eventually finding new clients among Russia's mafiosi. Ilya Zbarsky and Samuel Hutchinson, *Lenin's Embalmers* (London: Harvill Press, 1998).

31 Based on reports from a Korean news agency and Reuters, quoted in the Serbian daily newspaper *Borba*, 6 September 1994.

Figure 1.8. The eternal house on Red Square in Moscow that Lenin and Stalin shared—at least for a while. Stalin's body was transferred only when an instruction came from Lenin in a dream. This picture was published in 1931 as a postcard, now in the collection of the Children's Postcard Museum in Moscow.

A bizarre and less known transfer of religious toposes is also connected to Lenin's mausoleum. When Stalin died in 1953, Lenin's eternal resting place in Red Square became the home of both leaders—at least for a while.

Stalin's cult of personality started to deteriorate in 1956 with Khrushchev's famous secret speech at the 20th Congress of the Soviet Union's Communist Party. At a later party congress, when the campaign against Stalin had advanced, a female delegate announced that Lenin had come to her in a dream and confided that he was embarrassed to lie next to someone who had inflicted so much misery on the party. That gave the Congress an incentive to take Stalin's body out of the Mausoleum and bury it in the Kremlin Wall Necropolis in 1961.[32] This case is quite atypical for the twentieth century, even more so in a society that considered itself the embodiment of dialectical materialism. But it was consistent with a range of Christian legends. There are many stories of saints who came to people in visions and dreams with specific instructions on how to act.[33]

Processions were also re-established in socialist societies but under a different name: parades. Apart from the line that connects them to the special tradition of military parades, they also had a clear pseudo-sacral dimension. In such exhibitions of "Gesamtkunstwerk"[34] in the street, pictures and models of leaders were carried on special standards like those used to carry icons in communal religious processions. Mausoleums of leaders and places of important victories marked by public monuments became places of pilgrimage.

---

32 Katherine Verdery, *The Political Lives of Dead Bodies: Reburial and Postsocialist Change* (New York: Columbia University Press, 1999).
33 Maguire, *The Icons of Their Bodies*, 12–15, 42, 44.
34 The German word for creative work where different artistic media are combined in a single coherent form.

As in Christianity, in the para-religious cult of communism there were also heretics, those who strayed from the canonical path defined at party congresses. In photographs—historical documents— those who were thought to have betrayed the revolution were made to disappear by retouching. This phenomenon, described in literature, for example, by the Czech writer Milan Kundera,[35] had its roots in the distant past. Apart from examples from ancient Egypt, another that is especially interesting and surprisingly close to modern practices is a family portrait of Septimius Severus created around 200 CE, now in the collection of Berlin's Altes Museum. On it, the face of Geta, one of

Figure 1.9. Tondo of the family of Roman emperor Septimius Severus (egg tempera on wood, 199 CE, 30.5 cm diameter). A face thought to belong to the emperor's son Geta (center left) has been crudely blanked out. Photo credit: José Luiz Bernardes Ribeiro.

Septimius' sons, has been scratched out and covered with excrement. As his brother Caracalla ascended the throne, Geta was condemned to *damnatio memoriae*.[36]

The Icon in Serbia's Post-Socialist "Popular Awakening"

Yugoslav socialism was considered "something in between." At least this is what Yugoslavs believed. At any rate, it differed from the Soviet and Eastern Europe patterns, so visual manifestations of the cult of the ruler and the use of his icons were somewhat different as well.

The image of Josip Broz Tito, "the president with an unlimited mandate," was omnipresent but not too obtrusive.[37] (This description, quoted from the Constitution, could mean he is still president—more than two decades after his death—since his mandate was not limited by death, as we can conclude from a strict reading of this phrase.)

---

35 Milan Kundera, *The Book of Laughter and Forgetting* (1979 in Czech, 1995 in English).

36 Belting, *Likeness and Presence*, 106. *Damnatio memoriae* in Latin means "condemnation of memory," indicating a person to be "disremembered"—that is, excluded from official accounts.

37 Bojana Pejić, "Tito, ili ikonizacija jedne predstave" [Tito, or Iconization of a Performance] in *New Reading of the Icon*, edited by Dejan Sretenović (Belgrade: Center of Contemporary Art/Geopoetika, 1999).

In addition to being represented in images, there were also concessions to iconoclasm: the word "TITO" was created by arranging blocks of limestone or by planting seedlings on mountain slopes. It was also written on factory facades as well as on public and private buildings. The display of Tito's pictures in classrooms, courtrooms, hospitals, military barracks, and offices had become customary, even though the first legislation on the use of his image occurred relatively late, in 1977—in other words, while Tito was still alive.

Another law dealing with the same issues was passed after his death by the Socialist Federal Republic of Yugoslavia [SFRY] Assembly on 26 September 1984. Its exact title was "Law on the Use of the Name and Likeness of Josip Broz Tito." Unlike the first one, the more recent law stipulated prison sentences. It replaced "customary" and "voluntary" implementation with the obligation to exhibit images, and forbade the use of his likeness, name, or signature as trademarks.[38] This can be viewed as a final codification of a ruler's iconic representation—in this case, Tito's.

This law was not in force for long. And the manner in which his images disappeared discretely or, more often, noticeably and in a well-organized manner[39] could be a subject of study in the context of historical iconoclasm.

The way Josip Broz Tito was buried in May 1980 also differed from the norms of other countries in the socialist bloc. Despite later press speculations about a 1980 proposal that Tito's remains should be embalmed,[40] it is evident this was not what the party leadership had in mind, even for a single moment. This is confirmed by reports of the medical council. Their daily records of the last months of Tito's life were printed on the front pages of all Yugoslav newspapers to support the notion that an autopsy was not necessary.

And so Tito's body did not become yet another product of the best supplied biochemical laboratory in the Soviet Union, Moscow's Institute of Medicinal and Aromatic Plants, where a team was responsible for the preservation of Lenin's "mummy." Their list of accomplishments includes the preserved bodies of Georgi Dimitrov (Bulgaria's leader), Klement Gottwald (East Germany's leader), Hồ Chí Minh (North Vietnam's

----

38 Pejić, "Tito, ili ikonizacija jedne predstave," 115.
39 The pro-regime daily newspaper *Politika* published in 1991 (when Slobodan Milošević was in power) the news that a gigantic monument of Tito created by Frano Kršinić had been removed from the square in the Serbian town of Užice. The news coincided with the start of the removal. But during the process of removal, they found that the bronze figure was anchored more strongly than expected, so removal of the sculpture was postponed to the following day. *Borba* commented on this incident in "Politika izlazi u susret željama svojih čitalaca" [*Politika* fulfills the wishes of its readers].
40 Aleksandar Ćirić, "Punjeni komunisti" [Stuffed communists], *Vreme* (Belgrade: 8 August 1994).

leader), Agostinho Neto (Angola's leader), and other giants of the international workers' movement.

Nor was a smaller replica of the mausoleum in Red Square built for Tito in the center of Belgrade, as was done in Sofia for Georgi Dimitrov. Nevertheless, despite the distance from the Soviet model, we cannot say the House of Flowers (Tito's mausoleum) has no clear connection with ancient history, although officials presented it as an almost arbitrary choice for a tomb.

The burial of "common" people on their property or in a home garden instead of in a public cemetery is a custom that persists in some parts of the Western Balkans.[41] Janko Maglovski, probably the only researcher so far to observe the House of Flowers through the matrix of sepulchral customs,[42] concludes it isn't a grave of some ordinary person on his land (the land on which the House of Flowers was built wasn't Tito's property, but that's another subject). By burying a heroized person in a new grave, a *locus profanus* [a profane place] became a *locus religious* [a holy place]. Clearly, such a place would become a pilgrimage site, as was obvious to anyone who knew Belgrade in the 1980s. This location created a triangle: "the court," "the treasury," and "the grave"—an archetypal spatial arrangement that can be traced back to the Old Testament.[43]

The display of pictures of Tito wearing civilian clothes or one of his many martial uniforms was hardly the only form of cult behavior established during his lifetime. Perhaps even more important was the annual—or more precisely—the springtime mix of pilgrimage and procession called the Relay of Youth. This state "Juvenalia" coincided

----

41 Slobodan Milošević is buried in the garden of his family home in Požarevac.

42 Janko Maglovski, "Grob—Locus religious—Ideology" [Grave—Locus religious—Ideology], in *Sveske društva istoričara umetnosti Srbije*, no. 22 (Belgrade, 1991), 3–10.

43 In this case, "the court" is Tito's residence at present day 15 Užička Street (previously named Rumunska Street) in the most luxurious part of Belgrade, Dedinje. It was built as a family house by architect Aleksandar Acović in 1934. Tito moved into it in October 1944 after Belgrade was liberated from the Germans in World War II. Since then, it has been thoroughly reconstructed twice. The whole "Memorial Center" was radically reconstructed when Slobodan Milošević moved in with his family after he became the President of the Federal Republic of Yugoslavia. When NATO missiles hit it in the spring of 1999, this carried strong symbolism and was interpreted by the regime as an assassination attempt. The second point of the triangle—the treasury—could be either the Museum of Yugoslavia or Villa Mir [Peace House]. The Museum of Yugoslavia (also known as 25 May) was built in the early 1960s to store the presents Tito received. It probably has the largest collection of relay batons in the world. Villa Mir is a circular house officially called the "Memorial collection." It was built in the late 1970s as Tito's new residence, adapted for his old age. Tito never moved in (he died before it was completely finished), but Slobodan Milošević did after his house on Užička Street was demolished. He was arrested in this building in the spring of 2001, in the presence of a small number of his "defenders" and a large number of photojournalists who tried in vain to capture this moment. The third point—the grave—is of course the House of Flowers.

Figure 1.10. Some of the batons used in the Relays of Youth, as displayed in the House of Flowers. Photo credit: Simon Legner (CC BY-SA 4.0, Wikimedia), https://commons.wikimedia.org/w/index.php?curid=83600633.

with Tito's proclaimed birthday (proclaimed because the date was chosen for celebrating Tito's birthday among several dates given in his documents, even though 25 May was not among them). The ritual that culminated in a grand show in a football stadium changed through the decades. Its changing form meant that the federal relay (which replaced numerous local relays in the early years) created a certain "mystique of touch." It was a symbolic connection among the celebrant's subjects who would hand over the relay to the next carrier, thus connecting the whole country and emphasizing the unity of its regions.

Ideological inertia enabled these processions to continue even after Tito's death.[44] Nearly a decade later, a thoughtful and highly sophisticated art provocation ended this custom. When, according to the established plan, it was Slovenia's turn to host the Relay of Youth in 1987, a group called "New Collectivism" (part of the "Neue Slowenische Kunst" movement) won the design competition. They created a relay baton that looked nothing like traditional batons and weighed several kilos, which made it completely unsuitable to carry in a race. The relay was publicized with a poster which turned out to be a repackaged Nazi poster, as the ideological committees found out too late. That scandal marked not only the end of a long tradition—and foreshadowed the end of Yugoslavia as a federation of diverse republics—but it was also the only serious and well-grounded action of radically critical art in Yugoslavia during the 1980s.

Despite the lengthy development of Tito's cult in multiple contexts, and regardless of the two laws on uses of his image and identity, Yugoslavia's socialist "self-gov-

----

44 Pejić notes that in celebrations of Youth Day before 1980 images of Tito were rarely included, since the "original" was present. After 1980, the practice of substituting visual representations for the original began and over the years these became larger. Pejić, "Tito, ili ikonizacija jedne predstave," 114.

ernment" never built a consistent set of rules concerning the social role of visual representations of this important icon. The two laws regulated the use of Tito as a trademark more than they gave clear directions regarding the place of the ruler's portrait in society.

This lack of clarity persisted into the following epoch of a new leader, Slobodan Milošević. Yet apart from the lack of ideological direction in the marginal field of political iconography, the Milošević era has been characterized as an "anti-bureaucratic revolution"—or, as one writer called it, "a happening of the people"—marked by a complete lack of ideology concerning all aspects of society. Instead of ideology, there were simulacra. Thus, at times it looked like the main social concept was nationalism, but at other times it looked like a renewal of communist patterns. In reality, survival of the ruling circle was all that filled the void space for ideology.

Such a society quickly left its imprint on the arts. This was most visible in architecture, the art most directly connected to the social fabric. Since Yugoslav society didn't have any guiding idea, architecture didn't either, as it reflected the country of the time, including the suddenly generated capital of war profiteers. Serbian architecture in the era of Milošević was permeated by kitsch, primitive new-money projects that were highly eclectic and self-deluding in the belief that they belonged to the postmodern idiom. Entire neighborhoods of Belgrade were full of buildings with newly added top floors and Corinthian columns affixed to concrete facades—an accurate portrait of Serbia in the 1990s.

During the war which officially "didn't even exist" but which left countless ruins and massive civilian casualties, urban development quickly devolved into chaotic local conflicts with ever-changing goals. This was obscured by a return to the importance of icons—especially the return of the ruler's portrait as a cult image, as well as the renewed popularity of religious icons in secular public spaces. Because Marxist parties were officially atheist, religious icons had been sequestered for decades in religious institutions and the privacy of believers' homes. As was the case in earlier times in many Eastern European countries, icons now had a role in reinforcing the collective identity: they were timeless in style and content. More importantly, they were clear signs of a wish to differentiate the countries that had an Orthodox heritage from "the West" and emphasize a certain kind of ethnic authenticity.

Enlarged icons, together with the leader's image, became essential elements in mass meetings aimed at establishing a new government. Similar icons with the same function also appeared in mass meetings of the opposition parties. What is interesting is the interaction between two types of icon. In Serbia in the late 1980s, not only could one see pictures of Slobodan Milošević and religious icons next to each other on the dashboards of trucks and cars, but one could also find them in people's homes, where a cresset[45] was hung between a photograph of the President and a picture of the family saint.

Applying religious practices to profane images or to the leader's pictures took other forms as well. This photo shows a woman kissing a photo of Slobodan Milošević in the same way that a believer would kiss an icon in an Orthodox church. The picture was taken in Belgrade in December 1996, at a Socialist Party event presented as a spontaneous manifestation: the regime wanted to show that they, and most importantly the leader, still had the people's support despite months of protests against the Party's theft of the most recent election.

There are also scenes from the early days of Milošević's rule when people supported him more strongly. At the "Rally of Truth" in Belgrade's Ušće Park, one could see a para-religious trance recorded by a television camera: In an act of intimization of the ruler's picture which even a medieval king would envy, an old woman danced the waltz with a framed portrait of Slobodan Milošević.

Figure 1.11. Religious practice applied to a profane portrait: a woman kissing Slobodan Milošević's photograph at a meeting of the Socialist Party of Serbia in December 1996. To kiss the picture is to kiss the person pictured. Photo credit: Draško Gagović.

The return of the icon as a traditional cult image with a clear sacral purpose in the social environment was a new kind of misuse—a sacrilege not seen before that time. This sacrilege had different forms but common to all of them was that the instigators got the attention they wanted, profiting their cause as if these icons were propaganda tools.

In a strict sense, an icon cannot be separated from its liturgical function, so one might consider it a sacrilege even to display an icon in a museum, or to create it without a spiritual purpose.

Yet sometimes icons were displayed in places totally at odds with Christian moral principles. For example, the tradition of putting pictures of saints on war banners.

----

45 A cresset is a cup suspended as a lantern which holds oil or wax that can be lit for illumination.

Figure 1.12. Serbian Infantry flag (1853). Saint Andrew appears on the flag because the Principality of Serbia was recognized as a state on St. Andrew's name day in 1830. Photo credit: Ministry of Defense.

Figure 1.13. Constantine's Labarum, reconstructed by Eugene Ipavec for Wikimedia. The "Chi-Rho" symbol at the top is one of the earliest "christograms," intended to show allegiance to Jesus. In 324 CE the Labarum became the Roman Empire's official standard.

Saint Andrew, patron of the Karadjordjević dynasty (Serbia's royal family), appears on regimental flags of the Serbian Army.

On Bulgarian banners, the Mandylion showing Christ's face appears with the inscription "God is with us." Though it may be hard to determine whose side God is on when armies praying to the same God clash, the use of icons on military banners recalls an even older tradition—the military use of religious insignia like Constantine's labarum.[46]

However, such traditions don't justify one paramilitary formation's wall calendar published during the 1990s war in Bosnia—the unit called "Mandy's Lions" from Ugljevik. There one can find two icons for each month along with more than 80 group and individual portrait photos of the members of this not-so-large formation. Careful examination shows that all the photos were taken on the same day, and the same combatants appear in mutually exchanged uniforms, in different poses, and with different weapons. The members of this paramilitary unit are presented on the calendar as if they were models. The icons also have an inappropriate function—to give this little-known paramilitary group some "spiritual credibility." This kind of sacrilege isn't unique: starting in the 1990s, icons were used on wall calendars to advertise many different products. This is just a particu-

----

46 The "labarum" was a military standard which displayed the "Chi-Rho" symbol, an early "christogram."

Figure 1.14. Icons as the warrior/models' "heavenly pledge," below the center of a calendar created by "Mandy's Lions," a paramilitary unit from Ugljevik.

larly drastic example. The most frequent kind of sacrilege is trivialization.

In the last decade of the second millennium in Serbia, holy images or icons could be found on ballpoint pens, key rings, badges, notebook covers, cigarette lighters, and menus. The distribution of what an increasing number of iconographers create (often crudely copied from ancient designs) went from car hoods to bookstores. During the 1990s in Belgrade, there were almost no bookstores without at least one icon in the window—either painted by hand or photoprinted. And so the images to which one regularly paid special respect in churches and homes were increasingly found among scandalmongering publications and video cassettes with dubious content.

The social ambiance where an icon becomes a souvenir, something "authentic"

Figure 1.15. Unusual contexts: icons in the window of a Belgrade bookstore, grouped with video cassettes of Serbian movies, cookbooks, costume jewelry, etc. Photo credit: author.

to offer foreign visitors, is typical not just in Serbia. It is common in all post-socialist countries where Orthodox Christianity is the dominant religion. In the gift shop of the monstrous monument to Nicolae Ceaușescu's megalomania—the People's House (more about it in the following chapter)—which is almost a necessary destination for tourists visiting Bucharest, one cannot buy any brochure or book about that monument, or the people who ordered its construction, or Romania under the Ceaușescu couple. Not even a postcard. The only objects awaiting buyers in the glass cases are icons.

But probably the peak of icon misuse, as well as a completely new type of sacrilege, was their appearance on beer labels. One could almost say that to print an icon on a wine label would be *less* sacrilegious. Here are two examples of icons on beer labels. First is a reproduction of the White Angel from the "Myrrh Bearers" fresco in the thirteenth century monastery of Mileševo. The other shows a contemporary icon of St. Ilija (Elijah) reprinted without much skill on the label of Slavsko Piva, produced by Beogradska Industrija Piva (BIP). Those who put icons on beer labels surely wanted to establish some connection between this drink and national customs and traditions. But this is a false claim since beer brewing in Serbia is a modern import, not from the time they want to evoke.

40

Figure 1.17. A contemporary icon of Saint Ilija (Elijah) on the label of Slavsko beer (left), and "The White Angel" from a 13th century fresco in the Mileševo monastery, reproduced on the label of Bajloni-Weifert beer (right). After the Second World War, these breweries were nationalized and since the 1960s both operate as subsidiaries of BIP (Beogradska Industrija Piva, the Belgrade Beer Industry).

Figure 1.16. Display cases in the gift shop of Ceaușescu's People's House, Bucharest. Photo credit: author.

In the societies of the "Byzantine Commonwealth," icons were important symbols of faith inseparable from the liturgy. Therefore, one must wonder what an icon on a beer label symbolized in the context of Serbian society in the last decade of the second millennium. It was a society without any code of political behavior, marked by an ad hoc ideology based on elements completely lacking in depth and meaning. Therefore, everything was possible in it and nothing mattered. So, an icon on a beer label could be seen as just another juxtaposition in a vast matrix of arbitrary coincidences. However, if we put this phenomenon in a traditional matrix, we can see that mediation between the spiritual and material worlds takes place between beer drinkers and some imagined tradition. The ritual by which this symbolic exchange takes place is getting drunk.

2

Pathopolis

On 23 February 1997, scientists from the Roslin Institute in Edinburgh, led by Professor Ian Wilmut, announced the arrival of a new being whose birth might change the destiny of humankind. We should note immediately that this being wasn't human. Unfortunately for a large number of prophets, and especially for millions of readers of magazines such as the *Weekly World News*, and Serbian magazines like *Miracle, The Third Eye*, and similar mass-circulation publications, it wasn't the Devil either—at least, not at first sight.

The being was a sheep. She was named after a doll. Dolly the Sheep was the world's first cloned mammal. This success in the field of genetics brought us very close to the realization of nightmares which many science fiction authors have envisioned. The appearance of the first cloned humans was now just a matter of time.

It is an unsolved mystery why the cloning of people evokes the fear of a newborn who will be a replica of Adolf Hitler. Long before the successful cloning of a warm-blooded animal, films were made about the Third Reich's leader being cloned by his fanatical followers in Latin American enclaves.[1] However, according to some "reporters," the first person from the past whose clone will walk the earth will come from a completely different sphere.

On 20 January 2000, *Danas*, a daily newspaper in Belgrade, reported that "Swiss scientists are very close to the most sensational undertaking in the field of genetics. They intend to clone Saint Peter, Jesus' most loyal collaborator and friend..."[2] The text further states that the project will use DNA molecules preserved in the Apostle's bones.

----

1   For example, *The Boys from Brazil* (1978), based on a novel of the same name by Ira Levin.
2   Quoted from *Danas*, the most widely read newspaper in Belgrade. We can attribute the "most loyal" epithet to the superficiality of the journalists' knowledge of the New Testament, since even casual church-goers should know that Saint Peter denied his teacher three times when he was in trouble.

According to tradition, Saint Peter was the first leader of the early Roman church. His relics are in the Basilica at the Vatican, which was erected where Peter was crucified and buried in 55 CE. Scientists allegedly plan to insert a sample of his DNA into an egg cell and they claim that they've already chosen a healthy young woman to carry Saint Peter 2.0 for nine months under her heart. Unfortunately, her identity is concealed from the readers.

It is not clear from this brief report what Catholic Church leaders think about this revolutionary undertaking. As is usually the case with newspaper articles on the edge of credibility, one cited source is extremely supportive of the experiment but another considers it blasphemy. The article states that the Pope is "very angry and revolted." If that is the case, it is not clear who will unlock Saint Peter's reliquary and let lab technicians apply their scalpels and pincers to the holy relic looking for a high-quality cell. Maybe Vatican officials will decide to cooperate with the scientists to spite the protesters who, as the article states, demand an unconditional end to the project. Or maybe the scientists will decide to take Saint Peter's DNA without permission, conspiring with their countrymen from the Pope's Swiss Guard.

The scientists' quest does not stop with the re-creation of Saint Peter's body. Some of them expect the clone to retain Saint Peter's memory. Geneticist Ian Berkhof told the newspaper that "if this undertaking is successful, and I have no doubt it will be, we will soon know much more about Jesus and his work than we know now. We aren't creating just a simple copy of the well-known saint. The clone will be Saint Peter the Apostle himself. We hope to be able to stimulate his deepest memories using hypnosis."

Following up on the hope expressed in this story (rather than the fear expressed in sci-fi films), might there be some subject or group of subjects that preserve copies of memories that can be extracted to help us understand society's future? Is there an element that, by analogy with the DNA molecule, which contains all the information about yet-to-be-evolved beings, a particle which we could decode into a broad picture of the social organism? Not to revive it, but to see it, and not necessarily with the help of hypnosis?

Money as an Image of the State

Numismatists believe that by observing and carefully analyzing coin specimens and paper currency, one can reconstruct almost all aspects of the society that created and put them into circulation, not only based on their inscriptions but also by how they look and how they were made. This is because money is one of the faces of the state. We must not forget that apart from its economic function, money is a kind of *"Biblia pauperum"* [pauper's bible]. Even the illiterate generally understand the value of money. The target group of this medium is more or less everyone. And apart from unequivocal messages like the denominated value, money sends hidden messages. Rarely are those as obvious as the Masonic symbols on the back of the American one-dollar bill, a favorite of conspiracy theorists.

Money as a facilitator of trade or an intermediary in the exchange of goods results from the development of a market economy. In ancient societies, different kinds of goods fulfilled the role of money as mediators of trade. They could be considered a primitive type of money. (Interesting fact: the name of the national currency of post-soviet Ukraine recalls the time when the weight of silver was measured in *hryvnia*[3]). Primitive money was first used when people started to exchange one type of good for another, not because it itself could satisfy a need, but to serve as the means of payment for some third kind of good.[4]

In the evolution of money as a medium for trade, there was a civilizational turning point in the seventh century BCE: coins were introduced. King Alyattes of Lydia (who is thought to have reigned from about 635 to about 585 BCE) stamped his imprint on disks of electrum (an alloy of gold and silver). Traders in Asia Minor then stopped weighing each piece of metal because they trusted the Lydian imprint.

Compare Phillip II of Macedon's tetradrachm and a Celtic stater. You cannot explain the differences between them only by the different levels of artistry. The tetradrachm not only shows that the Hellenistic empire of Macedonia inherited its knowledge of art and craftsmanship from classical Greece, it also shows that as the ruler's portrait began to stand out clearly, absolute power over society shifted to him personally. The visual appearance of Phillip's coin gives the impression of a stable institutionalized environment, while the barbarian imitation (even though today we might consider it more esthetically exciting) makes us feel the opposite. By copying the template, they tried to claim some of the authority of the society that created the original. But we can also feel the instability and inadequacy of short-duration barbarian kingdoms.

We see a somewhat different background story if we compare Venetian coins from the end of the twelfth and the beginning of the thirteenth century with the first Serbian silver coins. In that case, the replica was remarkably successful—a bit too successful, as we shall see. Doge Lorenzo Tiepolo's *"grosso"* and Serbian King Dragutin's *"denaro grosso con bandera"* differ mainly in the titles and the identity of the

----

3   The *hryvnia* has been Ukraine's national currency since 1996.
4   Dragana Gnjatović, *Dobri i zli dinari: Funkcije novca i novčani isistem srednjovekovne Srbije* [Good and evil dinars: Monetary functions and the monetary system of medieval Serbia] (Belgrade: Jugoslovenski pregled, 1998).

Figure 2.1. The template, a tetradrachm silver coin minted around 320 BCE by Philip II of Macedon (top) and a Celtic stater (barbarian imitation, 1st century BCE, bottom). Photo credits, top: Vlado Kiprijanovski (photographer) and Maja Hadji-Maneva (author), Macedonia: Coins and History (Skopje: National Bank of the Republic of Macedonia, 2008), https://www.nbrm.mk/content/muzej/Macedonia_coins_and_history.pdf, and bottom: Auction VII catalog (Lot 18), International Coin Exchange Ltd. (Dublin: 2014), https://www.numisbids.com/n.php?p=lot&sid=720&lot=18

Figure 2.2. As if they were brothers: a Venetian "grosso" ("matapano" of the Venetian doge Lorenzo Tiepolo, top), and a Serbian "grosso" (King Dragutin's "denaro grosso con bandera," bottom).

ruler and the saint. There are almost no differences in the quality of material or craftsmanship,[5] although in the photographs here, there is a big difference in the amount of visible wear.

Until the 1270s in medieval Serbia, only barter or cattle were used in local trade rather than money. Primitive money in Serbia and other Slavic countries was canvas ("*platno*" in Serbian, hence the words "*plata*" [salary] and "*plaćanje*" [payment]). Still, as early as the beginning of the thirteenth century, Serbian rulers and the nobility recognized the benefits of using coins acquired through trade with other countries.

The first attempt to mint local coins was during the reign of King Radoslav (1227–1233). Radoslav's minting process, which was probably of small scale, depended completely on Byzantine designs.[6] After King Radoslav left the throne, the minting of money stopped in Serbia. It started again at the beginning of King Dragutin's rule (1276–1282/1316), but with the Republic of Venice as the role model.

Coin minting in Venice began between 1192 and 1202 while Enrico Dandolo was the doge, and stopped after 150 years under doge Andrea Dandolo. In twelfth and thirteenth-century Europe, only the dinar was minted, in small de-

----

5   In fact, Venetian coins were minted using silver from Serbian mines.

6   Vujadin Ivanišević, *Novcarstvo srednjovekovne Srbije* [The coinage of medieval Serbia] (Belgrade: Stubovi kulture, 2001).

nominations, which brought major problems in trade. Because of this, the appearance of "big dinars" (*grossus denarius*) was a huge success wherever they were minted. One of the first *grossi* was the Venetian *matapano*. The "head" side depicted Saint Mark giving a flag to the bareheaded doge, and on the "tail" side, Jesus Christ sat on a high-backed throne. Venetian *matapano* quickly became the preferred medium of payment in the eastern Mediterranean, since trade there was mainly controlled by Venice. Therefore, the first Serbian coins minted in large quantities (in Brskovo, Montenegro) were based on the *matapano*'s design.

Serbs were mentioned in Dante's *Divine Comedy* because of their money: in the nineteenth canto of *Paradiso*, where the souls of the righteous sing and fly and an eagle talks about God's unfathomable justice and the need for faith in salvation. The poet then gives examples of how rotten some Christian rulers were:

> ...two crowns have bastardized.
> And they, of Portugal and Norway,
> there shall be exposed,
> with him of Ratza,
> who hath counterfeited ill the coin of Venice.[7]

Ratza (Rascia in Italian) was the name of medieval Serbia's main administrative district. Hence the Serbian expression: "koji (dakle) loše upotrebljava venecijanski kalup" [Translator's note: in English, "which therefore uses the Venetian model badly"].

At the end of the thirteenth and the beginning of the fourteenth centuries, Venice passed laws punishing the circulation and use of Serbian coins.[8] Between 1280 and 1291, the law forbade money that *resembled* Venice's coinage, whereas between 1294 and 1322 the law forbade money of *worse measure*. It is a fact that successive issues of coins by Stefan Dečanski, and his son, Dušan the Mighty (Serbian kings from 1322 to 1355), showed decreasing quality and weight, which led to devaluation of the currency (inflation). This was most likely caused by excessive military spending and budget deficits, eventually ruining the money's value and contributing to "barbarization"—a pattern that links us unmistakably to the 1990s.

To interpret the relationship between a society and the physical appearance of its money, we don't have to go back to classical antiquity, to the Middle Ages, or look at the "greenbacks" which are a favorite target for those who despise the New World Or-

---

7   Henry F. Cary, trans., *The Divine Comedy of Dante Aligheri* (New York: P. F. Collier & Son, 1909).
8   For more, see Ivanišević, the chapter on "Vrednost srpskog novca" [The value of Serbian money], 36–37.

Figure 2.3. An icon of Yugoslavia's record-breaking hyperinflation in the 1990s: Serbian poet Jovan Jovanović Zmaj on a 500 billion dinar banknote. There is some symbolism in the fact that the face of the poet who wrote "Withering Rose Buds" ("Djulići Uveoci" in Serbian) marked the peak of the wave of "withering money." Photo credit: National Bank of Serbia.

der. There are many examples closer both in time and in geography.[9] First among them is the collection of multi-colored bills known as Yugoslav hyperinflation banknotes. These were printed at the beginning of the 1990s, mostly in 1993, the year that would be remembered in the "Third Yugoslavia"[10] for record-breaking inflation.[11]

But let us skip over the banknotes with the faces of renowned Serbian men. A few years ago, Predrag Čudić wrote an extensive and humorous essay about them titled "Serbian Romanticism."[12] The portraits of renowned men on the banknotes printed during hyperinflation contained, at least in the quality of their drawing, significant visual dignity. Nevertheless, they were put into a somewhat vulgar ornamental context: the used-up conventional forms and incongruence with the figurative sketches spoke to the social frame in which they were created.

----

9   All the data on banknotes from the Democratic Federal Yugoslavia, the Federal People's Republic of Yugoslavia, the Socialist Federal Republic of Yugoslavia, and the Federal Republic of Yugoslavia comes from Željko Stojanović, *Papirni novac Jugoslavije 1929–1994* [Paper money from Yugoslavia 1929–1994] (Belgrade: National Bank of Serbia, 1994).

10 Inaugurated on 27 April 1992, the "Third Yugoslavia" consisted of just Serbia and Montenegro because Bosnia-Hercegovina, Croatia, Macedonia, and Slovenia had seceded.

11 1993 ended with inflation in Serbia reaching an unprecedented 313 million percent *per month*, according to S. H. Hanke, "New Currency Boards Come to the Balkans," *Transition Newsletter* 8, no. 1, January-February (Washington: World Bank, 1997).

12 Predrag Čudić, *Saveti mladom piscu ili književna početnica* [Words of advice to a young writer or a literary novice], Library "Apatridi" (Belgrade: Radio B92, 1996), 143.

Figure 2.4. The premiere of "a peasant woman" on the one-million-dinar banknote. Photo credit: National Bank of Serbia.

Figure 2.5. Banknote issued in 1991 during the economic emergency declared by the much-hated Ante Marković. The "peasant woman" managed to keep her value—briefly—after 4 zeroes were eliminated from the denomination.

Figure 2.6. The second premiere pf the "peasant woman"—on the first banknote of the Federal Republic of Yugoslavia [1992-2003]. In lieu of a traditional national emblem, the National Bank of Serbia's logo is used.

Figure 2.7. Inflation accelerates: 100 becomes 100,000.

Figure 2.8. Further acceleration: the "peasant woman" on a 500 million dinar banknote.

49

Figure 2.9. Three degrees of the "peasant woman's" advance (on the back of the banknotes): From wheat to a sunflower, to the building of the Faculty of Agriculture in Zemun, a Belgrade suburb.

Although we can learn a lot from the renowned men humiliated by appearing on inflationary banknotes, the visual rhetoric of money was even more persuasive when faces of "ordinary people" were used: portraits of an anonymous woman, a girl, a young man, and a child. The smiling woman with a scarf wrapped around her head (whom we call the "peasant woman" for convenience) occurred for the first time on the one-million-dinar banknote issued on 1 November 1989 in the SFRY. After Prime Minister Ante Marković introduced market reforms and a new fixed-exchange rate policy based on the slogan "one Deutsche Mark for seven dinars" (against which most Yugoslavs united as one state enterprise after another went bankrupt even as inflation was briefly halted), the peasant woman was resurrected on the 100 dinar note in March 1990. And in 1992, she had the privilege of starting the banknote series for a new country—the two-member federation called the Federal Republic of Yugoslavia [FRY]—with the same denom-

Figure 2.10. The "weeping boy" also originates from the SFRY, on the 500 dinar bill. We will see him later on the 100 million dinar bill.

Figure 2.11. What do the backs of the "weeping boy's" banknotes suggest? First, that he fought with the Partisans, "through the woods and hills," as the old war-song says ...

Figure 2.12. ... then he went skiing (the backside of his first 1993 bill shows the ski lodge on Mount Kopaonik)...

Figure 2.13. ... and finally, he seems to have become an academic (the backside of his 100 million dinar bill shows the Serbian Academy of Science and Art's building).

ination, a 100 dinar bill. This was the first banknote without the much-hated communist emblem with torches, wheat, and the red star on top. Lacking an officially adopted heraldic sign for the new state, there is a freakishly stylized logo of the National Bank of Serbia next to the image. We will meet the woman with the head wrap two more times in the following year but the stylized swathe on the reverse side will change. How-

Figure 2.14. 100-dinar banknote issued in 1955 featured the "woman of Konavle". This series set the visual style of banknotes that would remain in circulation the longest in FPRY and SFRY.

ever, the theme stayed in the area of agriculture: in one version, there was a sunflower and in the other, the building of the Faculty of Agriculture.

The young man (whom we call the "weeping boy") was also born before the hyperinflation of 1993. He first appeared on 1 March 1990 on the 500 dinar note. We will meet him four more times.

But we can reach valid conclusions only if we look further back into the past: the money which was in circulation the longest in the Federal People's Republic of Yugoslavia [FPRY] and the SFRY, predominantly using variants of one color, appeared for the first time in 1955 when the famous "Woman from Konavle"[13] was issued on a 100 dinar note.

The series continued with other anonymous subjects (the reaping woman on 500 dinars, a miner on 1,000 dinars) and stayed in circulation until the appearance of banknotes with a different visual concept in 1985. An exception to the use of anonymous subjects was Ivan Meštrović's relief from the so-called "Vidovdan cycle."[14] This reproduction on the 50-dinar banknote satisfied the "Serbian-Croatian axis":[15] the subject is eminently Serbian but the author is a Croat who had different attitudes toward national feelings in different phases of his life.

---

13 Konavle is a Croatian region near Dubrovnik, known for the quality of the folk costumes worn by local women.
14 Vidovdan (St. Vitus' Day) is a religious holiday on 28 June in Serbia, dedicated to Saint Prince Lazar and the martyrs who fell in the Battle of Kosovo in 1389.
15 Balancing the Serbian-Croatian relationship was a sensitive but necessary consideration in the former Yugoslavia.

Figure 2.15. 50-dinar banknote issued in 1968 featuring an engraving of profiles from a series of relief sculptures made between 1906 and 1913 by Ivan Meštrović commemorating the Battle of Kosovo in 1389.

This axis of Yugoslav "brotherhood and unity" would also be satisfied by the personality of Nikola Tesla (a Serb who was born in Croatia), who would appear in this series of banknotes in a shape of a sculpture by Croat Frano Kršinić. Tesla would show up many more times on other banknotes. Writer Ivo Andrić also represented the republics' "axis of brotherhood," so he shows up on one of the last banknotes issued in the SFRY.

Tito's face did not appear on banknotes until 1985—that is, until five years after his death. This contrasts with the frequent use of his image on postage stamps, starting even before Yugoslavia's liberation from Germany: he appeared on a stamp issued by the other provisional state construct, "The Free Territory of Trieste" (1945–1954).[16] Tito's name rarely appeared on the stamps to identify his face, probably because his appearance was so well-known in Yugoslav society. On the other hand, it might be the result of European traditions in philately, pre-war Yugoslav, and even pre-Yugoslav Serbia, that the ruler (especially a crowned sovereign) appears on postage stamps without being named.

Issuing the banknote with Tito's image changed the visual tone in force for thirty years. It is a multi-colored banknote looking, at first sight, more superficial than previous notes, even though it had a watermark for the first time since World War II. Behind the frivolity offered by pastel ornaments, there was a cruel fact: the time of debt-

---

16 Tito's face appeared on a postage stamp for the first time on 21 February 1945. The painter Djordje Andrejević designed the series, which was initially denominated in Milan Nedić's dinars (Nedić was the Yugoslav Prime Minister who collaborated with the Nazis during World War II). In May of the same year the series was re-denominated in dinars from the Democratic Federal Yugoslavia. See *The Catalogue of Postage Stamps of Yugoslav Countries,* Vol. II (Belgrade: Bureau for Postage Stamps, 1976).

Figure 2.16. Tito's face appeared for the first and only time on a Yugoslav banknote (but not on coins) as late as 1985, five years after his death.

or's socialism was ending.[17] This was an insight of the very person presented on the obverse of the banknote. Accelerating inflation was starting to show the weakness of the country's economic construction. In addition, an embarrassing mistake marred the first batch of banknotes put into circulation: the year of Tito's death was indicated as 1930, not 1980.

Explicitly revolutionary symbols and slogans were missing from the dinar banknotes, from which we conclude that the heritage of revolution was simply taken for granted. However, the same cannot be said for genres of socialist development: the banknotes often feature references to agriculture, shipbuilding, or industrialization. We can, but do not need to, attribute conservativism to the designers of banknotes. In fact, the currencies of most countries tend to be dominated visually by combinations of ornamental motifs intended to thwart counterfeiting, while also evoking the skills of engravers from past centuries.

The denomination of the 1985 Tito banknote was 5,000 dinars. It appeared in the era of advanced "necrocracy," the rule of the dead President, at a time when the coun-

---

17 Socialist Yugoslavia had a higher standard of living than other Eastern Bloc countries thanks mainly to loans the country obtained from Western countries. Unfortunately, the loans were used to fund current consumption rather than being invested in infrastructure or production capability. This pattern continued after Tito died as economic growth faltered, labor unrest spread, and unemployment rose. By 1988, Yugoslavia had the highest foreign debt per capita of any European country. Glenn E Curtis, ed., *Yugoslavia—A Country Study*, Area Handbook Series (Washington: Federal Research Division, U. S. Library of Congress, 1992), https://www.loc.gov/resource/frdcstdy.yugoslaviacountr00curt_0.

try's political leadership wanted to solidify his memory and associate themselves with "the greatest son of the Yugoslav peoples and nationalities." In that period Tito's portrait acquired new public prominence. It had never been part of stadium decorations during celebrations of his birthday when the living "original" was still present. In a completely different way than Tesla and Andrić, Tito's face on the banknote satisfied a "generally Yugoslav" or "transnational" concept.

The next step up from 5,000 dinars, in currency denomination, was not 10,000, as might be expected, but 20,000, which showed that inflation was already growing. On the obverse of the banknote, there is a miner again. Brown and dark tones dominate the picture. Like the previous miner, the model's name was unknown (people had nicknamed him *Som* [Translator's note: in English, the catfish]; and TV shows and documentaries were made about him). But unlike the old miner, the new miner had somewhat generic facial features. The old miner was smiling, to show how happy Yugoslavs were with the post-war construction of socialism. In contrast, the new miner is pensive, frowning a bit, maybe even worried. The old miner looks the holder of the banknote in the eye, which we can interpret as expressing confidence and trust. The new miner stares into the distance. The way this archetypal proletarian is rendered seems to hint at the forthcoming chaos and disenchantment.

This series of bills started with Tito's 5,000 dinar note and continued with the miner and other anonymous characters on other denominations. Despite small visual

Figure 2.17. The miner on the banknote of a socialist society on the rise (1965) is looking right into your eyes with a smile. The face radiates trust and hope for a better future.

Figure 2.18. The miner from the end of socialism (1987) seems worried. His gaze is locked into the distance. Was he seeing something that those who had him in their pockets didn't see?

Figure 2.19. A gallery of the anonymous faces on Yugoslav banknotes in the year of hyperinflation (1993). Although there were two authors of these drawings, one of them being among the most prominent Serbian painters, there is almost no recognizable difference in style or quality: the subjects' feeling of loss and neutrality of expression dominate the pictures. That neutrality masked the intensifying conflicts of national and party nomenclatures which grew into war.

changes, this series remained in circulation until the end of the second millennium, though now serving just half of the Federal Republic of Yugoslavia.

As devaluation accelerated, the series of planned banknotes was interrupted with two new bills responding to the "war against inflation." As a rule, every country has sketches prepared of banknotes which can be put into circulation at critical moments. But the mint which in 1993 would be able to issue one series per week was not yet so well-trained. For the first time since the 1940s, explicit revolutionary iconography appeared on the currency in the form of images of memorials steeped in socialist modernism, the sculptural idiom of the 1960s and 1970s: Dušan Džamonja's "Monument of Revolution" on Kozara, and Miodrag Živković's "Monument to the Battle of the Sutjeska and Šumarice" in Memorial Park, appear on the backsides of the bills whose appearance coincided with the anniversary of the Battle of Kosovo (1389–1989) and the introduction of a new style of political rhetoric. Both memorials are embedded in amalgams of geometrical, floral, and geographical ornament. The incoherence of these motifs suggests an attempt to revive already dead values, to resurrect themes eroded by time.

Maybe it was a coincidence, but these bills also advanced federal Prime Minister Ante Marković's program of monetary reform, which included eliminating four zeroes from the currency's denominated value. Therefore, the designs appeared simultaneously in two versions, as 50 and 200 dinar notes interchangeable with 500,000 and 2,000,000 dinar notes. Spenders had to rely on their knowledge of current prices to understand which dinar value applied.

Figure 2.20. The banknotes issued in 1990 provide visual evidence of the radical monetary reform strategy of Ante Marković (SFR Yugoslavia's last Prime Minister) for turning inflationary money into stable money. These two banknotes (500,000 and 50 dinars) not only had the same design, they had the same value, and both were used for a short period interchangeably as four zeroes were cut from the denomination.

Figure 2.21. "Monopoly" money: Nikola Tesla on a poorly printed banknote with no serial number. One of the last scions of the 1993 hyperinflation.

Hyperinflation was the predictable result of the increasingly accelerated printing of banknotes. At the same time, more unpleasant color combinations appear on the bills and the quality of the printing decreases (at one point, offset printing replaced intaglio printing). Finally, the banknotes were issued without serial numbers, probably the only such case in the world.

A warning continued to appear by inertia on all bills issued by the mint stating that counterfeiting is punishable by law. But as the volume of banknotes increased and their value decreased, the whole country slipped into a situation where all laws became senseless. Since the value of what we could hardly call money anymore continued to evaporate, who would bother to counterfeit it? The paper that looked like money was just one of the elements in a complex system organized by the state to benefit the members of the governing oligarchy. In this way those pieces of paper acquired certain alchemical powers.[18]

But let us return to appearances and iconography. When the need for political correctness ended and the two-member federation of Serbia and Montenegro was created with a simpler composition of nationalities, portraits of renowned men who did not balance the "Serbo-Croatian axis" began to appear on the banknotes: linguist Vuk Karadžić, Prince-Bishop Petar Petrović Njegoš, poet Jovan Jovanović Zmaj, physicist Mihajlo Pupin, poet Djura Jakšić, Prince Miloš Obrenović, revolutionary Karadjordje, geographer Jovan Cvijić, etc. By the end of 1992 and in 1993 they quickly took turns with the peasant girl, the weeping boy, the miner, etc.—the nameless characters already familiar to the citizens.

The general visual impression of inflationary bills from the late SFRY (1945–1992) and early FR Yugoslavia (1992–2003) brings these products close to the paper tokens used in the game of "Monopoly." What is "Monopoly?" It is a game of hoarding money and real estate played on a board with dice and counters. There are additional elements of luck in this imitation of privatization, such as cards that enable social climbing and getting out of jail free, but it also has the possibility of sudden bankruptcy. If we add firearms, smuggling, and pyramid schemes masquerading as savings banks,

Figure 2.22. The Latin alphabet is missing from the banknotes signed by Bank Governor Dragoslav Avramović (1994), even though, as many forget, it too was a writing system historically used by Serbs. The switch may reflect a conviction that foreigners didn't need new dinars or that Serbs didn't need to deal with foreigners—at least not those who cannot read Cyrillic. One more premiere: For the first time these bills have the coat of arms of the Federal Republic of Yugoslavia.

---

18 There is an outstanding study of inflation and its connection with pseudo-private pyramidal savings banks: Mlađan Dinkić, *Ekonomija destrukcije, Velika pljačka naroda* [The economy of destruction, a great robbery of the people]. The first edition was published by VIN in 1995, later editions by Stubovi kulture (both publishers in Belgrade).

it could be an accurate picture of post-socialist Yugoslavia. The money appropriate for such an environment was already present.

"Avram's" dinar[19] stopped the rampant inflation. It debuted 1 January 1994 although the 1, 5, and 10 dinar banknotes would appear sometime later and without the signature of their creator, Bank Governor Avramović. The New Dinar's value was tightly connected to the German Mark and had only the signature of the vice governor on them. The change in name of the currency was de facto unconstitutional since in the Serbian Constitution, the monetary unit is specified as the "dinar," not the "new dinar."

The first series of new bills had minor changes in their general visual appearance, but no change of characters: the 1 dinar featured botanist Josif Pančić, Tesla was on the 5 dinars, and on the 10 dinars there was Njegoš, the Prince-Bishop of Montenegro. But as early as March in the same year, the transitional forms were replaced by more permanent designs. On the new banknotes signed by the popular Governor (who was invited into the Serbian Academy of Sciences and Arts because he got inflation under control), the 1 dinar banknote was cancelled and replaced by a coin. Tesla on the 5 dinar bill was rejuvenated, and Djura Jakšić appeared on the 20 dinar note. Two more interesting facts: for the first time on the obverse of these bills there is the coat of arms from Žabljak Yugoslavia.[20] Fact number two: This is the first and only money of Yugoslavia (all three states, in fact) on which only the Cyrillic alphabet was used.

As this "stable money" started to lose value, too, new denominations appeared in June and October 1996: namely, 50 new dinars (with Prince Miloš Obrenović) and 100 new dinars (with linguist Dositej Obradović). The other alphabet identified in the Constitution (Latin) returned on them, but the Governor disappeared and his deputy remained alone again.

Avramović's "stable money" was embraced by the public as visible evidence that the never-ending spiral of inflation had halted. But the release of psychological pressure hid the deeper fact that the introduction of the new currency was detrimental to the citizens' living standards. After a long period of empty shelves, goods became available again, but at prices several times greater in real terms than they had been (previous prices had been temporary and more or less fictitious anyway). Nevertheless, the initial popularity of the new banknotes brought about interesting uses of them in an electoral campaign.

In the 1997 presidential elections, the campaign of opposition candidate Vuk Drašković, leader of the Serbian Renewal Movement, was guided by the slogan "One

---

19   Named for Dragoslav Avramović, Governor of the National Bank of Serbia. His nickname in Serbian was the same as the Biblical character Abraham.

20   The FRY, 1992–2003.

for All." His campaign managers understood the effectiveness of subconscious associations. The charismatic "king of demonstrations" (Drašković) changed his image over time, from the untamed bohemian writer with long, tousled hair to a strong competent leader with neatly trimmed beard. For another round of vitally important elections (practically all of them were such in the 1990s), Drašković's beard and hair were shortened, and a tie appeared as a new accessory. The remolding of his image and three-quarter profile on posters and other propaganda materials were meant to form a clear association with Njegoš's face on Avram's new 10 dinar banknote, which had been in circulation for nearly three years. The difference was that the Prince-Bishop wore a traditional Montenegrin cap and costume.

Figure 2.23. Subconscious association: remove the traditional cap and coat from Prince-Bishop Petar II Petrović-Njegoš (as represented on the 10 new dinar bill, left). Replace them with a modern suit and you see presidential candidate Vuk Drašković (right).

One of the first steps in society's attempt to re-invent itself after the regime change on 5 October 2000 was the introduction of new banknotes. The new authorities obviously understood the symbolic importance of money. The dinar became the preferred means of payment once again (it had given way to the US dollar and German Deutschmark during hyperinflation, and then to the "new" dinar). This time the state was intent on making everything proceed without a mistake. But since the Serbian dinar (which supplanted the Yugoslav dinar) was not adopted by Montenegro, the name *Yugoslavia* gradually lost meaning in the two-nation partnership.

"Dinkić's dinar"[21] was without a doubt the first currency in this region advertised on billboards. The slogan went: *"A new dinar for a new era."*

All the famous personalities represented on banknotes in the 1990s were men. Aware of this fact, Serbian National Bank officials decided to put a woman on the 200 dinar bill:

----

21 Mlađan Dinkić was the Governor of the National Bank of Serbia from 2000 to 2003.

Figure 2.24. "A New Dinar for a New Era": it is not common to advertise banknotes on billboards. Still, as the first visible sign of change, this advertising action was well received. Photo credit: Dušan Šević

painter Nadežda Petrović. Issued in 2001, her banknote was protected with a hologram, suggesting that Yugoslavia had finally become a modern European democracy.

Linear gravure stylization of the portraits that graced all of the bills was abandoned. This was due to the fact that the bills were offset printed, rather than intaglio printed, making them easy to counterfeit with scanners and color photocopying, which happened very quickly, if we are to believe journalists. Watermarks were used for protection instead of complex ornamentation. Other security features were hidden codes and metallic threads embedded in the paper.

Figure 2.25. This 200 dinar banknote featured the painter Nadežda Petrović, the first named woman (not just a female stereotype) to appear on Yugoslav currency.

Figure 2.26. With the introduction of "Dinkić's dinar," photo-offset printing replaced intaglio-engraved printing.

The choice of motifs for the 20 dinar banknote demonstrate the power of inertia. As already said, despite the dinar being valid only in Serbia, it retained the name and thus the myth of Yugoslavia, and used iconic images referring to a state rejected by most of its citizens. It also used artwork by an artist who was now a foreigner—the Croat Ivan Meštrović. The statue of Njegoš shown on the backside of the bill was installed in the new Mount Lovćen mausoleum designed by Meštrović (replacing Njegoš's old and modest chapel near Jezerski Peak).

It is interesting that the view of Meštrović's sculpture on the 20 dinar bill "amputated" the eagle above the poet's head—possibly because the eagle looked like something from the façade of a Third Reich Security Office. This made it controversial in the late 1960s and early 1970s, a time of social and ideological turmoil in Yugoslavia.[22] At that time, as always in Yugoslav socialism, rational arguments were overturned by party politics. But Meštrović remained on the banknote, thanks to the popularity of his esthetic interpretation of Vidovdan.[23] The survival of Njegoš can be explained by

Figure 2.27. Montenegrin motifs on a 20-dinar bill not valid in Montenegro. The composition consists of a page from the Octoehos in Cetinje (former capital of the Kingdom of Montenegro), a view of Mount Lovćen in Montenegro, geometric stylization of the mausoleum designed by Ivan Meštrović, and the sculpture of Njegoš without the eagle over his head. The graphic stylization of Njegoš' right leg in the national costume, combined with a suitable view, invited certain lewd interpretations.

---

22 For a complete dossier of texts published in the press and in expert periodicals about the controversy surrounding Meštrović's sculpture, see *Art, a Magazine of Fine Arts and Criticism,* nos. 27–28, July–December (Belgrade, 1971).

23 As noted earlier, Vidovdan is a national religious holiday memorializing Saint-Prince Lazar and the Serbs killed in the battle against the Ottoman Empire in Kosovo in 1389. In the years before World War I, Mseštrović created a series of powerful sculptures (the "Kosovo Cycle") to commemorate this event and designed a temple to house them. The temple was never built.

the patriarchal and national-epic values still dominant in Yugoslav society.

It seems that money trouble is a permanent part of this region. The trouble can be divided into at least two types. On the one hand, there are doubts projected by the issuing country onto the design canvas as visual confusion. On the other hand, people cannot get enough money, no matter how it looks and how susceptible it is to inflationary rot.

Belgrade as a Patchwork City

Money is just one medium expressing a society's character. A much more complex but equally descriptive medium is architecture—or more precisely, architecture in an urban environment. Why urban? Simply because in cities space is regulated by government, just like money and the economy. Government influence is much less decisive in rural environments.

Cities are materializations of relationships in society. The influence of the state and its ideology on architecture and urbanism has been analyzed in many different contexts.

Figure 2.28. Meant to create scandals: a frontal view of Meštrović's sculpture of Njegoš in the Lovćen Mausoleum. Above the poet's head there is a large eagle which is omitted from the 20-dinar bill. Photo credit: Mark Creedon - https://www.polarsteps.com/MarkCreedon/3889812-europe-2020-2021/31185575-cetinje

ferent contexts. Speaking of Hippodamus (the first urban planner), Aristotle said that his merit was the recognition that "the city is the picture of its social order." Lewis Mumford made a similar observation: houses speak and act no less than the people inhabiting them. Mumford also remarked that those in power have always had a weakness for cities. Cities were in fact their reflection.[24]

The symbolism embodied in the architectural plans of totalitarian regimes is particularly suitable for deciphering thanks to their defiant simplicity. Thus, scholarly exhibitions of "totalitarian art" in recent decades have tended to focus on architecture rather than, for example, sculpture or painting. One such exhibition was the thoroughly

---

24 Lewis Mumford, *The City in History* (London: Penguin Books, 1961).

prepared *Art and Power: Europe under the Dictators, 1930–1945* at the Hayward Gallery in London (1995).

When studying Nazi architecture, one cannot ignore the fact that an unfulfilled artist, Adolf Hitler, was a dominant influence in shaping official visual expressions of the German spirit. Besides, like many past tyrants, he had a "court architect"—Albert Speer. In Speer, Hitler found a reliable implementer of his ideological framework for construction projects based on racial identity, neo-paganism, the resurrection of German mythology, and an all-pervading megalomania. At the 1937 Party congress, Hitler confirmed his ambition to build "the greatest building in German history." He stressed that mankind's most important cultural creations are made of granite and marble, because they offer stability in a world of change and transience.[25] In the same speech he stated that colossal works would "present the highest confirmation of the political power of the German nation."[26]

Figure 2.29. Watercolor of a Viennese street scene attributed to Adolf Hitler, who was known to have earned a meager living prior to World War I making and selling such paintings copied from postcards. Authenticating specific works by Hitler is no longer possible because of the large number of fakes authenticated by fake experts.

Such a vision of architecture as propaganda inevitably includes elements from classical architecture to evoke the durability of Rome's power. But a careful analysis of imagined or realized constructions shows that elements of modern architecture, and even more so, urbanism, inform National Socialist architecture. If one looks at Speer's North-South axis for Berlin, ignoring the scenographic and operetta layers, it is apparent that his concept was very close to Le Corbusier's radical projects.

---

25 Quoted from the essay by Iain Boyd Whyte, "National Socialism and Modernism," in the exhibition catalog for *Art and Power—Europe under the Dictators, 1930–1945* at the Hayward Gallery (London: Thames and Hudson, 1995), 262.

26 Whyte, "National Socialism and Modernism," 262.

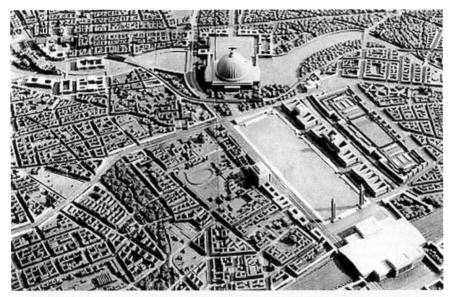

Figure 2.30. Model of Germania and Volkshalle, a project by the Nazi architect Albert Speer for central Berlin (~1938). For generations people believed that supreme power resided in the sky. The huge dome of Germania was meant to represent the sky brought down to earth, thus identifying Berlin as the world's supreme power.

The blatancy of the leaders' ambitions makes it easy for us to read the architectural concepts of totalitarian societies. When dictatorships tried to manifest specific national styles in their architecture, projects were always created within a limited time frame and often involving an integrated plan. That, too, makes exegesis simpler. It is more challenging to decode the message of whole cities that are sediments of a sequence of changing social circumstances through a long history. Belgrade offers such a challenge, but we will try to "read" it anyway and see what it can teach us.

Archeologists claim that Belgrade is very old. However, this is not evident at first sight. Of all the advantages a city can have, Belgrade is left only with a good location. Nowadays one cannot see very old important buildings there. To read Belgrade, one must start from a fact which many people overlook, either accidentally or on purpose: throughout most of its history, Belgrade was a military camp, a lookout station, and a border post for longer than it has been a capital.

According to Mumford, at the dawn of civilization, cities were created as representations of the cosmos, a way to bring the sky down to earth. Then, during their development and duration, they became pictures of the possible. Although Belgrade wasn't founded as early as the ancient cities of Mesopotamia and Anatolia, it is nevertheless a "picture of the possible." And since what is "possible" in this part of the world has

65

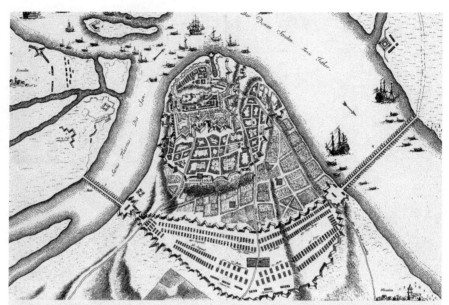

Figure 2.31. "Ground Plan of the City and Fortress of Belgrade in 1717" (detail) by Pieter Schenk (Library collection, University of Darmstadt).

changed radically in recent centuries, today's Belgrade is a conglomerate, a collection of bizarrely mixed and entangled layers.

When reading a city, one notices existing features more than missing features. And yet Mumford quotes Emerson, who believed a city lives through remembrance. In Belgrade in the 1990s, to the extent that there was an ideology at all, it was built on references to the past—remembrances. But many examples show that the references were highly selective, guided by what was useful for politics in the present; the rest was consigned to oblivion. It is important to note that the mechanism of amnesia operates not only on the ancient and currently unwanted past, but on much that happened yesterday.

The notion that Belgrade, and the whole of Serbia, evolved at the crossroads between East and West is repeated often in many different forms. Of course, such a simplified description can be applied to Austria, Turkey, the Caucasian countries, and sometimes even Russia. However, strong evidence for it can be found in disappeared layers of Belgrade architecture.

The history of Belgrade begins with the large fortress of Kalemegdan. Built by the Scordisci, a Celtic tribe, it was first mentioned in 279 BCE as "Singidunum." For centuries the local population lived entirely within its walls. After it was captured by the Romans, Singidunum became a border post on the military frontier between Rome and barbarian Central Europe. It was captured by the Ottomans in 1521, and recaptured by the Austrian army in 1717, when Belgrade was still little more than the fortress and its local resource base.

Apart from Kalemegdan and the buildings that were (or partly still are) inside it, one of the first large buildings built in the area outside the fortress was the so-called "Rice Palace" [in Serbian, *Pirinčan palata*].[27] It was long thought to be the residence of Prince Eugene of Savoy, who led the Austrian army to victory over the Turks at Singidunum in 1717. But a careful analysis of historical records indicates that he only lived in the area for a short time. A second theory is based on the observation that *"Pirinckhan"* in Turkish means something like "rice center," which suggests that the building (or an earlier construction in the same place) had an economic function that predated the Austrian victory. In any case, it became the residence of Serbia's Governor, Prince

Figure 2.32. A sketch of the Rice Palace by Felix Kanić as it appeared in 1860, before the local population had pilfered most of it for building materials. This drawing was published in the newspaper Politika in 1930 when what remained of the building was removed: http://politikin-zabavnik.co.rs/pz/content/beograd-koga-vise-nema?page=5497.

Alexander of Württemberg, until the Ottomans reconquered the area in 1739. They let the building stand unoccupied as its fine stonework was gradually plundered. Until recently, one could still find perfectly shaped consoles and capitals from the Rice Palace in the backyards of shabby houses in Belgrade's Dorćol district.

The ruins were described in the short story "Buena" by Hajim S. Davičo, an important but long-forgotten Belgrade writer from the second half of the nineteenth century:

There were dark and somber ruins of what was once a military palace resembling the ruins of ancient Roman buildings, something which in enlightened

----

27 Dušan Popović, *Beograd pre 200 godina* [Belgrade 200 years ago] (Belgrade: Geca Kon a.d., 1935), and various authors in Zdravko Antonić, ed., *Istorija Beograda* [History of Belgrade], Vol. 1 (Belgrade: Balkanological Institute, Serbian Academy of Sciences and Arts & Draganić Publishing House, 1974). See also Pavle Vasić, *Barok u Beogradu 1718–1739* [Baroque in Belgrade 1718–1739] (Belgrade: PhD thesis, 1974).

countries would still be preserved as precious ... If there is someone of today's middle-aged Belgradians who did not walk along the thick walls of the Rice Palace as a child and who hasn't once seen the moonlight over the river bed bordering Jalija[28] through its fallen windows, that person cannot imagine how terribly damaged is this part of Belgrade, which the rays of the rising sun illuminate earlier than any other. Created and gifted by nature with the most favorable conditions, meant to be not only a place for gardens and orchards but also an entrance to the town, a wonderful climb to the city, the most beautiful wharf on the Danube—the Jalija neighborhood has instead been turned into a storage area for the forwarding of all types of freight.[29]

Figure 2.33. The Bajrakli Mosque is the oldest sacred building on the territory of Belgrade today.

The ruins were finally removed in 1930. This was reported in a front-page story in the newspaper *Politika* titled "Demolition of the Old Pirinčana" and subtitled "Ruins that have stood in the middle of Belgrade for 190 years."[30] The Rice Palace was at what today is 10–12 Cara Dušana Street. A multi-story building was built on the site and is still there.

The heritage of Oriental constructions wasn't any luckier. Out of some eighty mosques,[31] only one survives today—the Bajrakli Mosque. Completed in 1688, this is the oldest sacred building that remains on the territory of Belgrade.[32] This plus two *türbes* ["tombs" in Turkish] are all that is left of the long Turkish presence and their construction of cult buildings.

---

28 Belgrade's lost Jewish neighborhood.
29 Hajim S. Davićo, *Priče sa Jalije* [Stories from Jalija], Vasa Pavković, ed. (Belgrade: Centar za stvaralaštvo mladih, 2000).
30 M. S. P., "Rušenje stare Pirinčane" [Demolition of the old Rice Palace], *Politika*, 8 November 1930, 1.
31 The Ottoman travel writer Evliya Çelebi (17th century) said there were even more, but he liked to stretch the truth.
32 Ljubomir Nikić, "Džamije u Beogradu" [Mosques in Belgrade],*Godišnjak grada Beograda* 5 (Belgrade 1958); Divna Djurić-Zamolo, *Beograd kao orijentalni grad pod Turcima 1521–1867* [Belgrade as an oriental town under the Turks 1521–1867] (Belgrade: Museum of Belgrade, 1977).

Figure 2.34. Sheikh Mustafa's tomb (before reconstruction) at the intersection of Višnjićeva and Braće Jugovića streets in Dorćol. Originally built in 1784 and restored by the Turkish government in 2011-12, this is the only surviving remnant of the place where the first session of Serbia's Governing Council met in 1807. The number "1389" scribbled on the wall is a political slogan referring to the Battle of Kosovo. Photo credit: Klovovi, 2010 (Creative Commons license 4.0).

Another complex is connected to one of these two *türbes*—Sheikh Mustafa's at the intersection of Višnjićeva and Braće Jugovića streets. This *türbe* is a remnant of the *khanqah* [Translator's note: dervish meeting place] in whose yard it used to be. The *khanqah* is important in Serbian history for at least two reasons. First, after his arrival in Belgrade at the beginning of the nineteenth century, linguist Dositej Obradović lived there.[33] The second reason is that in 1807 the first session of Serbia's Governing Council met in the *khanqah*.[34] A society that cares about its past would mark the site of such an important event. The lack of such a marker speaks volumes about the nature of the Serbian "national awakening" in the 1990s: it was just theater to hide the real nature of the regime which robbed so much that it lost any moral credibility.[35]

The search for Belgrade's missing elements could go on much longer, but what is left in today's urban tissue offers enough insight into what people generally call *genius loci*. Most importantly, Belgrade is characterized by uncontrolled construction and non-selective destruction. Different influences that are still present make the city diverse, so we can say without fear of contradiction that Belgrade is a collage or "patchwork city" with dissimilar building styles put together like patches on a tattered garment. The stylistic incompatibility of elements standing next to each other give Belgrade its unique character.

----

33 Serbia's first Minister of Education, Obradović was a key figure in the national and cultural renaissance. He co-founded the first colleges to teach teaching methods (pedagogy) in Eastern Europe.

34 Branko Vujović, *Beograd u prošlosti i budućnosti* [Belgrade in the past and future] (Belgrade: Draganić Publishing House, 1994), 162–163.

35 After the Serbian editions of this book were published, the Turkish government funded the reconstruction of Sheikh Mustafa's *türbe* starting in 2011. See Gordana Andric, "Turkey Breathes New Life into Serbia's Ottoman Relics," *Balkan Insight* (16 December 2010), https://balkaninsight.com/2010/12/16/turkey-breathes-new-life-into-serbia-s-ottoman-relics/.

The area around St. Michael's Orthodox Cathedral is a good place to start reading the city because it can be characterized as a kind of spiritual center. Designed by Adam Friedrich Kwerfeld, the construction of St. Michael's was finished in 1840.

Built in the Classical style with some Baroque details, it clashes visually with Princess Ljubica's Residence, which is across the street. Erected seven years before the cathedral, the Residence has some traditionally European features but it is obviously built in a Balkan style with Byzantine concepts bequeathed to us by the Turks.[36]

A third disparate element stands between the Cathedral and the Residence: the Building of the Patriarchate. It was built at the location of the old Metropolitanate between 1934 and 1935 based on the project of Russian architect Victor Lukomsky. It is yet another in a series of attempts to create the long-wanted "national style" in architecture by invoking the local medieval heritage.[37] Despite differences,

Figure 2.35. The Tower of St. Michael's Orthodox Cathedral is a significant vertical in Belgrade. Photo by Dragoljub Zamurović (Creative Commons license 3.0).

Figure 2.36. Princess Ljubica's Residence, on Kneza Sime Markovića street.

---

36 Vujović, "On St. Michael's Cathedral and Princess Ljubica's Residence," 176–179.
37 Vujović, "On St. Michael's Cathedral and Princess Ljubica's Residence," 176.

Figure 2.37. Building of the Patriarchate. Photo by Marko Djoković.

the Patriarchate's dome is an obvious quote from the symbolically significant Serbian Patriarchate of Peć.[38] It rises above a thick mass in the middle of the building which contrasts with the almost absurdly slender columns flanking it, while the eastern façade (facing St. Michael's) is divided into side wings, a portico, and a chapel apse. These internal inconsistencies, visible from both near and far, seem to reflect the Serbian Orthodox Church's continuing uncertainty about whether to modernize. The relationship between the vertical tower of St. Michael's and the squat mass of the Patriarchate is visually one of the strongest in Belgrade. We might even say this is the center of the city's spatial and stylistic collage.

We can get an even clearer sense of chronological and stylistic sedimentation if we look at the street between Princess Ljubica's Residence and the Patriarchate. On the corner there is the house of trader Spasoje Stevanović, with its playful contours and perfectly proportioned corner bay windows.[39] One can connect the façade with shapes from St. Michael's, but it is also clear that Spasoje Stevanović's house is visually and stylistically incompatible with all the surrounding buildings.

This example of the typical architecture of a new wealthier class stands next to the tavern named "?" (*Znak pitanja*—Serbian for question mark), one of the rare remaining representatives of nineteenth-century Balkan construction in the "post and petrail" manner.[40] Behind the building, in the place where until the 1930s there was the tavern's twin (another tavern called "Ičko's House"), a typical 1930s residential building was built, with coldly rational early modernist façades that had already become an architectural cliché.

----

38 An autocephalous patriarchate from the fourteenth to the eighteenth century in Kosovo.
39 Vujović, "On St. Michael's Cathedral and Princess Ljubica's Residence," 180.
40 Vujović, "On St. Michael's Cathedral and Princess Ljubica's Residence," 181–82. "Post and petrail" is a system of construction in which timber frames are filled with bricks or plaster.

2. Pathopolis

Figure 2.38. The contrasts never end: the National Bank of Serbia, designed in Neo-Renaissance style by Konstantin Jovanović, stands next to the SIP building, probably the most successful implementation of Le Corbusier's ideas in Belgrade. Photo credit: National Bank of Serbia.

Going up the street, another residential building fills the whole block. It was built between 1954 and 1956 according to Milorad Macura's project.[41] Under the rubric of "a higher living standard," the building was intended for officials in the Ministry of Foreign Affairs. This house, also known as the "SIP building," is probably the most successful implementation of Le Corbusier's ideas in Serbia. One researcher wrote that its "modernistically baroquized exterior architecture, with its jagged polychrome canvases, its proportions, the rhythm of numerous floral balconies and terraces, expresses the effort to defer to the laws of esthetic order of its surroundings."[42]

In the next block, the progression is completed by the National Bank of Serbia. This 1889 representative palace is the most important work of architect Konstantin Jovanović, son of the first Serbian photographer and famous lithographer Anastas Jovanović. The National Bank was built in Neo-Renaissance style with rustically chiseled stone blocks on the ground floor, lighter tympanums above windows on the first floor, and very light windows on the second floor, with an expressed horizontal division, profiled wreaths (with the final one being especially flamboyant), and accentuated portals.[43]

----

41 Mihajlo Mitrović, *Novija arhitektura Beograda* [Newer architecture of Belgrade] (Belgrade: Publishing House Jugoslavija, 1975), 99.

42 Mitrović, *Novija arhitektura Beograda*, 99.

43 Vujović, "On St. Michael's Cathedral and Princess Ljubica's Residence," 183–84, and Ljubomir Nikić, "Arhitekta Konstantin Jovanović" in *Godišnjak grada Beograda* 4 (Belgrade: City Museum, 1957).

In the next block, between an anonymous house built before World War II and a bulky building whose main façade faces the Belgrade "cardo,"[44] there is a department store called Robni Magazin. It was erected in 1907 according to Viktor Azriel's plans as the first modern department store in Belgrade.[45] Its decorative elements and glass façade make this building one of the most successful examples of the Secession style in the Balkans.

As we can see, this brief walk provides a conspicuous polyglossia: In just over 200 meters, there are six completely different stylistic formations, mainly in their most representative forms. Similar patchworks including additional styles extend beyond the city center.

Figure 2.39. The Robni Magazin department store (1907). Photo credit: author.

This unplanned diversity on the streets of Belgrade is overlaid with interventions of the 1990s, when "the Serbian people got their dignity back," in the words of an eminent writer who did not live long enough to see the results of his diagnosis. Of course, when reading the recent urban layers, one should consider all the elements: the war, extreme redistribution of wealth, pauperization, lobotomy by mass media, the behavioral models offered by soap operas, the criminalization of government, and many more. Therefore, after going a few decades into the past, we must describe the layer added by the decade following the so-called "anti-bureaucratic revolution"—which, if we are to believe the TV stations controlled by the regime, ended in a year of renovation and construction.

Urban Downfall in the Shadow of War

The word "pathopolis" is taken from Lewis Mumford, who took it from Patrick Geddes.[46] It originated as a definition of a stage in the development of the city of Rome. Speaking of Rome in the time of the last emperors, Mumford stresses the general pov-

---

44 "Cardo" is a Latin term used by Roman city planners for the main north/south street of a city.
45 Vujović, "On St. Michael's Cathedral and Princess Ljubica's Residence," 128.
46 Specifically, from Patrick Geddes, *Cities in Evolution* (London: Williams & Norgate, 1915).

erty combined with endless circus games. Half the city's population regularly attended the circus and theater arenas. During the time of Claudius, the number of holidays when the games took place exceeded two hundred per year. This marked the transition from Parasitopolis to Pathopolis. During the reigns of Nero and Caligula, Rome reached the next level—Psychopathopolis. According to Mumford, only one level was left, and Rome was to reach it a bit later—Necropolis, the city of the dead.[47]

There was a brief historical moment when Belgrade put out its hand to take the baton from Rome. If Constantinople was "the second Rome," and Moscow was the third (after the October Revolution, when Moscow fell under the control of heretical Bolsheviks and many Russians emigrated to the former Yugoslavia), someone had a wild idea: to suggest to King Alexander Karadjordjević to become the crowned patron of "the fourth Rome." The proponents of this idea must have missed another old argument: In the biography of Despot Stefan Lazarević,[48] a Bulgarian writer living in Serbia, Constantine of Kostenets (also known as Constantine the Philosopher) noted that Belgrade "was truly on seven hills."[49] According to Constantine, this was not only necessary to constitute a new incarnation of Rome, it was also a bond with the "eternal city" of Jerusalem.

Although Belgrade developed from a military station and was a border town many times, it proved a suitable place for the imperial pretensions of others. We must not forget Belgrade was the capital of the ruler who enjoyed being seen as some uncrowned head of the ecumenical empire of the barefoot, which was then called more innocently "the Non-Aligned Movement."[50] One can even see an echo of this superiority complex in an attempt by the 4th Congress of the then-ruling Socialists to promote Belgrade as the informal capital of the "resistance to the New World Order," or in the initiative of the political club called JUL to create "a permanent forum of egalitarian parties and movements."[51]

Despite significant differences, some features make Belgrade in the 1990s recognizable as a pathopolis: One could compare Rome's sadistic games and state-sponsored anesthesia with Belgrade's omnipresent "apolitical entertainment" TV stations,

---

47 Mumford, *The City in History*, 234.
48 Lazarević ruled Serbia from 1389 to 1427. Most significantly for our story, he moved Serbia's capital from Kruševac to Belgrade and rebuilt its fortifications.
49 Constantine of Kostenets, *Život despota Stefana Lazarevića* [Life of despot Stefan Lazarević], ed. Gordana Jovanović (Belgrade: Publishing Houses Prosveta and SKZ, 1989), 101.
50 The "Non-Aligned Movement" was a forum of 120 developing countries that sided neither with the USA nor the USSR during the Cold War. Its founder was Yugoslav president Josip Broz Tito.
51 Dušan Radulović, "Nesvrstani, drugi put" [The non-aligned, a second time], *Vreme*, no. 479, 11 March 2000, 40. JUL (Jugoslovenska Udružena Levica, the Yugoslav United Left) was a political club led by Slobodan Milošević's wife Mirjana Marković.

Figure 2.40. The new building of Radio Television "Pink" in the upscale neighborhood of Dedinje. The prize it won from a prestigious architectural review brought it to the center of a short yet sharp dispute because the building was erected without a permit. Photo credit: TV Pink.

which, interestingly, were owned and led by people deeply involved in politics—allies of the ruling parties. Prominent in their programs was music. But funnily enough, the few foreign music videos these stations broadcast did not originate from the countries to which their owners were politically close: There were no videos from North Korea, China, Belarus, or Iraq, just as the owners of these TV stations did not drive cars made in those countries but from the countries that would lead the NATO aggression against Serbia. The building of Radio Television "Pink," erected in the heart of a posh residential area, Dedinje, could find itself comfortable in any Western European capital. Its vocabulary of architectural forms does not lag behind the current level of architecture in the developed world.[52] Still, it is unlikely that a new TV studio could be built in some other city's zone of the highest living standards—without permission.

---

52 This building, the work of architect Aleksandar Spaić, found itself in the focus of public attention during the 23rd Salon of Architecture in Belgrade. At the end of February 2001, it received one of the most important professional acknowledgements from the most prestigious review of architectural creations. One jury member publicly distanced himself from the decision, explaining that "the building does not fit the surroundings" (which could be accepted as true), but also giving reasons outside the domain of architecture. Consciously or unconsciously, he focused on the investor, who was a media magnate of the Milošević era, as well as the values that TV Pink promoted. For some people, these considerations overshadowed the success of the building's design. Some even raised the possibility of radically enforcing the city's land use rules by demolishing this structure because it had been built without permission. See Borislav Stojkov, "U pohvalu nezakonitosti—arhitektura između estetike i etike" [In praise of illegality—Architecture between esthetics and ethics], *Politika*, 7 April (Belgrade, 2001).

2. Pathopolis

Most of Pink's programming consists of local and foreign game shows, talk shows with celebrity guests, phone-in shows, dance concerts, and music videos. And these productions, with a few exceptions and catastrophic failures, were mostly of high professional standard. Such programs, especially the lyrics and iconography of popular music videos, formed the values given by Pink as reference models. That framework is called "turbo" or "Pink culture," and serious studies are being written about it.

This specific model of complete and casual surrender to the imperatives of never-ending fun as the ultimate value was transferred to politics. Obedience to the authorities of fun slid easily toward those who fostered the carefree world—i.e. successful politicians. Together with criminals who were the other half of that world and consumers of their own TV shows, they were modeled according to the fashion imperatives

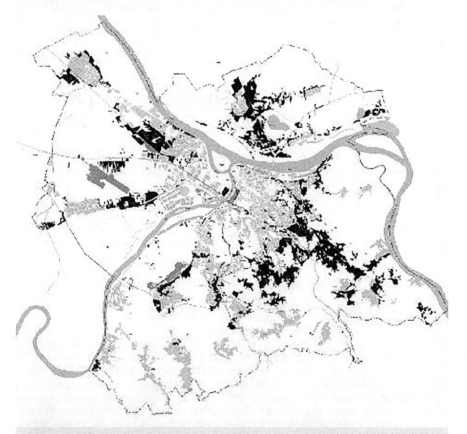

Figure 2.41. Map of Belgrade showing "informal settlements" in black. According to UN-HABITAT statistics from 2006, 43% of the structures used for housing in Belgrade were constructed illegally. Figure source: UN Human Settlements Program, Four Strategic Themes for Housing Policy in Serbia (2006).

Figure 2.42. A "street" in Kaluđerica, Belgrade's largest and fastest growing "informal settlement," 6 km from the city center. Community activists created a Facebook page ("Naša Kaluđerica"—in English, Our Kaluđerica) for residents to report problems and ask for help. This photo was posted anonymously in 2015 with the comment that streets in Kaluđerica are only asphalted just before elections and not again until the next election.

and values of the "Pink universe," which therefore represented an important propagator and validator. The superior technical quality of these TV productions, and their imagined alignment with Western role models, offered the illusion that the broadcasts were happening in some normal, even successful country, and not in a state banished from the world community, in which people scavenged through trash bins.

In all manifestations of "Pink culture" one can see an ambivalent attitude toward the city. On the one hand, it was glorified as the source of fashion, trendy night clubs,

Figure 2.43. Infiltration of the "old-new style" into the heart of the city: architectural details to spice up that cheap old box. Photo credit: author.

restaurants, and brands; on the other hand, it was presented as a dangerous and sometimes arrogant environment that needed to be conquered and everything erased from it that brought unwanted doubt. Therefore, the ideal ambiance for "Pink culture" was in the "informal" neighborhoods on the outskirts of cities.

All Serbs remember the moral of an old hit, almost a perennial, from the time when this type of music was innocently called "newly composed (folk) music": the song in which the singer curses "the girl from the city," the way in national epic poetry they used to curse cunning Latin girls who were also city residents. This stratum of the population, which in the 1970s and 1980s built its homes near cities but still far enough from them, finally had the opportunity in the 1990s to show in practice its repressed feelings toward cities by shooting at Vukovar, Dubrovnik, and Sarajevo. Although there was no chance to "move Pale to Avala,"[53] it seems that another strategy was used to conquer cities—the strategy of infiltration.

The City as a Forum

However, the city has a character completely different from rural docility and suburban disorder: The city is a forum created as a synthesis of an *agora* [a gathering place] and an *agon* [a struggle or conflict]. How does that synthesis fare in Belgrade?

The authorities tried to defend themselves from the forum created by student protests in the winter of 1996–97 (which usually began in the square in front of Belgrade University's Faculty of Philosophy) by deploying steel sheets as a barrier. The first sign that mass demonstrations could repeat in the fall of 1999 brought about the closing of the same plateau with metal construction fences, although no construction works started there months after they shackled the area. During the protests in 1996–97 and in the years to come, the "metal fence" role was given to police officers with their full equipment. At the height of the protests, the whole city center was a forbidden zone for both pedestrians and vehicles. There were also times when, despite the wishes of the inhabitants, areas of the city were closed for local residents and filled with more pliable people brought in from smaller Serbian towns—people used as scenery to appear to be supporting the leader and joined by an unusually large number of policemen in uniforms and civilian clothes. These officers took care that the new arrivals would not get lost in the city and become victims of aggressive locals. Such actions created traffic congestion during every congress of the Socialist Party of Ser-

---

53 Pale: a municipality in Bosnia under Serb control. Avala: a mountain near Belgrade. The author is making an oblique reference to the fact that many Serbian refugees from Bosnia flooded into Belgrade during the 1990s to escape the war, creating some tension between "the village people" (from places like Pale) and those who grew up in Belgrade.

Figure 2.44. Poster published during the 1996-97 student protests. Photo credit: archive of the protests compiled by University of Belgrade students

Figure 2.45. Police form a barrier to prevent protesting students from advancing through Belgrade. Photo credit: protest archive assembled by University of Belgrade students.

Figure 2.46. The Temple of Saint Sava on the Vračar plateau is one of the rare objects erected at the end of the 20th century that changed the city's silhouette. Construction began in 1935 but halted in 1941, until restarted by a third author–architect Branko Pešić–who adapted the plans of two pre-war masters, Nestorović and Deroko. Photo credit: https://commons.wikimedia.org/wiki/Category: Temple_of_Saint_Sava_front#/ media/File:Belgrade_-_panoramio_(10).jpg

bia or large gatherings at protest rallies and counter-meetings. Whole city districts were paralyzed for days. People could neither park their cars in front of their houses nor come and go when they wanted. (They also had to remove TV antennas from the roofs when ordered, so that a movie director favored by the regime could develop his epic cinematographic visions. According to a foreigner who was a member of the movie crew, this was unthinkable in any other European city.) The "reserved spaces" sometimes included a ban on the parking of all cars except those which belonged to members of the Socialist Party of Serbia.

Of course, taking into consideration other parameters than architecture, we are left with the question: How does Belgrade compare to other cities? According to research by the American consultancy William Mercer (quoted by the Sense news agency and reported by Serbian daily *Danas* on 9 February 2000), Belgrade was twelfth on the scale of quality of life in metropolises. Unfortunately, this was a list of cities with *the worst* quality of life. The list took four hundred indicators into account, including the level of health care, safety, public transport, possibilities to use free time, etc. New York City received 100 points while Belgrade received 38.9. There were about fifty cities whose index was above 100, meaning that their quality of life was better than New York's. At the bottom of the list there were only two cities outside Africa: Baghdad and Belgrade. Luanda (Angola), Ouagadougou (Burkina Faso), Kinshasa (Zaire), Bamako (Mali), Niamey (Niger), and Addis Ababa (Ethiopia) were ranked higher than Belgrade. However, life in Brazzaville and Khartoum was considered worse than in the capital of Serbia.

As we can see, the period that began with "bringing back dignity to the Serbian people" did indeed transform the capital. The number of large buildings erected in the 1990s in Belgrade can be counted on the fingers of one hand. One of those preceding this period—and the only one that seriously changed the silhouette of the city—is the Temple of Saint Sava.

The prehistory of the construction of this temple is long and complex.[54] The conditions of the architectural competitions (held in 1904–05 and 1926) directed the solutions toward the cancellation of every relationship with vernacular tradition. They also led the memorial temple of the saint who founded the autocephalous church toward the spatial concept of Hagia Sophia in Constantinople. Unlike Studenica,[55] Hagia Sophia has no direct relationship with the medieval Serbian tradition. In the second competition, Bodgan Nestorović's design won second prize. Among the other proposals was Aleksandar Deroko's. The church whose construction started in 1935 amalgamated these two solutions.

The whole competition, and the compromise which was the outcome, were topics of heated debate in expert circles,

Figure 2.47. Plaster models by architects Aleksandar Deroko (top) and Bogdan Nestorović (bottom) show their proposed designs for the Temple of Saint Sava submitted to the design competition. But the jury found all entries in the competition unsatisfactory. Five years later, they decided that Nestorović's 2nd prize design should be integrated with Deroko's entry.

especially among Belgrade's then-eminent modern architects. World War II stopped the construction and attempts to continue it after the war were thwarted by the unrelenting communist regime. Construction of the temple resumed in the mid-1980s on a dominant and historically symbolic plateau in Belgrade. For this occasion, the temple acquired its third author—Branko Pešić, the architect who designed the unashamedly modern 24-story office tower "Beogradjanka"[56] for the city center (built between 1969 and 1974). If we analyze the situation in more detail, it is clear that something

----

54 For the prehistory of the temple's construction, see Branko Pešić, *Spomen-hram Svetog Save na Vračaru u Beogradu, 1895–1988* [The Memorial Temple of Saint Sava on Vračar in Belgrade, 1895–1988] (Belgrade: Archbishop Assemblies of the Serbian Orthodox Church, 1988).
55 A twelfth-century Orthodox monastery in central Serbia.
56 "Beogradjanka" means "Belgrade Woman."

Figure 2.48. The Belgrade Palace (colloquially known as Beogradjanka), designed by Branko Pešić, the architect who also completed the design of the Temple of Saint Sava in Serbo-Byzantine revival style. Photo credit: https://forum.beobuild.rs/threads/palata-beograd-beogra%C4%91anka.4714/page-11#post-881103

that has had three different authors who worked on the same project, but neither together nor at the same time, has no single author as its creator. Therefore, we conclude that the largest building in Belgrade bears no signature of any master.

The fact that there was a sudden continuation of the construction after so many vain efforts by the church deserves comment. Despite the leading regime-applauding poet who shouted: "We are building the temple—the temple is building us!" and thereby unconsciously resurrected rhetoric from the construction of the Brčko-Banovići railway,[57] the Temple of Saint Sava represented the first visible sign of a break with Titoism in the urban and overall social landscape. In the great social regrouping, which was in preparation but still not yet visible, the only party in power realized it would need help from the church to navigate the turbulence that was imminent. When it allowed this construction, it got the patriarchate's help in the long run but in delicate circumstances. One could argue that the technologically innovative erection of the temple dome on the ground coincided with the swelling of immoderate and instrumentalized national enthusiasm. But far from it, this construction was actually the first trace of the break with Titoism in the city's visual identity.

The break assumed different forms and therefore was reflected in different ways in the urban tissue of Belgrade. The time of Titoism coincided with enthusiasm for post-war modernism. Every wave of modernization in the Balkan societies ended up unfinished, at least in the arena of architecture. Still, one might say that certain permanent and periodic campaign preferences of socialist Yugoslavia to be recognized as part of the developed world produced visible results that went beyond ideological

---

57 Construction of this railway in Bosnia was the first Communist Youth labor action after World War II.

Figure 2.49. The development of New Belgrade not only fulfilled the desire to create an ideal city of socialist modernism, it was also an attempt to finish and balance Belgrade's urban tissue which had been decentered by historical forces. Photo: Wikimedia Commons.

needs. For example, the construction of New Belgrade across the river from "old" Belgrade not only fulfilled the desire to create an ideal city of socialist modernism, it was also an attempt to finish and balance the urban tissue of Belgrade decentered by the exigencies of history. At the same time, this was also an attempt to join Belgrade with another historic urban core—Zemun.[58] Although all the most important administrative buildings of reconstructed Yugoslavia were planned for the New Belgrade side of the river Sava, the old part of the city was not left without representative buildings of modern architecture, both public and residential.

As mentioned above, cancelling modernism and its heritage was one of the ways to break away from the era of Tito. Without wasting a single second, the most important protagonists of this time would harshly settle their accounts with modernism in the press and in their memoirs, most of them having been secretaries, presidents of

---

58　Zemun is a town close enough to Belgrade to become absorbed as a surburb when New Belgrade developed between them. Its historical importance was as the farthest outpost of the Austro-Hungarian Empire when Belgrade was still part of the Ottoman Empire.

committees, theorists of self-government, Tito's biographers, delegates, and those who were "just following orders." As we would see, some of the cancellations had quite unusual manifestations.

The Museum of Contemporary Art is one of the rare edifices in the Yugoslavia of both Tito and his successors which was constructed specifically as a museum (between 1961 and 1965). Architectural designers Ivan Antić and Ivanka Raspopović used the privileged location by the river as best they could: They multiplied a crystal unit which is also the basis of the system of cascade distribution of natural light. In almost all reviews of Serbian post-war architecture, this building is recognized as one of the highlights.[59]

Figure 2.50. The Museum of Contemporary Art in Ušće park, New Belgrade. Photo credit: Museum of Contemporary Art website - https://msub.org.rs/zgrada-muzeja-savremene-umetnosti-2/?lang=en

At the beginning of the 1990s, during the "cadre cleansing of cultural institutions," the museum's director was replaced by a painter whose most important recommendation was that he had organized an art colony in his native village. The institution in which one previously could see exhibitions of international stature by Yves Klein, Emil Nolde, the Bauhaus, Fluxus, Robert Smithson, and Barry Flanagan (among others), almost immediately lost its curators, and its programs were quickly reduced to the level of a provincial house of culture. At the same time, signs in the Cyrillic and Latin alphabets appeared on the Museum's marble façades. Unfortunately, both signs had the same typographic error.

---

59 Mitrović, *Novija arhitektura Beograda*, 21.

Figure 2.51. The letter "M" was accidentally reversed in both the Cyrillic and Latin signs added to the Museum of Contemporary Art. Photo credit: author.

When illiteracy appears on the sign of a private shop, it can be seen as the shop owner's problem. But when it occurs on the façade of a nationally important cultural institution, it becomes evidence of institutional incompetence, and an implicit criticism of the state's cultural policy. We could be ironic and say that the museum's new management realized that the work they were exhibiting was not of museum quality, so they felt a need to convince people that the building was not, for example, a casino, department store, or grain silo. But if we avoid irony, we must conclude that putting a flawed inscription where the architects intended none to be shows disrespect for the building's conception.

This suggests a strange similarity among the republics of the former Yugoslavia, almost ten years after their bloody divorce: on the tombstone of Croatian President Franjo Tudjman (who died at the end of 1999), the letter "N" was accidentally inscribed in reverse, as the Croatian press noted at the time.[60]

Figure 2.52. Original form of the Children's Hospital on Tiršova Street. Photo credit: Milan Zloković (via the Milan Zloković Foundation).

---

60   Milorad Ivanović, "Feleriâni grob faraona" [The pharaoh's faulty grave], *Blic News*, no. 21, 22 March (Belgrade, 2000), 22.

Primitives may want to annul modernist architecture but there is a more persistent phenomenon: the defacing of modernism by the addition of building annexes. Let us start with the most drastic example: the Children's Hospital in Tiršova Street. Guides with the widest range of tastes describe it as a building which "takes a special place in the developmental flow of Serbian architecture of the twentieth century."[61] It was the work of Professor Milan Zloković and when originally constructed (between 1936 and 1940), it probably presented the best-realized building of its kind in this part of Europe.

Extensively damaged when Belgrade was bombed during World War II and poorly maintained thereafter, the annexes it obtained in the early 1990s successfully transferred it to a place where the architectural principle of improvisation is still dominant. It is significant that this major intervention remained anonymous: no author dared to sign the rebuilding of Zloković's work, which remains a clear example of the internal destruction of Belgrade's architectural heritage in the 1990s.

The dispute about this project emerged from expert architecture circles where such rebuilding was regarded as a crime. It was refuted with the pathetic explanation that children were dying, just as the regime-controlled media used the excuse that Serbian children were suffering, in order to justify the savage destruction of Croatian and Bosnian towns with artillery. Investors in the hospital's transformation hid the fact that it was possible to construct a new building in the yard, just like local investors in the wars on the territory of the former Yugoslavia hid the information that it was possible to find nondestructive solutions for all of the Balkan peoples including Serbs.

The construction of additional stories on buildings is a well-established phenomenon in Belgrade. The population influx was always strong in the capital city, and in

Figure 2.53. Alterred form of the Children's Hospital on Tiršova Street. Photo credit: Milan Zloković (via the Milan Zloković Foundation).

----

61 Vujović, "On St. Michael's Cathedral and Princess Ljubica's Residence," 290–91.

the 1950s and 1960s, many stories were added to older residential buildings. But from the perspective of the 1990s, the earlier interventions were modest and discrete, driven mainly by the addition of attics to undistinguished buildings with flat roofs. However, densification of the city was not limited by the supply of flat roofs or undistinguished buildings. Extensions were applied to houses from the beginning of the century, interwar buildings with apartments for rent, multi-story residential constructions from the 1970s, as well as those that were recently built. Imaginative and heterogeneously added stories even decorate houses on the main city square.

Figure 2.54. Extra floors added to a building in Belgrade. Photo credit: Instagram/malo_smo_nadogradili

Two Alpine cottages, surrounded by flowers, were built on the flat roof of a multi-story building which forms part of the first view upon arrival in the old part of Belgrade. These became symbols of Belgrade's epoch of improvised superstructures. In one of the numerous polls in which citizens mostly expressed disgust at this form of urban lawlessness, one dissenting voice rang out: it belonged to a lawyer with an office in the building topped by the cottages. The lawyer said that now he has no difficulty in explaining to people where his office is and the cottages provide a kind of free advertising for his practice.

Figure 2.55. As incorrigible individualists, people do not only seek greater height as the way to add living space. There are more imaginative solutions. Photo credit: author.

87

These two houses even provided an argument in a brutal campaign by the then-ruling "red and black" coalition[62] against the local governments led by their political opponents. But let it not be forgotten that this practice started long before red and black extremists ceded power grudgingly, under enormous pressure, after losing control of Belgrade in the local elections. According to the head of a city in central Serbia, it was a former Minister of Construction—a senior official of the ruling Socialist party, SPS—who allowed the construction of additional stories in the central part of the city. He changed the law on the construction of additional stories and the transformation of common spaces into new apartments, in order to legalize the illegal expansion of his own apartment. Such a moral giant now severely criticized the "urbanistic chaos" for which he blamed the later municipal authorities.[63]

Figure 2.56. Two Alpine vacation homes were erected on the flat roof of a multi-story building becoming the first sight one sees approaching the old part of Belgrade from the bridge on Brankova Street. They have become a symbol of the time of complete urban anomie. Photo credit: author.

On the one hand, cities are places that allow and reward expressions of individuality. On the other hand, they require certain standards of behavior, including respect for neighbors and subordination of personal desires to the common good. Therefore, two vacation homes on a rooftop present a picture of change in the urban fabric—a sign that suburban primitivism has started to infiltrate the city.

Somewhere between primitivism's attempt to undermine modernism by imposing additional unregulated stories and modernism's own banalization lies the phenomenon of construction clutter. Josip Plečnik's Church of Saint Antony of Padua on Bregalnička St. was built starting in 1930-32 though some parts were added much later.[64] Despite not being finished according to the plans of this great Slovenian master of architecture

---

62 Following the 1997 elections, the Socialist Party of Serbia (SPS), the Yugoslav United Left (JUL), and the Serbian Radical Party—the so-called "red and black" coalition—formed a short-lived "national unity" government.

63 Interview with Milena Milošević, then head of the Municipality of Vračar, in *Vreme*, no. 479 (11 March 2000), 20–21.

64 Vujović, "On St. Michael's Cathedral and Princess Ljubica's Residence," 294; Marjan Mušić, "Plečnika u Beogradu" [Plečnik in Belgrade], *Zbornik za likovne umetnosti Matice Srpske* [Fine arts collection of Matica Srpska], no. 9 (Novi Sad: 1973).

(the dome he designed for this church was never constructed), it is without doubt one of the most valuable buildings of modern architecture in Belgrade. Saint Antony's is also of great importance as a record of Plečnik's achievements: of his many buildings designed and depicted with circular floor plans, this is the only such work which actually got constructed. Local experts greeted this temple as "the first monumental sacral object in Belgrade."

Plečnik's churches and his other constructions are essential stops in design lovers' visits to Ljubljana and Prague. In Belgrade, however, illegally constructed objects surround Saint Antony's on all sides leaving no space for a proper view. The entrance hall, which is a masterpiece by a genius who almost handcrafted the details of his objects, can hardly be seen at street level.

Modernist architecture in Belgrade has not only been degraded by added decorations and functional expansions but by deliberate destruction. Serbian politics in the 1990s, based on conflicts with neighboring republics and efforts to spite the mighty, finally came to the point where most of the world became its enemy. The NATO bombing which started in March 1999 destroyed more works of modern architecture than all the enemy and allied bombings during World War II. The list of valuable structures

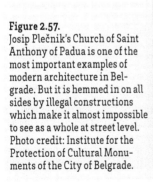

Figure 2.57.
Josip Plečnik's Church of Saint Anthony of Padua is one of the most important examples of modern architecture in Belgrade. But it is hemmed in on all sides by illegal constructions which make it almost impossible to see as a whole at street level. Photo credit: Institute for the Protection of Cultural Monuments of the City of Belgrade.

destroyed by the bombing is long, but on it a special place belongs to buildings of recent heritage, usually targeted because of their function.

In Novi Sad, the building of the Provincial Government and Assembly of the Autonomous Province of Vojvodina was hit. It was the most mature work of Dragiša Brašovan. Then his anthological Air Force Command Building in Zemun was attacked. In Belgrade they damaged Ivan Antić's Secretariat of Internal Affairs.[65] His two other buildings (the Museum of Contemporary Art and the Children's Cultural Center[66]) were collateral damage when nearby structures were hit.

On the last night of April and again on 8 May 1999, several cruise missiles hit Nikola Dobrović's buildings: the Army Headquarters and the Federal Ministry of Defense. On 29 April, the Avala telecommunications tower was destroyed. It was the work of architects Uglješa Bogunović and Slobodan Janjić. These were symbols not just of modernism in architecture but of life in Belgrade.

The buildings of the Federal Ministry of Defense were erected between 1953 and 1963.[67] With their shapes, the buildings make a sharp cut compared to the surrounding (also monumental) objects erected mainly in the spirit of historicism. The size of these constructions on both sides of the street make a clear spatial metaphor in which the cascading shape of the two buildings presents the form of a canyon. It was well-known that the reference was to the canyon of the river Sutjeska,[68] the most important hub of the mythology of the Yugoslav national liberation struggle. The materials,

Figure 2.58. Panoramic view of the damage caused to Dobrović's Federal Ministry of Defense buildings by NATO bombing. These were the strongest signature of socialist urbanism in the tissue of old Belgrade. Left standing as a reminder of the bombing, they were finally demolished in 2015. Photo credit: Adam Jones (Creative Commons Attribution-Share Alike 2.0 Generic license - https://commons.wikimedia.org/wiki/File:Panorama_of_Buildings_Damaged_in_1999_Kosovo_War_-_Belgrade_-_Serbia_(15803615912).jpg

----

65 Today known as the Palace of Serbia.
66 Then called *Dom Pionira* [Pioneers' house].
67 Vujović, "On St. Michael's Cathedral and Princess Ljubica's Residence," 239, and Nikola Dobrović, *Eseji, projekti, kritika* [Essays, projects, criticism] (Belgrade: Faculty of Architecture of the University of Belgrade and the Museum of Architecture, 1998).
68 Nemanjina Street is a traffic artery connecting the main railway station and Slavija Square, where vehicles "flow" between the cliffs of Dobrović's red canyon. There was even an initiative—eventually dropped—to rename the street as Sutjeska Boulevard.

combined with the discretely placed toposes of the modernist jargon, and the overall movement of the masses which (paradoxically) connects and pacifies the energies of neighboring buildings, make this complex an architectural masterpiece.

The TV tower on Mount Avala was an even stronger symbol. It not only made the local architects proud, the construction engineers dealing with statics were pleased with its logical yet innovative design.[69] The idea of a foundation penetrating directly into the ground was replaced by a tower standing on a tripod. The three legs connected to a long concrete box with a triangular section, which at a certain height was expanded into a "flying" core where visitors could enter the concrete vertical and take elevators up to an observation deck.

Just before 9 pm on 29 April 1999, the first of two laser-guided depleted-uranium missiles struck one of the Tower's legs, causing the whole structure to collapse. The goal of the attack was to stop the transmissions of Radio-TV Serbia, as the station's wartime broadcasts were the regime's most powerful tool of social influence. After the loss of the tower, a new system for distributing government broadcasts was quickly implemented using microwave relays.

Nevertheless, the loss of such an iconic structure was a huge psychological blow. If one had to choose

Figure 2.59. The Avala TV Tower: probably the most powerful embodiment of the idea of progress in the Former Yugoslavia. Photo credit: Avalski Toranj.

an image that embodied the idea of progress in the former Yugoslavia, this would have been, without a doubt, the Tower of Avala. It had merged with a story about a mountain in a nostalgic poem by Serbian writer Miloš Crnjanski and ebullient Slavophile inscriptions by Konstantin Josef Jireček about a mountain hovering over Belgrade. We should note that even without the structures erected there in the twentieth century, Avala was a symbolically powerful place that served the memory of Vidovdan.[70] King Alek-

----

69 Vujović, "On St. Michael's Cathedral and Princess Ljubica's Residence," 335; Mitrović, *Novija arhitektura Beograda,* 41.

70 Vidovdan is a Serbian national and religious holiday on 28 June, the date when the Serbian army lost the Battle of Kosovo against the Turks in 1389. This historical event, which stopped Turkish expansion into Europe, is an important element of Serbian identity.

sandar's royal sculptor, Ivan Meštrović, was credited with blowing up the freshly reconstructed medieval fortification on the top of Avala with land mines.[71] (Truth be told, the fort was Turkish. Therefore, some justification would be found by Milošević's television for that destructive gesture from long ago.) On the site of the fortification, Meštrović erected the negative of Cyrus the Great's Tomb: the Tomb of the Unknown Soldier.

The other part of the story about the continuity of Yugoslavia is told by the second prized object on Mount Avala. If Meštrović's monument, with only one granite slab added and discretely hiding the name of the donor, remained a military shrine for the whole of Yugoslavia, then the modernist needle of the TV tower was a shrine that covered Yugosla-

Figure 2.60. The collapsed TV tower on Mount Avala. Photo credit: TANJUG.

via with radio waves. This engineering marvel exceeded the scale of Avala: the tower was at an elevation higher than the tomb, thus making clear the hierarchy of two Yugoslavias (the royal and the communist).[72]

What made the TV tower's construction deeply socialist, however, was its basic needlessness and the megalomania it represented. For its function—signal distribution—it would have been sufficient to have an antenna on a metal pole stuck into the ground. However, in addition to its unique profile, the tower had a "panoramic" restaurant where people used to go as some kind of pilgrimage. But due to the lack of logic in putting a restaurant on a mountain tower, making it uneconomical, this hospitality business failed. (As Serbs say: "Every miracle lasts three days.")

But the tower itself remained as a sign of new, more communicative times dominated by television. It surged above the city and the clusters of holiday homes nearby. In socialist Yugoslavia, as well as in other countries of the Eastern bloc (where they looked much poorer and were called "dachas"), such houses were a form of savings, a store of capital for people who did not trust banks. The tower stood until the infor-

---

71 Đurđe Bošković, "Grad Žrnov" [The city of Žrnov], *Starinar* 3, no. 15 (Belgrade: 1942), 74–91.
72 The lower elevation of the royal tomb could be interpreted as inferiority to the communist tower.

Figure 2.61. Left: the "CK" building (headquarters of the League of Communists) before being damaged by NATO missiles in 1999 (photographer unknown). Right: the same building, repaired and renovated as the "Ušće Business Center" (photo by Jelena Irić).

mation pouring out of it grew from low intensity propaganda into war hysteria. In the end, the hysteria scattered down Avala's slopes.[73]

The recent building that Belgradians mourn the least was the so-called Ušće Business Center (featured on the cover of this book). Behind its "transformed" name is a 24-story building originally designed by Mihailo Janković, Mirjana Marjanović and Dušan Milenković, and constructed in 1964.[74] Few people remember its original name: "the Palace of Social Organization." Instead it was known as "CK." The initials stand for *Centralni Komitet* in Serbian: the Central Committee of the League of Yugoslav Communists. The twelve Tomahawk missiles fired at this modernist, visually minimalist, yet protruding building (thanks to its prominent location) pierced the very heart of Milošević's political power—his party's headquarters—which also symbolized the continuity between the "old" communist and "new" populist regimes. The "new" regime was allegedly pluralist and democratic, and aside from the police and adminis-

---

73 In 2002, the Journalists Association of Serbia proposed building an exact replica of the Avala TV Tower on the same spot. Radio-TV Serbia endorsed the project, helped publicize it, and organized various fund-raising events. Over one million euros was raised during the next four years and reconstruction started in December 2006. The new tower is 204.68 m tall, 2 meters taller than the original, and like the original, it attracts more than a hundred thousand visitors each year.
74 Vujović, "On St. Michael's Cathedral and Princess Ljubica's Residence," 321–322.

Figure 2.62. The Federal Secretariat of Internal Affairs on Kneza Miloša Street is one of the rare "socialist realist" buildings in Belgrade. An urban legend says it was built with stones from Tito's prison camp for his ideological opponents. Photo credit: author.

trative apparatus it inherited intact, the "new" one took over the "old" party's property, including this unpopular building.

Speaking of old, the last traces of old Yugoslav heraldry on the façades of public buildings in Belgrade were the bronze coats of arms on the Military Museum and the gates of the Kalemegdan fortress. They were taken away without much fuss right after the proclamation of a new, smaller Yugoslavia. The same traces of old Yugoslav heraldry remained on another building hit with cruise missiles: the Federal Secretariat of Internal Affairs. This building is one of the rare "socialist realist" architectural creations in Belgrade. An urban legend says it was built with stones shipped from Goli Otok,[75] the prison camp where Tito put his ideological opponents. It was designed in 1947 by architect Ludvik Tomori as the only building on which such a coat of arms sculpted in green granite was initially planned. All other coats of arms of socialist Yugoslavia on Belgrade façades were later additions to much older buildings, replacing previous heraldic marks.[76]

"Targeting" in the Urban Environment

In the sphere of propaganda, many responses to NATO's air attacks can be described as willful "self-targeting." As is generally the case with closed social systems, the message sent by the "targets"[77] was read differently inside and outside the country. Concerts in public squares and later on bridges in the evenings when the bombing

---

75 The Barren Island.
76 Marko Popović, *Heraldički simboli na javnim zgradama Beograda* [Heraldic symbols on the public buildings of Belgrade] (Belgrade: BMG, 1997).
77 Oddly enough, the English word "target" was used, not the Serbian word "cilj."

usually started were presented to the public and in the media as manifestations of the well-known "Serbian defiance." At the same time, they were seen abroad (and by some parts of Serbian society, such as the church) as completely irrational festivals celebrating the destruction of human and material resources. We could also observe the blatant hypocrisy of a criminal regime acting as a victim. Of course, this *innocent victim of a regime* had nothing to do with the large-scale expulsion and killing of other peoples by the Serbian army and paramilitary forces, or the destruction of property in other republics by fire or grenades.

Among the more amusing displays of "popular resistance" was the campaign of "yogi levitators" using meditation to deflect NATO aircraft. Huge canvas targets were also draped over the cages of animals in the Belgrade Zoo, to stress that even the animals in Serbia were ready to be sacrificed.

Figure 2.63. Large canvas target draped over an animal cage at the Belgrade Zoo, showing even Serbia's animals were ready for the "aggressive NATO war machine." Photo credit: author.

A particularly pathological manifestation consisted of decorating the bombed tower of the Central Committee's headquarters in Ušće with string lights to greet the year 2000.

On a more intellectual plane, a lengthy text drafted by doctors, writers, and intellectuals close to the Milošević regime titled "To the Coherence and Invincibility Committee" was published without a trace of irony in the weekly magazine *NIN*,[78] which likes to think of itself as Serbia's *Newsweek*.

The tradition of placing small and large memorial plaques was also revived. The memorial plaque on the fence of the factory "21 May" in Rakovica is among the smaller

----

78 Nikola Vrzić, "Komitetu za koherentnost i nepobedivost" [To the coherence and invincibility committee], *NIN*, 6 May 1999, 24.

ones—or at least among the cheaper ones. There was a grand opening to install it with ruling party officials present on a day which people were uncertain about whether it was still a public holiday or not: 7 July, the Day of the Uprising of the People of Serbia. On that day in 2000, the factory workers (who were not even informed about the event) expressed disapproval of the plaque, which described their factory as a tombstone and included uninformed mistakes, such as references to the "President of England" and the "Secretary of America," which made it even more embarassing.

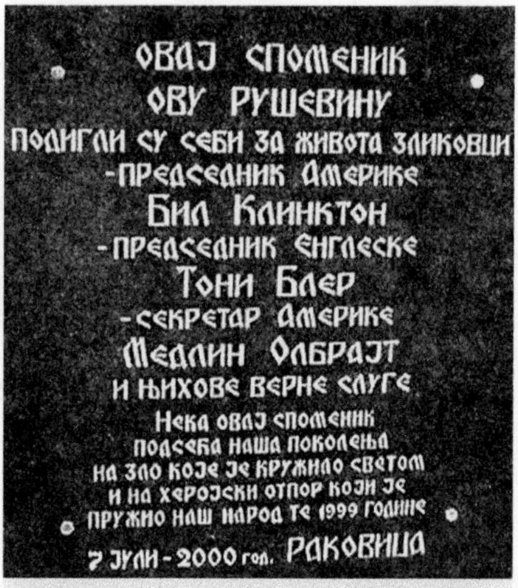

We Won (1): Medals as Reflections of an Incoherent Ideology

At the beginning of Radoje Domanović's *Stradija*,[79] after a lot of wandering around the world at the behest of his father, a traveler finds the heroic land of his forefathers—"the land of a famous and happy nation to whom God gave a great and rare kind of happiness: in their language, there is a completely correct grammatical rule making the land and its people proud: the letter *K* in front of the letter *I* always becomes the letter *C*."

Figure 2.64. Memorial plaque on the "21 May" factory in Rakovica typifies the low quality of state propaganda. Translation of the text:

"This tombstone, this ruin, was erected by villains during their lives: the President of America Bill Clinton, the President [sic] of England Tony Blair, the Secretary of America [sic] Madeline Albright, and their loyal servants. May this monument remind our posterity of the evil that circulated over the world and the heroic resistance of our people in the year 1999. July 7, 2000, Rakovica"

The descriptions of the landscape, the river, and the fortress on the hill leave no doubt: The unnamed capital of the long-sought-after motherland is Belgrade. The first contact with the inhabitants of the town is the hero's introduction into a series of bizarre situations. All the passers-by carry medals, diagonal sashes, and stars. Some "have so many of them that they cannot even carry all of them on their clothes, so they pull along carts full of medals . . ." The hero attracts the attention of the gathered folk: they are disgusted by a man who did not receive any decorations in sixty years.

Even a century after the first publication of *Stradija* in serial form in *Srpski književni glasnik* [the Serbian Literary Herald] in 1902, things have not changed much. There-

---

79 "The Land of Tribulation."

fore, Radoje Domanović's satires can still be considered contemporary literature: not only *Stradija,* but also *Vodja* [The leader], *Danga* [The stigma], and *Kraljević Marko po drugi put medju Srbima* [Prince Marko among the Serbs for the second time].

After the breakup of the former Yugoslavia in the early 1990s, the decorations of this state became obsolete, and the medals were not bestowed anymore. Yet the former Yugoslavia's coat of arms could still be found on personal documents (passports, ID cards, driver's licenses) issued long after this symbol had lost its validity.

But after the "victory" over NATO in 1999, during the period of "renovation and reconstruction," there was an orgy of new medals which were distributed to compensate for the historic break, and Domanović's relevance was restored. In the new system of awards, decorations, and honors given in the final years of Milošević's rule, a hybrid was created which did not take into consideration the traditions of the two countries that the Žabljak constitutions formed into the Federal Republic of Yugoslavia.[80] At the apex of the pyramid of new awards, there was the ruler's *Badge of Honor.* As we shall see, the way it was made into a collage reveals a lot more about Milošević's ideology than the creators of this valuable object could even guess.

The social history of awarded decorations is long: The first medals for merit appeared in antiquity and re-appeared during the Middle Ages. The oldest still-awarded traditional medals today are the British Order of the Garter (established in 1348), the Danish Order

Figure 2.65. Some of the medals awarded by the Socialist Federal Republic of Yugoslavia, starting in 1943. Photo credit: Pinki via WikiMedia (CC BY-SA 4.0).

----

80 Žabljak is a small town in Montenegro where the Federal Executive Council adopted a new constitution for a new state in 1992—the Federal Republic of Yugoslavia, which consisted of Serbia and Montenegro. In other words, these two republics of the former Yugoslavia decided to form a joint state rather than become independent from each other. But the delegates who voted to transform the SFRY into the FRY had mandates that were invalid, because they were elected in the SFRY as early as 1986. This was Slobodan Milošević's way of maintaining the illusion of continuity between the SFRY and the FRY as its successor. The Žabljak constitution was in force until 2003.

of the Elephant (established around 1460), and the Portuguese Order of the Tower and Sword (established in 1459). The French Legion of Honor was established in completely different circumstances in 1802. Our old medals (Serbian and Montenegrin) were created mainly according to the design of local artisans in famous jewelry stores, mostly in Vienna. After 1914, they were made in France and Switzerland. Between the two world wars, some medals were made locally.

With their shapes and elements, local insignia from the nineteenth and the first half of the twentieth centuries relied on the well-known European tradition of honorific decorations. The key element in

Figure 2.66. The Star of the Serbian Order of Miloš the Great. Photo credit: Robert Prummel (via Wikipedia, CC BY-SA 4).

nearly all of them is a cross, whereas the stars of the first two degrees have eight points. An exception was a medal awarded for a short time—the Order of Miloš the Great[81]—consisting of the Prince's face in an oval, with higher degrees having a 12-pointed star. The dominant colors and enamel on the medals are of red, blue, and white—just like the national tricolor.

The Order of the Cross of Takovo is the oldest medal of the Principality of Serbia. Proposed by the Minister of Internal Affairs, the Council of Ministers decided on 24 March 1865, to establish this order to mark the fiftieth anniversary of the Second Serbian Uprising. On 22 May 1865, Prince Mihailo Obrenović signed the decree establishing the cross and the silver medal as the forms of the award.[82] At the celebration held in Topčider, the Prince pinned crosses on the chests of survivors of the Second Serbian Uprising, which had started in the village of Takovo. The text of the decree did not describe the cross, but the press reported at the time that the medals were forged from Prince Miloš's first cannon and then gilded.[83] Since medals of such quality could

---

81 Miloš the Great (Prince Miloš Obrenović).

82 Mila Piletić, *Medalje jugoslovenskih naroda u 19. i prvoj polovini 20. veka* [Medals of Yugoslav peoples in the nineteenth and the first half of the twentieth centuries] (Belgrade: Military Museum, 1987); Desanka Nikolić, PhD., *Naše medalje do 1941* [Our medals until 1941] (Belgrade: Military Museum, 1971).

83 We can see that symbolic value outweighed the material value of the decoration artefact. But in the case of the only modern Serbian crown molded from Karadjordje's cannon, we have the "mystique of the matter."

Figure 2.67. The Order of the Cross of Takovo—the oldest medal of the Principality of Serbia. Photo credit: Robert Prummel (via Wikipedia, CC BY-SA 3).

Figure 2.68. The Order of Karadjordje's Star was introduced to mark the 100th anniversary of the First Serbian Uprising. Basically, it replaced the main order of the dethroned Obrenović dynasty.

Figure 2.69. The Order of the White Eagle survived the change of dynasties in 1903. Just like the Order of Saint Sava, it is mostly for merits in education, culture and religion.

not be made in Serbia, their creation was delegated to one of the best Viennese goldsmiths. Unsigned sketches were also kept, based on which one can conclude that the first Serbian photographer and lithographer, Anastas Jovanović, provided the conceptual design for the Cross of Takovo. This is confirmed by the telegraph correspondence between the goldsmith in Vienna and the Board for the Celebration of the 50th Anniversary of the Uprising.[84]

But there is a discrete contradiction in the cross's design. The medal consists of two crosses: one, covered with white enamel, is the Maltese cross, while St. Andrew's Cross is placed between its arms to commemorate Saint Andrew's Assembly on 12 December 1858. This assembly proposed that Prince Alexander Karadjordjević should abdicate and invite former Prince Miloš Obrenović to return to Serbia and assume the throne once more. The paradox of it all is that St. Andrew the First-Called was the patron saint of the rival Karadjordjević dynasty.

The Order of Karadjordje's Star is a very clear compensation. It was introduced to mark the one hundredth anniversary of the First Serbian Uprising but it essentially re-

----

84 Piletić, *Medalje jugoslovenskih naroda,* 21–32.

placed the main order of the dethroned Obrenović dynasty. As with the previously described medal, there is a certain contradiction. This time it is between its name and appearance. Although the Order is called a "Star," it is clearly a cross, despite having a circle of small rays between the arms of the cross.[85]

The Order of the White Eagle, however, survived the change of dynasties in 1903.[86] Just like the Order of Saint Sava, it is mostly for merits in education, culture, and religion. After the May Coup, it was redesigned only by changing the monogram on the reverse of the medal with the year that the order was founded. Like the two already mentioned, it also had a wartime version with swords. The newly formed Kingdom of Serbs, Croats, and Slovenes (later called Yugoslavia) took over the medal system from Serbia the same way it took over the Karadjordjević dynasty. The real and total change of the medal paradigm started during World War II.

In January 1942, the Supreme Headquarters of the People's Liberation Partisan and Volunteer Army of Yugoslavia (as they called it in the first phase of the war) established the Order of the People's Hero. On 15 August 1943, Josip Broz Tito issued a "Decree on Decoration in the People's Liberation Struggle," which contained the nucleus of the later system of medals. That same autumn, the Second Session of the Anti-Fascist Council for the National Liberation of Yugoslavia in Jajce (Bosnia) confirmed the Decree and started work on designing the first medals. Djordje Andrejević-Kun and Antun Augustinčić provided the sketches. The following spring, Augustinčić took the plaster models to Moscow by airplane. Based on those models, by the end of June 1944 the first series of partisan medals were fabricated at Moskovskiy Monetny Dvor.[87]

Figure 2.70. Order of the People's Hero, produced in Russia in gold for newly socialist Yugoslavia. Reliance on the Soviet model continued even after Tito's political break with the USSR.

One can clearly see the Russian influences: instead of a triangular sash (as with the Order of Karadjordje's Star), there is one with five angles. The stars are also

85 Piletić, *Medalje jugoslovenskih naroda*, 41–49.
86 Piletić, *Medalje jugoslovenskih naroda*, 32–35.
87 Stojan Rudež, "Medalje bivše SFRJ" [Medals of the former SFRY], *Službeni list SFRJ* [Official gazette of the SFRY] (Belgrade, 1987).

five-pointed. Since the system of medals in the former Yugoslavia was established during and right after World War II, the dominant artistic expression could be defined as socialist realism. As such, they very quickly became visually recidivist since as early as 1948 Yugoslavia's state art began departing from this idiom and entered the realm of socialist estheticism, supporting abstraction and modern forms.

The post-war medals also eliminated the system of ranks. Instead, there were distinctions based on gold, silver, and bronze wreathes. In other words, they borrowed the coding used in sports competitions.

A bit isolated and lonely in the medal universe was the Order of Saint-Prince Lazar.[88] Established in 1889 by the last member of the Obrenović family to mark the five hundredth anniversary of the Battle of Kosovo, this medal had only one rank: only

Figure 2.71. Only the king and the crown prince had the right to wear the necklace and medal of the Order of Saint-Prince Lazar. Photo credit: Kolomaznik (Wikimedia Commons, CC BY-SA 4.0).

the king and the crown prince of full age had the right to wear it.The creation of the conceptual design for this medal was given to Mihailo Valtrović, the first educated researcher of Serbian medieval antiquities, founder of the magazine *Starinar*, director of the National Museum, and leading advisor on ceremonies in both the Obrenović and Karadjordjević courts. At the time, the crown did not exist as an artifact. It showed up after 1903 for the coronation of Petar I Karadjordjević. On the medal of Prince Lazar, the crown was shaped like a Byzantine dome *stemma*. Creation of the medal was not delegated to the Viennese workshops where all other medals had been made. Instead, either one or two copies of this necklace (we cannot say for sure) were made by Nicolay & Duncker, a famous manufacturer of gold jewelry from the city of Hanau in Germany.[89]

----

88 Piletić, *Medalje jugoslovenskih naroda*, 38–40.
89 Since the medal was to be worn by the king and the crown prince of full age, it is possible that two copies of the necklace were made. Still, considering the value of the materials and the cost of production, it is hard to say today if there was another in addition to the one seen in royal portraits. A copy worn by the royals was exhibited in the military museum in Kalemegdan. In October 1944 it disappeared, together with other valuable objects.

2. Pathopolis

As the president of Yugoslavia, Josip Broz Tito had the personal flag of a sovereign. Conceptually, this flag was the same type as that of the pre-war Yugoslav kings from the Karadjordjević family. It was square, with the same colors as the national tricolor, with a trim consisting of multiple triangles in the same colors (blue, white, and red). The only difference was that in the middle of the white area there was the coat of arms of the new Yugoslavia with five and later six torches. As a Marshal, Tito wore the marshal's insignia, which in theory, others could also wear if they attained that highest rank. According to the Medal Award Act at least, there was no decoration of honor which only he had the right to wear as leader of the country.

However, at the beginning of 2001, a Belgrade tabloid revealed that in the project to redesign the state symbols and decorations of honor, there was one which was unfamiliar to the public:

> Without question former President of the Federal Republic of Yugoslavia Slobodan Milošević, in November 1999, hung on his own chest the Medal of Jugoslavia weighing 637 grams of gold.[90]

The phrase "without question" in that sentence catches the eye as an unconscious motto of the entire Milošević era, acknowledging the oriental non-transparency of his despotic rule. The text then explains that the medal's value is estimated to be about 30,000 Deutsche Marks and consists of a necklace and a star:

> The necklace is made of 14-karat gold and consists of twenty identical 27x27 mm pieces on which there are the monogram and coat of arms of the Federal Republic of Yugoslavia (placed one after another), then a central holder 41x41 mm in size on which a 21x21 mm monogram is mounted. The integral parts are connected in a chain, the total length of which is 110 cm.

The conceptual designs of the necklace and star were taken over from the medal system of the former SFRY but with certain changes: The SFRY coat of arms was replaced with the FRY coat of arms on a red enameled base. On the medal star, ten diamonds 2.7 mm in radius were implanted along with five zircons 3 mm in radius.

Further along in the text one learned that since the Institute for Manufacturing Banknotes and Coins did not have a developed capability to process gold, they partnered with a jewelry manufacturer named "Majdanpek" for this project.

---

90 *Blic*, Belgrade, 16 January 2001, 6.

Finally, the article implied that there was a certain Law on FRY Medals stipulating that this decoration of honor was automatically given to the President of the FRY at the start of his term—even though this law seems to have been adopted after Slobodan Milošević took office. It did not indicate if he was obliged to give this state jewelry back when his mandate ended.

We can see from the precise published description that, like the rest of the medal system, but also like the ideological framework of Milošević's governance as a whole, completely incompatible elements were amalgamated. The very need to introduce a sovereign medal on a necklace says enough about the self-regard of the person possessing it, which exceeded even Tito's.

We can add that the pendant hanging from the chain is most likely a rudimentary (and heraldically remodeled) imitation of the Order of the Great Yugoslav Star which never hung on the chest of a foreign sovereign who was a real friend of our nationalities and peoples. Its overall appearance seems to have been established by the last member of the Obrenović royal family but the medal was also worn by the Karadjordjević family. From all this, we can conclude it is an example of a medallion collaged together from scraps just like the whole heraldic and medal system of the time, which says a lot about the scrappy and inconsistent ideological system causing it.

Almost all post-socialist countries, including the countries close to Serbia (like

Figure 2.72. Order of the Great Yugoslav Star. Photo credit: Borodun (via WikiMedia Commons (CC BY-SA 4.0).

Figure 2.73. Serbia's heraldic coat of arms (1947–2004), designed by Đorđe Andrejević-Kun.

Slovenia and Croatia), created visual identities with state symbols as one of the first steps after becoming independent. Still, a long time after the dissolution of the former Yugoslavia, the country which remained afterward lacked such a set of symbols. This was a country with an unclear name, unestablished borders, and an anthem that caused at least half its citizens to hoot and whistle when it was performed. It had a flag from which the red star was removed in a basically unlawful way, despite there being an almost universal consensus. And its provisional federal and republic coats of arms were remnants of the former socialist times (with two sheaves of wheat, a star, and a cog wheel). Thus, the Serbs began the third millennium.

What we could only imagine or guess at from descriptions in the press was confirmed when the public was finally able to see Milošević's Order of Yugoslavia—under very strange circumstances. As a kind of afterthought to a press conference hosted by the Republic Ministry of Internal Affairs on 13 June 2001, a box with the gold chain was presented. The topic of the press conference was how to clarify the relationship between the Serbian Army and the police regarding responsibility for crimes committed against Albanians in Kosovo before and during the NATO intervention, as mass graves were being discovered one after another. And so, the precious symbol of power found itself right next to its frightful consequences: a refrigerator truck with eighty-six human corpses sunk in the Danube near a police training center in Batajnica.[91]

Unfortunately, the public will never know if the creators of this unique hybrid of pre-war and post-war state jewelry also wanted to emulate the old law limiting possession of the Order of Prince Lazar. Since the badge of the Order was also for the crown prince, maybe a copy was supposed to be given to Marko Milošević.[92] The badge's appearance is completely consistent with the taste of the social circles in which Milošević Junior moved. Gold chains were a status symbol of "tough guys" from Belgrade: the more gold you had, the better. It is hard to imagine that an ambitious and adventurous young man like Milošević's son could find a better status symbol than a gold necklace weighing nearly 700 grams with a pendant decorated with diamonds.[93] But things did not turn out well for the ruling family.

----

91 Batajnica is a village that became a remote part of Belgrade. See the BBC Monitoring Service report about the news conference in "Serbian Minister Comments on Exhumed Bodies," reprinted in *Global Policy Forum*, 13 June 2001, https://archive.globalpolicy.org/intljustice/tribunals/2001/0613yugo.htm.

92 Slobodan Milošević's son, about whose privileged success his mother boasted.

93 On the same day that the newspapers reported on the Interior Ministry's press conference, one of the newspapers ran an article headlined: "The President without the Badge" (*Glas javnosti*, 14 June 2001). The reporter dryly stated that Milošević's successor would not wear the badge on a necklace because a recent amendment to the FRY's Medal Award Act had erased this provision. Surely it was just a coincidence.

New Houses for New People

As already mentioned, at the time of misery prevalent in the 1990s, Belgrade did not get many new public buildings. The same cannot be said for private construction initiatives. This applies especially to the thin layer of society which realized that the dark times of war are the best for putting scruples aside and making money. All kinds of war profiteers, government commissioners for dirty business, happy winners of favorable loans or various import quotas, informants, and local mercenaries found it was the perfect time to build a house.

Not even in the shadow of the bombing did people stop constructing healthy, good-looking, and tough houses for healthy, good-looking, and tough people—the people of a new time. Let us not forget that the "BambiLand" amusement park[94] in Požarevac, owned by the young ambitious businessman Marko Milošević, opened while the residents of Yugoslavia were experiencing tense and sleepless nights.

There was also a massacre of modern architecture in the location which is certainly the most desirable in Belgrade—the neighborhood known as Dedinje. Interwar villas were "redesigned" according to the requirements of modern times and some flat roofs were slanted. Some art studios on Senjak Hill built in the 1960s not only changed their owners but also their appearance and purpose. According to their new owners' requirements, they mostly turned into residences with tall fences in Serbian-Roman-Latin-American-dictator style.

Figure 2.74. Hiding the grandeur of one's house is an established trope in societies with large disparities in wealth. Such disparities are sometimes misunderstood as the mark of a high degree of economic development. Photo credit: author.

---

94 BambiPark (or BambiLand in English) is an amusement park in Slobodan Milošević's hometown. Funded by the Municipality of Požarevac and the Bambi biscuits factory, it was built as an imitation of Disneyland. Slobodan Milošević opened it before the 2000 elections and his son Marko managed it until his father's extradition to the ICTY Tribunal in the Hague in 2001.

Buildings with flat roofs in the modernist idiom are perfect for partition and the addition of more floors. A flat roof is not just a structural decision. It identifies the owner as part of an international movement, the living current of architectural style.[95] It was an obvious choice between the two world wars when most of these villas were created.

On the other hand, the reshaping of villas on Dedinje, along with the addition of nonflat roofs, could be seen as a visible contribution to Serbia's rejection of modern Western norms and the "New World Order." By deforming houses, a new relationship with the local was established.

Dedinje was one of the most desirable residential areas for the new elite who unscrupulously, and sometimes with threats of violence, pushed out the remaining members of the population that built villas before World War II. They even pushed out the heirs of those who, wearing Partisan uniforms, effectively restructured the original population of Dedinje in 1945.[96] Thus, Dedinje clearly shows the microgeography of power in Serbian society at the turn of the third millennium as it did in earlier years.

Unfortunately, the most notable examples of the new stylistic expressions in Dedinje's architecture are usually inaccessible to those who want to document them photographically, because roving police units protect the area and react negatively to strangers with cameras.

Figure 2.75. A villa in Dedinje "redesigned" according to the requirements of modern times. A few villas under state protection were irretrievably destroyed with such "embellishments." Photo credit: author.

---

95 Ljiljana Blagojević, "Moderna kuća u Beogradu (1920–1941)" [The modern house in Belgrade (1920–1941)], published by Zadužbina Andrejević (Belgrade: Biblioteka Akademija, 2000), in Serbian with an English summary.

96 Some communists confiscated private properties after World War II and moved into old Belgrade villas.

Figure 2.76. Built in the 1960s, art studios on Senjak (a hill near Dedinje, now full of mansions and embassies) changed their owners as well as their appearance and purpose. Photo credit: author.

Figure 2.77. Apart from the benefit of drainage, a slanted roof gives a house a more traditional look. Photo credit: author.

Figure 2.78. A large house increases the owner's social status. Photo credit: author.

The largest houses belong to post-socialist magnates and powerful families. So, this subcategory could be named the "Karić style."[97] The Karićs have devastated a number of houses with partition walls and the construction of additional stories and

---

97 The Karić brothers were especially close to the Miloševićs, which gave them unique opportunities to develop profitable businesses in banking, manufacturing, broadcasting, real estate, telecommunications, etc. By the mid-1990s they were said to be the richest family in Yugoslavia.

balustrades, changing the profile of this part of Belgrade, including a few villas protected by law. The public scandal about a revoked authorization for wall paintings in one of their palaces gave the public a brief glimpse of their lifestyle—if not to see the unfinished bad art, then at least to learn about the planned renovations. It seems that the female artist they engaged suffered a range of humiliations when she was judged not good enough by her employers and their artistic advisors. Therefore, for the exterior of one of their palaces, they chose a somewhat better creator: Michelangelo Buonarroti. As seen from above the semi-fortress wall, their balcony is decorated with casts of Michelangelo's David and the an-

Figure 2.79. A wrought iron gate bigger than a house. Photo credit: author.

tique sculpture of goddess Aphrodite. And to remember better this meeting between the Old Testament, Renaissance, and Hellenic traditions on the balcony's balustrade, everything is doubled.

Instead of a detailed analysis of the giant residences built for the Karić family, it is enough to see their family/corporate coat of arms. One detail that stands out immediately is the date "1763," featured above the word "Peć" in the center of the em-

Figure 2.80. Casts of Michelangelo's David and a Greek sculpture of Aphrodite adorn the balcony of a Karić mansion in Dedinje. Photo credit: author.

Figure 2.81. The Karić family's coat of arms. Note the date "1763,"suggesting the design is 250 years old.

Figure 2.82. Evidence of a centuries-old connection between the Ming and Karić dynasties? Chinese vases with a Serbian family's coat of arms in the window of an antique store/branch bank. Photo credit: author.

blem. In 1763, heraldic traditions barely existed for Serbs, and in Peć (the Karićs' home town in Kosovo) heraldry was as common as internal combustion engines in Aztec villages. The Karić family's pretense of antique nobility is hardly credible.

The "mishmash of signs" continues with the Karić family coat of arms appearing on a Chinese vase in the window of an antique shop/branch bank on Kralja Petra Street. There, fake heraldry finds support from a fake antique, thus closing a circle and sealing the bond of friendship between the Karić and Ming dynasties.

Not only the social class which "fared well" under Milošević, but the whole of Serbian society gradually found itself in an environment where almost all status symbols, and even most consumer goods, were fake. In wealthy countries, the Rolex President watch is a recognizable accessory demonstrating the wearer's status. In a Belgrade weekly, an advertisement openly offered a convincing replica "from abroad." Thanks to this ad, anyone who wanted to present themselves as a person ready and able to pay 12,490 Deutsche Marks for a watch could do it for just 130 Marks.

Buyers of this "replica of the highest quality" (or those who own a stolen original) were also likely to drive the newest German limousine or Japanese SUV.[98] Because of

---

98 SUV = Suburban Utility Vehicle, a "muscular" vehicle design favored by Belgrade's criminals and nouveau riche.

Figure 2.84. Two palaces erected next to each other in Dorćol, probably without permission. They exemplify the "new architecture," dislocated from function and sources of the styles, but sometimes of surpassing originality. Photo credit: Dušan Šević.

NAJKVALITETNIJA uvozna re-plika ROLEX PRESIDENT-a, težiša, zvuk, kruna na ključu, kućište od brušenog čelika, President narukvica i sve ostalo potpu-no identično.

Ugrađen japanski mehanizam i Hardlex staklo, Anti-Shock, High–Precission, kvarcni sa liti-jumskom baterijom i rokom trajanja baterije od najmanje 5 godina.

CENA REPLIKE JE SAMO 1,1% OD CENE ORIGINALA /replika 130 DM – original 12490 DM/.

Količina ograničena, moguće na-rudžbe i rezervacije. Isporuka pouzećem.

Figure 2.83. Newspaper adver-tisement for a fake Rolex watch. The society in which counter-feits have the right to be coun-terfeits with pride cannot see anything unusual about this ad.

laws, insurance for such cars was "cancelled" (a clever euphemism for the ancient and brutally correct word "stolen"—invariably from a Western country). These were driven or surreptitiously transported into the Kingdom of Darkness where Interpol had no author-ity. Less successful citizens were doing something similar: Stalls in public markets were full of "Levi's" from Novi Pazar,[99] as well as pirated CDs of music or computer software and VHS tapes of movies mass-duplicated in Bulgaria or Serbia. If they smoked, they smoked fake cigarettes (usually a Ukrainian brand la-beled "Marlboro"). If they drank, they drank Bulgarian or North Korean "Johnnie Walker"—claimed to be from Scotland, of course.

The prevalence of inauthentic identity symbols, ranging from clothes to politics, inevitably encour-aged inauthentic architecture, and vice versa. In a world inspired by fairy-tale TV programs, these buildings belong to their environment only ostensibly. Their functionality was so limited that they hardly qualify as homes. They are more like sculptures, materialized fantasies, urban anecdotes.

---

99 A town in southwestern Serbia well known for sewing, dressmaking, and clothing production.

Figure 2.85. Multi-story buildings increasingly acquired new pseudo-traditional elements, like angular roof towers. Such houses are basically materializations of fairy tale castles for "heavenly people." The phrase "heavenly people" is used as a synonym for Serbs.

Banal displays of this "new historicism" were not limited to single-family homes in Dedinje or elsewhere. Collective multi-family/multi-story buildings increasingly acquired new pseudo-traditional elements, like angular roof towers. Such elements are a victory for ready-made "traditionalism" over the impersonality of ready-made "modernism."

Celebrity Charlatans

Something important to this narrative but not mentioned before was the presence of personalities on the most popular TV stations in Serbia in the 1990s who predicted the future, as well as amateur historians who made fantastic claims about Serbia's remote past (the more remote the better). In addition to political leaders, "business people," singers, actors, athletes, and professionals active in the para-economic/para-

Figure 2.86. "Cleopatra" being interviewed. Photo from her Facebook page. TV Pink says many popular singers contributed money for her sex change operations.

life around us, there were people like Cleopatra, the first of a whole flock of oracles, fortune tellers, healers, shamans, and clairvoyants. Having left behind her original name (Duško Ilić), the original spelling of her new name ("Kleo-patra") and her gender (she was born male),[100] Cleopatra became one of the biggest media stars in the decade of the country's wars, tragedies, and eventual disintegration.[101]

During the 1990s, the glass screen of the television took the place of a *tepsija*[102] in which renegade janissaries used to "catch stars" to forecast the weather and reveal what is to come. With help from Cleopatra and her many rivals and successors on the one hand, and various fake historians, archeologists, and ethno-geneticists on the other, and thanks to the relentless promotion of these two types of social and mental scum, the present was effectively cancelled and replaced by the near future or distant past.

The fact that people on TV were predicting the future was always convenient for the Milošević regime and became part of their propaganda (sanctions will be lifted, the bombing will stop, the American President will get AIDS or at least break a leg). But that was only the surface of this complex operation. A more important goal was creating a conditioned reflex which could at any moment shift your eyes away from the real causes of misery.

Similar to the fortune tellers were the charlatans, hugely promoted in the media, who determined that Serbs came to Earth from Sirius, invented the "Vinča" alphabet,[103] and authored the Old and New Testaments. The officialization of charlatanism started in grand style in 1985 with the loud promotion all over Yugoslavia of a local translation of Roberto Salinas Price's book *Homer's Blind Audience*.[104]

Figure 2.87. The Mexican book that opened a portal of mystification which grew to monstrous size in the Balkans.

----

100 TV Pink, "Naša Najpoznatija Proročica Je Nekad Bila Muško!" [Our most famous prophetess was once a man!], https://www.pink.rs/domaci/257151/nasa-najpoznatija-prorocica-je-nekad-bi-la-musko-kleopatra-se-zvala-dusan-bavila-se-muzikom-a-evo-kako-je-izgledala-foto.
101 Cleopatra's Facebook page describes her as "the Balkan prophetess, crowned queen of the prophets," https://www.facebook.com/balkanskaprorocicakleopatra.
102 *Tepsija* is a shallow pan used for baking. In the epic folk song "Of Recent Times" (which the author quotes in the above text) the future could be foretold by pouring water from the Danube into a *tepsija* to "catch the stars."
103 Vinča is a Belgrade suburb known for neolithic archeological excavations. The "Vinča" alphabet has been claimed to be the world's oldest.
104 Published in San Jerónimo Lídice, Mexico, by Casa Huicalco in 1980, and in Belgrade by Izdavacka Radna/TANJUG in 1985.

In it, this Mexican amateur historian ridiculed Heinrich Schliemann[105] and those who believed him. Price instead identified Troy's location as a small place called Gabela near the Neretva river delta in Bosnia-Hercegovina. People who had never heard of Homer's epics suddenly felt important because they were *Trojans*. The well of mystification that opened at that moment led to the growth of buried social conflicts which evolved into a set of wars and over time became a ravine where illiterate lovers of the "Vinča" gathered. They were ready to kill for the sake of the Cyrillic alphabet even when they did not know it well. Then there were those who thought the antiquity of their ethnicity was vital to their present status, as well as experts who either publicly or secretly supported (or by simple inaction enabled) the spread of myths about the past of our people and pseudo-scientific syntheses of history and astrology. Many beliefs that came from such myths materialized as plaster or concrete lions beside gates, eagles on fences, and other sculptural forms.

Interlude: How the Past Travels

Over thirteen decades ago, near a fountain on a steep Belgrade street, a boy had a quarrel with Turkish soldiers about whose turn it was to pour water. A fight started and, as in a Hans Christian Andersen or Grimm Brothers fairy tale, a young apprentice named Sava was left lying on the street, wounded, his jug broken, next to two dead fellow citizens. What ensued was a heavy artillery bombardment of Belgrade from the fortress of Kalemegdan. After an avalanche of tumultuous events, the so-called "Great Powers" decided that the Ottomans should leave Kalemegdan and this brought Serbia's liberation. In the 1920s, thankful descendants renewed the Čukur fountain and decorated it with Simeon Roksandić's sculpture.[106]

Figure 2.88. Čukur fountain on Dobračina Street commemorates an incident that led to Ottomon troops shelling Belgrade from Kalemegdan in 1862. In response, the "Great Powers" decided the Ottomans should leave Belgrade, resulting in Serbia's independence. Photo credit: author.

---

105 Schliemann was a nineteenth century German amateur archeologist who tried to identify the physical locations of Troy and other places mentioned by Homer in the *Iliad* and *Odyssey*. His excavations produced some convincing evidence.

106 Vujović, "On St. Michael's Cathedral and Princess Ljubica's Residence," 150.

Figure 2.89. Fountain without water at the corner of Balkanska and Kraljice Natalije Streets. Photo credit: author.

Figure 2.90. The fountain's female figure echoes a relief sculpture on a nearby façade, which itself echoes a sculpture by Djordje Jovanović. Photo credit: author.

More recently, at the corner of Balkanska and Kraljice Natalije Streets,[107] you can see another decorative creation. We do not know if the fountain has any name, or if its creator feels like an artist, or if the nymph's bustline reflects the stone mason's need to get away from morbid themes for a moment.[108]

Still, if we take a walk through this area and notice decorative details on the mostly dilapidated façades, we will see that the author of the relief on the newly built fountain found his inspiration on the lintel of a nearby house in Balkanska Street: The creator made the façade come alive with a prone female figure in high relief, repeating the allegorical figure of "Sava" made by the famous sculptor Djordje Jovanović in 1908.[109] In this way we can trace the journey of a motif through time and gender in a relatively limited space.

When we place this journey in a coordinate system of historical turning points, we can sense a pattern. In 1862 Belgrade was bombed. After that came liberation, and people erected a sculpture with prone figure on a fountain with no running water. In 1999 Belgrade was bombed and a fountain with a prone figure was created without running water. We have yet to see if what happened afterwards[110] was really another liberation.

---

107 Kraljice Natalije was the street's original name. Under communism it was called Narodnog fronta [Street of the National Front].

108 What the author means is that the sculptor has remodeled the young boy Sava (from the Čukur fountain) as a young girl.

109 *Vajarski radovi akademika Đorđa Jovanovića* [Sculptural works of academician Djordje Jovanović] (Belgrade: Royal Academy, 1933).

110 That is to say, the changes after Milosević.

Požeška Street as a Manifesto of "Anti-bureaucratic" Architecture

I believe a meticulous analysis of Belgrade's architecture after 1945 would show that every phase of Yugoslav socialism brought a unique kind of modernism, that is, every socialist five-year plan or later reform left small but visible changes in the modernist idiom. Thus, for example, across from the Belgrade Fair building and next to Dragiša Brašovan's huge state printing house (erected right after World War II), apartment blocks remain as the only example in Belgrade of a standard state design for residential buildings. The apartments had no kitchens, because it was assumed that under socialism, people would eat in state kitchens. Of course, people soon found that their anachronistic desire to eat meals in private had not disappeared, so makeshift kitchens in the individual apartments replaced the service provided communally.

If we go back through the history of different phases and reforms of Yugoslav socialism, and include external influences in these changes, we would notice a correlation between "guidelines" and "viewpoints" with changes in building construction style. Since architecture is one of the most expensive and technically complex artforms, the imprints of ideology generally appear with a delay. But if we were to look for the social formation that most quickly reached agreement with the city's visual identity, it

Figure 2.91. This block of flats across from the Belgrade Fair and next to the State Printing house is the only example of normative socialist residential design in Belgrade. Photo credit: author.

would be without a doubt the so-called "anti-bureaucratic revolution."[111] The current state of Belgrade is the result of an untamed swelling of rigged-up constructions.

We can take Požeška Street as a realized manifesto of "anti-bureaucratic architecture." Before the radical transformation in the 1960s, it was an idyllic street on the outskirts of the city, full of yards with greenery. Then as the city grew, residential buildings were erected on both sides of the street, giving a certain serious rhythm and monumental air to the whole area. This rhythm was based on large cubic volumes of multi-story residential buildings alternating with much shorter buildings of commercial purpose. However, this rhythm was destroyed by a decision to "improve" this part of the city—just as social values were destroyed by the decision to "give dignity back" to our citizens.

Truth be told, we need to note that before the city began to expand, Požeška Street was a gateway to *Ibarska magistrala*.[112] Some models of the street's radical "adaptation" were already being tested in settlements next to this important road to the south. Elements of the architectural language had begun to appear on inns and houses of Yugoslav expats working in Germany, as well as on "graveyard homes"—mausoleums sometimes better decorated and equipped than houses for the living.

The original Požeška Street was brought about by urbanistic thinking when people still believed in certain principles and a social ideology. However, adaptation occurred in a time that lacked specific thoughts about cities or houses. Instead, anything was acceptable but nothing was important. American and European postmodern architecture was widely discussed in Serbia but understood and replicated quite superficially. There used to be some rationale that held decontextualized fragments together in a postmodern construction, even if it was strange. Now there was no rationale at all. In this way, the architecture of Požeška Street and agglomerations like it were similar to the politics of when they were created. In the same way that columns with capitals, slanted roofs, balustrades, glass curtains, and other familiar elements lost their original meaning and purpose, ideas like "nationalism," "communism," "patriotism," and "market socialism," which were cited by Serbia's ruling regime in the 1990s, hid empty spaces. Unfortunately, this did not mean the totality lacked deadly potential.

The first phase in the reshaping of Požeška Street was to build annexes. Clean modernist residential cubes not only got taller, they were "decorated." Thus, objections to the unfussiness of modernist architecture were expressed. By this time we

---

111 The "anti-bureacratic revolution" included a series of public rallies organized by the ruling party which helped it strip authority from disobedient local leaders as Milošević tightened his grip on power.
112 State Road 22, commonly known as the Ibar Highway, connects Belgrade with central Serbia.

Figure 2.92. The first step in the reshaping of Požeška Street was the construction of annexes on the residential buildings built in the 1960s and the introduction of "ornaments" to temper a "too overt" modernism. One could say that ready-made "post-modernism" attacked ready-made "modernism." Photo credit: author.

all knew that ornamentation was not in fact a crime.[113] However, it is a crime to impose ornamentation on buildings that don't need it. A "zig-zag" organization of windows placed the construction close to the 1990s set of values: If a time of relative abundance leads to asceticism in architecture, it was logical that flamboyant houses should become more desirable in times of poverty.

The initial rhythm of a regular alternation between residential and business buildings, giving the towers and their apartments access to sunlight, was nullified by filling in the open spaces. In-fill buildings were created during a short period of "anti-bureaucratic" enthusiasm, without any coordination. And so at one moment between two skyscrapers, we would see a tall new office building, and just a bit further away, sandwiched between two tall buildings there would be a rigged up little house, nicely built as befits a private pharmacy. The general concept of filling in the empty spaces between isolated buildings continued to absurdity: Between two houses, recently constructed according to the same project and already close together, there was a new intervention—the kiosk.

In such a crowded ambiance, street life flourished. While huge department stores were empty and failing, the world of trade poured onto the sidewalks. Already narrow pedestrian paths were further narrowed by rows of kiosks and stalls so that Požeška, like many other streets, became a kind of oriental souk. Trade capillarization brought about even smaller units: selling from the hoods of cars and out of cardboard boxes. These could be considered a diminutive type of kiosk. Flea markets expanded and became habitual. An orgy of smuggling, selling in the grey market, and illegal currency exchange

---

113 Contrary to Adolf Loos, the Austrian architect who famously declared ornamentation in architecture to be a crime.

were the result of sanctions and regime policies in the early 1990s. At the
same time, "informal commerce" enabled the government to buy social
peace. The primitive "liberalism" of the
flea market and kiosk resulted from the
disappearance of regulation.

Without any doubt, the kiosk was
the most important architectural form
of the Slobodan Milošević era. A ubiq-
uitous phenomenon, it has been extensively studied and there were con-
tests for the best designs. Požeška
was hardly the only place where they
were found: They existed in all parts
of the city, even in places that one
would think were impossible.[114]

Figure 2.93. Street life flourished but architecture suffered as streets became more crowded and
less regulated. Photo credit: author.

However, one recent variant surpassed all classifications—the expandable kiosk.
A kiosk can expand in several ways. Linear expansion is surely the most prevalent: At
the most basic level, a kiosk with extensions (such as front- and side-facing surfaces,
with a possible roof extension) evolves to the next level by adding a Turkish roller shut-

Figure 2.94. The proliferation of kiosks was the dominant feature of urbanism
under Milošević. Photo by
Nataša Anđelković.

----

114 See Nataša Anđelković, "Jugoslavija, socijalizam, nostalgija: Hoće li opstati čuveni crveni kiosk
sa viršlama u Beogradu?" [Yugoslavia, socialism, nostalgia: Will the famous red hot dog kiosk in
Belgrade survive?], BBC, 19 June 2021, https://www.bbc.com/serbian/lat/balkan-57512704.

ter. Then by, let's say, putting a display freezer or open stalls outside, it conquers the pedestrian zone, to the point where the sidewalk gets so narrow that consumer by-pass is made difficult.

Another variant is a kiosk expanded across a gap. This is achieved by occupying locations some distance from the kiosk, first with moveable, and then, in the second phase, with immoveable objects. At a suitable moment, a roof appears above the components, also covering part of the sidewalk. This creates a small shop unavoidable for passers-by.

This expansion of a kiosk from its initial core (in this case, a shed) to a second core (with a connecting roof) doesn't last. Systematic monitoring would show that such kiosks change their purpose and appearance easily, in an almost guerilla-like fashion—for example, from a cold-drinks stand to a chess club, to a fish store, then a locksmith's shop—although these specializations are often only fronts for the real business: selling liter bottles of petrol illegally. The propulsive activity of reselling petrol (typically brought in from Romania) was possible thanks to sanctions and the Milošević regime's mismanagement of the economy—hence the stickers from the final anti-Milošević campaign, saying "Puk'o je"[115] next to a picture of a plastic flask of "Super Premium"—quite a bizarre contradiction.

The Way Something Is Written Is as Important as the Content– Maybe Even More.

Graffiti has existed in various forms since the beginning of literacy. Regardless of how a message is written on a more or less visible surface, it is meant to be seen. Among the oldest remaining graffiti are those from the prison in Pompeii. The archaeology of ancient Rome confirms the early origin of a subspecies that still exists today: toilet graffiti.

Many buildings and well-known sites, and even masterpieces of wall painting, are marred with inscriptions made with some sharp object, marker pen, or paint. Most spectators today would consider such marks to be vandalism. But then again, one can take graffiti seriously as part of the historical record, a medium providing unique insights into the feelings of ordinary people. This applies both to ancient and to modern graffiti.

Civilization's development roughly aligns with the accelerating development of technology. The span between how hard it was to inscribe limestone or marble, and how easy it is to spray color from an aerosol can, proves that progress has not ignored the requirements of graffiti. New technologies have not only brought quicker execu-

---

115 In colloquial English, "He's finished."

Figure 2.95. The readiness of Serbian society for change after a decade of Milošević is summed up in the graffiti which says "Maki is each one of us." Photo credit: author.

tion but have also increased the potential for pictorial sophistication. Consequently, in the 1980s a uniquely urban form of street art developed, which eventually won recognition from galleries and museums.

The readiness of Serbian society for change, after more than a decade of Slobodan Milošević, was summarized in the graffiti "Maki je svaki" [Translator's note: "Everyone is Maki"]. Bogoljub Arsenijević Maki, an icon painter from the town of Valjevo, became a symbol of rebellion in 1999 when he brought a note of radicalism into Valjevo's protests while the opposition was still characterized by despondency. After they beat him up in prison and he spectacularly escaped from the Maxillofacial clinic, Maki played a vital part in the October 2000 protests.[116]

And so when a majority of advocates of political change got over their threshold of fear, when they finally reached a consensus, the 5th of October happened.[117] One of the focal points of public hatred in Belgrade was the chain of perfume shops named SCANDAL, with goods imported from the hostile and decadent West. It belonged to

----

116 Dragan Bujošević and Ivan Radovanović, *5. oktobar: 24 sata državnog udara* [5 October: 24 Hours of the Coup], Press-Document No. 10 (Belgrade: Media Center Library, 2000). The book appeared quickly after the events it depicts and had enormous market success. In it, Maki was presented as a Serbian synthesis of Robin Hood and a kamikaze pilot (see the chapter "Maki's Cocktail").

117 It sold well but Bujošević and Radovanović's book did not receive adequate criticism, probably thanks to the overall euphoria. Written in a sensationalist manner with many elements of pathos, either consciously or not, it established the new mythology of 5 October based on patterns deeply rooted in national epic poetry. The opposition leader saying goodbye to women and small children on their doorsteps right before the "major battle" was reminiscent of the nine Jugović brothers saying goodbye to their beloved wives (and old Jug-Bogdan, their father, as the tenth) before they went to the Battle of Kosovo in 1389. These nine brothers and their father are mythical characters in a famous national poem "Smrt majke Jugovića" [The death of Jugović's mother]. Supposedly, they all died as martyrs.

Figure 2.96. Tear gas replaced the smell of perfume as one of the SCANDAL shops was vandalized. Photo credit: Draško Gagović.

Figure 2.98. The graffiti on the SCANDAL shop says: "Complain to Your Dad" and "Blow your Dad." Photo credit: Draško Gagović.

Figure 2.97. Poster at the entrance to the SCANDAL shop combines the 5-pointed communist star with pictures of Partisan women from the epoch of socialist realism, and this message: "SCANDAL wishes you a happy holiday." Photo credit: Draško Gagović.

Milošević Jr. In March 2000, the windows and contents of one of his shops were subjected to a spontaneous, almost Dadaist action in an atmosphere full of tear gas. On the left and right sides of the shop entrance, posters using familiar communist symbols wished its esteemed clients a happy holiday.

On the morning of 6 October 2000, the SCANDAL shop on Terazije square was trashed. Unambiguous political messages were left as graffiti.

Graffiti messages or pictures are sometimes applied by stencil to façades, especially if it is necessary to have many copies of the same text or drawing. This technique is much older than spray paint, as we can see in what is probably the oldest graf-

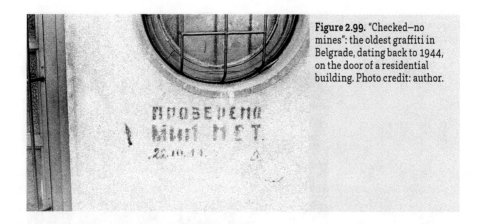

Figure 2.99. "Checked—no mines": the oldest graffiti in Belgrade, dating back to 1944, on the door of a residential building. Photo credit: author.

fiti in Belgrade, with a clear historical provenance (the stenciled words date from October 1944): "Проверено мин НЕТ. 22.10.44." ["Checked—no mines." It was stenciled on the door of a residential building after Russian soldiers checked it for mines that German soldiers might have left behind.] This phrase was absorbed into Belgrade slang after the war.

The use of stencils was taken up by Otpor,[118] a political movement created by students during the 1996-97 protest rallies. Its formation was announced by stencils of a stylized fist that appeared on the façades of buildings throughout Belgrade. As they gained public support, Otpor's fist became a visual mantra of rebellion against Milošević's regime. Otpor is properly credited with energizing the effort to overthrow Milošević on 5 October 2000.

The strength, humor, elusiveness, and finally triumph, of this movement (more about it later) encouraged other political formations, and even traditional political parties, to try to emulate their successful use of graffiti.[119] After the October 2000 regime change, a humorless imitation by the Socialist Party (SPO), main loser in the elections, appeared on Belgrade's façades. They tried to re-assert their existence with a stenciled symbol that mimicked both Otpor's fist and their own party's three-finger salute.

All messages—be they political, local, regional, or commercial—require the recipients to be at least somewhat literate. But in a country where literacy is low, care is needed to protect a special kind of literacy: the ability to read and write in Cyrillic. And within that literacy segment, there were special preferences. The content of what was written became almost secondary to the style of lettering.

---

118 *Otpor* means "resistance" in English.
119 Graffiti remains an important political tool in Serbia. But as it has been co-opted to a large degree by political parties, it is now seen as a less authentic expression of public sentiment.

Figure 2.100. By multiplying a simple nonverbal sign on thousands of façades, Otpor used a classic "urban guerrilla" tactic to suggest they were everywhere. Here, one of their activists demonstrates how the stencils were used with a spray can. Photo credit: Video Nedeljnik (ViN) footage in "Bringing Down a Dictator," a 2002 film by York-Zimmerman, distributed by the International Center on Nonviolent Conflict.

Figure 2.101. A re-worked Otpor symbol was used by the Socialist Party (SPO) in an attempt to jump on the youth movement's bandwagon by using spray cans and stencils. Photo credit: author.

The first public inscription a traveler—let's say a foreigner—arriving by airplane would see in Belgrade's airport is an advertisement for Karić Bank. This inscription (which on its left had a smiling sign of the New World Order: the McDonald's logo,[120] next to the Karić family's crest) asserted something of the national identity—albeit shifted into a foreign (Latin) alphabet. A foreigner who, despite everything, flew into Belgrade during the short sanction-free periods in the 1990s would see the alphabet of the Miroslav Gospel[121] as soon as he or she arrived.

The "Miroslav" typeface became particularly popular in the 1990s. It can be seen all over Serbia, in public inscriptions, advertising slogans, and on printed materials of

----

120 The beginning of the NATO bombing in March 1999 caused a spontaneous but well-organized action to destroy foreign embassies and cultural centers. Fast food restaurants were also targets—especially McDonald's, whose opening in March 1988 had been celebrated as a significant, even cultural event. Unhidden pride materialized as a bronze plaque on the façade of the first McDonald's restaurant opened in a communist country, in Belgrade. An action to save the restaurant in a state of war was directed toward persuading potential attackers that it was "our" property, not American, and when those appeals failed, McDonald's switched to the Cyrillic alphabet. The Golden Arches logo also got a small *šajkača*, the cap which is a part of the traditional national costume.

121 The Miroslav Gospel (in Serbian: *Miroslavljevo jevandjelje*) is an illuminated book-manuscript created in 1186. It is a masterpiece of illustration and calligraphy as well as one of the oldest documents written in Serbian. Today it is in the collection of the National Museum in Belgrade.

123

Figure 2.102. A Latin version of "Miroslav" lettering on the advertizement for Karić Bank is foreigners' first encounter with Belgrade—at the exit from Customs in the airport. Photo credit: author.

АБВГДЂЕЖЗИЈКЛЉМНЊОПРСТЋУФХЦЧЏ

(б) АБВГДЂЖЗИЈКЛЉМНЊОПРСТЋ

ŽŠČĆ ЏШ 1234567890 УФХЦЧЏШ

Figure 2.103. The Miroslav typeface was constructed by Panta Stojićević in 1921.

all kinds. Panta Stojićević devised it in 1921 when the printing foundry "Slovo" requested its design.[122] By 1922 it was already widely used. It is a sans-serif stylization of the Cyrillic alphabet and obtained its name after someone decided that it resembled the lettering in the Miroslav Gospel.

Created at the end of the twelfth century, the Ductus of Miroslav's lettering isn't unique since it was probably the product of two scribes with somewhat different handwriting styles. Nevertheless, both used the same medium—a sharpened quill—to record the dynamics of penmanship. Attempts to turn the script's qualities into machine calligraphy, and lately into a computer font, often led to typographic disaster and humiliation of the alleged model whose name was taken for its title.

---

122 Mitar Pešikan, *Naša azbuka i njene norme* [Our alphabet and its norms] (Belgrade: Vukova zadužbina, NIP *Politika*, Zavod za udžbenike i nastavna sredstva, 1993).

Figure 2.104. Two pages from the Miroslav Gospel.

Even if we agree that this font arrived with the last wave of the Secession style, and as such "looks good" on façades from that period (for example, on the attic of the Society for the Embellishment of Vračar) it looks quite banal on more modern buildings.

Figure 2.105. Building of the Society for the Embellishment of Vračar on Njegoševa Street. The "Miroslav" typeface is more convincing on older buildings. Photo credit: author.

Figure 2.106. On contemporary (not to mention postmodern) buildings, the "Miroslav" typeface looks like a caricature. Photo credit: author.

125

Figure 2.107. "Miroslav" lettering shows up even on traffic signs: for example, a "no parking" sign on Kneza Miloša Street. The quotation marks around Poland's name suggest it is not a real country. Photo credit: author.

That is even more true for inscriptions that accompany traffic signs. If we take the sign in front of the Polish Embassy as an example, we see an inadequate logo ("No Parking") complemented by a typographic error: the name of the country is in quotation marks. It is unclear whether this great Slavic country received the status of uncertainty reserved for those whom the government and mass media don't like (so sneering phrases like "the so-called 'opposition'" are used) because Poland joined NATO or if it was just the normal illiteracy of the authorities in charge of road marking.

The "Miroslav" font was even sucked into political fights over street names. After Tito died in 1980, graduates of his political school in Kumrovec[123] and some of the baton bearers from the annual Relay of Youth launched a first wave of "de-Tito-ization" with the energy of converts. This brought about the removal of many monuments honoring the late Marshal and a massive change of street and public-square names all over Yugoslavia. Belgrade was no exception: "Maršala Tita" was the name of the city's main street. In this case, a Solomonic solution was found in the street's new name, "Srpskih Vladara" [Translator's note: "Serbian Rulers Street"]. Thus, the imprint of the street's former namesake survived in an indirect and camouflaged way. However, we do not know if the authors of this new name realized that apart from various "national" rulers, they were also honoring Serbia's foreign rulers, including Austrian emperors, Ottoman sultans, and Germany and its World War II allies.

More recent fights over street names have explicitly involved "Miroslav" lettering. When democratic opposition parties won control of many local governments (to the dismay of the far-left coalition which remained in power at the republic level),

---

123 In the political school in Tito's birthplace Kumrovec, communist politicians used to learn socialist theory. The school looked like a fancy hotel with two conference halls, 145 bedrooms, a sports hall, a cinema and a bomb shelter.

this led to parallel deployments of street signs with conflicting old and new names. In Belgrade, for example, "Srpskih vladara" (the street's post-Tito name) was written on signs using the "Miroslav" alphabet, which has populist connotations, whereas the same street's even newer name (actually a revival of its pre-Tito name, "Ulice Kralja Milana"[124]) was printed on signs using the sans-serif block lettering that was the earlier norm for street names, to emphasize the continuity of the "civic order."

Figure 2.108. Duelling street names: a new street name in Belgrade is actually the old one (printed in the "Miroslav" typeface) and the oldest one, from before World War 2, is the latest one (printed in sans-serif block letters). Photo credit: author.

The sudden renaissance of "Miroslav" lettering in these new times testifies to the wish to find something "authentically Serbian" in the Cyrillic alphabet that Serbs share with other nations. It also had the function of evoking medieval times, when Serbia was a powerful, happy, idyllic country—as was believed and as TV programs said. However, this alphabet also confirms an unnatural relationship with tradition, a relationship based on superficial knowledge, even willful ignorance. The dishonest promotion of tradition did not stop with a specific typography. It spread to a whole spectrum of abuse of traditions committed in overt and covert ways. The regime's main idea was that Serbs were "a heavenly people" and atrocious consequences arose from that.[125]

----

124 The name in English would be King Milan Street, named for Milan I, who ruled the Kingdom of Serbia from 1882 to 1889.

125 The idea of Serbs as "a heavenly people" can be traced back to the battle of Kosovo, but it attained its most potent form in "Propast Carstva Srpskoga" [Downfall of the Serbian Empire], a poem published in *Srpske narodne pjesme* [Serbian folk songs] by Vuk Karadžić (Vienna: Staff of the Armenian Monastery, 1841). Aleksandar Pavlović explains: "At the beginning of the poem, a falcon (actually Saint Elijah) comes from the holy city of Jerusalem, carrying a letter from the Virgin to Emperor Lazarus [Prince Lazar]. In the letter, she offers him a choice between the earthly kingdom and the heavenly kingdom: if you choose the earthly kingdom, lead your army into battle and you will win; if you choose the kingdom of heaven, build a church in Kosovo and give communion to your soldiers because you will all perish. Lazarus decides that the earthly kingdom is transient and the heavenly one is eternal, and therefore chooses the latter and dies in battle." A. Pavlović, "Kako su Srbi postali nebeski narod" [How the Serbs Became a Heavenly Nation], *Odiseja*, 7 October 2019, https://odiseja.rs/kako-su-srbi-postali-nebeski-narod/. Since the poem says Lazar chose heavenly because "Earthly is for a small kingdom," the recently canonized Bishop Nikolaj Velimirović recast the story in imperialist terms in 1942: "Aj, ta Velika Nebesna Srbija!

Figure 2.109. Above the graffiti, the shop's hand-painted sign uses "Miroslav" lettering to advertise "Textile Goods" and "Intellectual Services." Photo credit: author.

The "Miroslav" alphabet is not only used in public inscriptions. Quite naturally, it found a place in trade, where public and private properties meet. The Karić Bank's use of a Latinized variant has already been noted. But in the late 1990s in Belgrade, small shops are sometimes found in makeshift buildings graced with surprising hand-painted signs: in addition to "Textile Goods," apparently one shop sells "Intellectual Services." What that means, we do not know, but they, too, use the "Miroslav" alphabet.

Selling through kiosks as the primary retail channel clearly affects advertising services. An ad or sign painted by hand in the urban landscape bravely stands against the technological superiority of a video or inkjet-printed billboard in the same way that Alpine cottages on a multi-story apartment block are both delightful and defiant.

Ona predstavlja već odavno ostvareni ideal Velike Srbije" [Oh, that great heavenly Serbia! It represents the ideal of Greater Serbia which has long been considered]. N. Velimirović, *Sabrana dela* [Collected Works], Vol. 5 (Šabac: Glas crkve, 2013), 651–684. The War Crimes Tribunal in the Hague prosecuted Slobodan Milošević and others as "part of a common scheme, strategy or plan on the part of the accused to create a 'Greater Serbia,' a centralized Serbian state encompassing the Serb-populated areas of Croatia and Bosnia and all of Kosovo, and that this plan was to be achieved by forcibly removing non-Serbs from large geographical areas through the commission of the crimes charged in the indictments." *Decision of the ICTY Appeals Chamber*, paragraph 8 (The Hague, 18 April 2002), http://www.icty.org/x/cases/slobodan_milosevic/acdec/en/020418.pdf.

Challenging the polished, soulless images of modern billboards, hand-painted ads are the keepers of a specific art tradition now found mainly at fairs, circuses, amusement parks, traveling menageries, and small businesses.

Of course, advertising a distinctive national identity did not stop with the "Miroslav" alphabet. A small fast-food kiosk promotes patriotic gastronomy with a hand-painted, wall-filling ad. Under a headline affirming Serbianness, a white eagle is shown bearing the Serbian coat of arms, its claws reaching down toward a pair of "*pljeskavicas*"[126] in buns (Figure 2.111).

Advertising billboards mostly present visions of desirable purchases admitting us to a world we are supposed to envy. Young attractive people sip coffee and smile, beautiful girls and handsome guys go to the seaside for an endless holiday, and modern appliances tempt us with their sleek styling. The look of Belgrade was fundamentally changed by the deployment of large numbers of billboards in the late 1990s. Not surprisingly, their size and location were as weakly regulated as housing construction had been earlier. Unfortunately, these high-power marketing tools were set loose in an economy that hardly produced anything. There-

Figure 2.110. A hand-painted ad (in this case, for a car wash) evokes the spirit of old times. Photo credit: author.

Figure 2.111. A small kiosk offers patriotic gastronomy: even the national symbol wants their pljeskavicas.

---

126 "Pljeskavica" is a spicy minced meat patty similar to a large hamburger.

Figure 2.112. A billboard advertises itself. Photo credit: Dušan Šević.

fore, it was not unusual to see a billboard advertising itself, because in many places there were fewer clients than rentable surfaces. The same can be said for companies offering modern advertising services.

The growing number of billboards in a society where people had less and less to spend on the products advertised brought a new dimension to the city's visual landscape: These clean, radiant screens are sometimes in stark contrast to the dilapidated urban objects surrounding them. Thus, paradoxically, they make Belgrade look more modern but also more impoverished.

Interlude: The Fine Art of Image Destruction (Iconoclasm Revisited)

The expression of political positions by modifying or destroying images began in Serbia at the same time as political competence, and it came from the very top.

The inspiration for "re-processing" the character of Ante Marković[127] on his 1990 election poster probably came from the same circles who wrote letters signed with

----

127 Ante Marković was the last prime minister of the former Yugoslavia, who decreased inflation from 56% a month in November 1989 to 2.4% a month in March 1990. Marković cut foreign debt

Figure 2.113. The simplest way to attack someone—in this instance, Ante Marković, candidate in the 1990 Yugoslav elections—is to present them as Hitler by adding simple elements to their picture.

false names[128] denouncing the Federal Yugoslav Prime Minister in *Politika's* daily "Odjeci i Reagovanja"[129] column. The simple and always applicable method of adding a mustache and a specific hairstyle to transform someone into Hitler (this being the most unimaginative transformation possible) has been used on the images of almost everyone who put their face on a campaign poster.

Disfiguring faces, whether they come from the sphere of politics or some other realm, is a very old practice (as was noted in the context of ancient Rome's *damnatio memoriae*). Sticking needles in dolls to harm a person via sympathetic magic is a related practice, usually associated with voodoo cults, thanks to numerous movies. But it was also one of the most common accusations made during the Inquisition, as can be found in the interrogation records. However, it is older than even the Middle Ages as dolls stuck with needles have been found in ancient Egyptian tombs, not to mention broken and bent lead figurines found in ancient Greek tombs.

----

in half, quadrupled the country's foreign currency reserves, and made the Yugoslav dinar the only convertible currency in Eastern Europe. He also aspired to get Yugoslavia into the European Economic Community. But nationalist political forces thwarted his plans. On 18 December 1989 in a speech to the Yugoslav Assembly (parliament) he said: "We will pay for our illusions with poverty, spiritual poisoning and a peripheral role in Europe." B92/Blic/Vesti, "25 Godina od Ostavke Ante Markovica Zablude cemo Placati Siromastvom" [25 years since the resignation of Ante Marković: We will pay for our mistakes with poverty] (Novi Sad: Portal 021, 20 December 2016), https://www.021.rs/story/Info/Srbija/151875/VIDEO-25-godina-od-ostavke-Ante-Markovica-Zablude-cemo-placati-siromastvom.html.

128 It may be unique in the world that someone who is a state representative "debunks" his government's president in writing, signs it with a pseudonym, and then brags about it in his memoirs. See Borislav Jović, *Poslednji dani SFRJ: Dnevnik* [The last days of the SFRY: A diary], 2nd edition (Belgrade: Politika, 1996). In the early 1990s, Jović was Serbia's representative to the Yugoslav Federal Presidency.

129 "Impacts and Reactions."

2. Pathopolis

The cult of imperial paintings and sculptures in ancient Rome differed to some extent from the early Christian period, equating the person represented with the representation itself. This is why an emperor's statues and portraits were honored. The diffusion of imperial portraits into distant provinces meant the emperor was present in every corner of the empire. Although it may seem anachronistic, this practice continued deep into the twentieth century, as can be seen in "the rule of service" in the former Yugoslavia's national army. Soldiers who took the Oath of Enlistment had to look Tito's picture in the eye while saying the oath. During indoor classes, the soldier had to put his cap on his desk with the five-pointed star facing Tito's picture, so the picture could see it.

The craze of systematically destroying pictures—whether they represented people in politics or not—spread a few times like a contagious disease through parts of Europe. The first such wave lapped over the Byzantine Empire in the seventh and eighth centuries. Although the theology of the image was only defined after the Eastern Orthodox Church defeated iconoclasm, speaking rationally we can assess the entire conflict which shook the empire to its core as more cultural than theological. Iconoclasm recognized the power of visual representation as the root of the problem.

Of course, there is a big difference between individual iconoclasm and iconoclasm as an organized campaign, but certain qualities can be ascribed to both. These emerge when the person in the picture loses the status of a representation and the picture is treated as an actual person, either in a wave of social frenzy or as the result of some personal pathology.

Elections in the Urban Landscape

The first elections in post-war Yugoslavia were held in November 1945. These elections for the Constitutional Assembly added a concept to the Serbian language that would outlast the new one-party voting system: the "blind box."[130] All elections held later under socialism lacked the true competitive spirit of Eros: you always knew who was going to win.

The Berlin Wall fell in November 1989. Following this symbolic event, all Eastern Bloc countries underwent political changes. Despite every attempt to replace multi-party elections with some hybrid form—or avoid them altogether—the governing party of Yugoslavia could not resist the wave of change sweeping across Eastern Europe. Therefore, a few months after multi-party elections were held in Slovenia and Croatia,

---

130 After World War II, there were many illiterate people in Yugoslavia. During elections, instead of circling a candidate's name on paper, a voter would put a rubber ball in one of the boxes. Each box represented one candidate and the winner was the person whose box contained the most rubber balls. The "blind box" contained the votes of the undecided.

the first multi-party elections were held in Serbia after nearly half a century. Even though the regime in power kept its hands tightly on all levers of social control, elections brought a return of competition, which had important impacts on the visual environment. Party rallies became public events, especially in cities, and the important role of posters was restored. Plus, a new medium arrived: television. And so, cities were transformed during electoral campaigns—albeit just temporarily. In the late 1990s, when Belgrade was covered with billboards, these temporary changes were intensified.

The Socialist Party of Serbia came into existence as a merger between the League of Communists of Serbia and the Socialist Alliance of Working People of Serbia—that is to say, the party and its long-constructed "outer circle" were integrated. The merger happened on 17 July 1990, after a successful "mobilization of the people" and a series of "Truth Rallies."[131] The unification provided an illusion of change while maintaining continuity of personnel and ideology—and keeping the party's grip on the apparatus of government. Among the dozens of party propaganda themes, a focus on the leader's personality was primary: On the cover page of *NIN* (which at the time was a political magazine obsessed with the leader's persona and the destiny of Serbs living in other Yugoslav republics), there were, without any comment, photographs of Felipe González Márquez, François Mitterrand, Helmut Schmidt, Willy Brandt, and Slobodan Milošević. This was clearly meant to suggest that Milošević and his party were comparable in ideology and practice to the other giants of modern Western European socialism—or more precisely, social democracy—and not communism, as the party's "enemies" claimed.

On one of the fliers handed out before the first multi-party elections in 1990, the interested public could learn that:

The Socialist Party of Serbia is the real choice for those of you:
- Who want to live in peace, not in nationalistic hatred and conflicts
- Who want a more peaceful future for your children instead of uncertainty and the threat of a fratricidal war
- Who want to live well from your work
- Who want society to help you when you need it
- Who find the condition for your own freedom in the freedom of someone else
- Who are for democratic dialogue and tolerance
- Who are for the values of progressive Europe, for coming closer to the most progressive socialist powers.

---

131 "Truth Rallies" were organized by Slobodan Milošević to promote his party's political views to the other republics of the former Yugoslavia. They were also a covert effort to pressure Slovenia, which was already planning to secede from the Yugoslav union.

Figure 2.114. Campaign banner of the reconstituted Socialist Party of Serbia in the multi-party elections of 1990. The slogan says: "WITH US, THERE IS NO UNCER-TAINTY–PEACE, FREE-DOM, SUCCESS." Note the symbols combining a 5-pointed star with a picture of a rose. Photo credit: Draško Gagović.

But leaflets were not the only medium the authorities used to address the people. Besides posters and TV promotions, electoral slogans were also spread by outdoor banners: "With us, there is no uncertainty." This carefully calculated expression relied on social inertia, and with good reason.

In keeping with the changing projection of the party's image, from "traditional communist" to "modern democratic socialist", the party's logo evolved in a specific trajectory during the 1990s. In the first multi-party elections, the five-pointed star was still featured, but it had a stem, which made it vaguely resemble a rose when seen from far.

The second phase of the logo's transformation introduced the silhouette of a rose superimposed on the star (see the campaign banner in Figure 2-114), while in the third phase, in the late 1990s, after a radical contemporization of the Party's visual identity, reference to the star completely disappeared and the rose was barely insinuated–it became just an abstract monogram.

Skillfully combining nationalist rhetoric with communism-redefined-as-socialism, the SPS appealed to voters from incompatible target groups: communist

СОЦИЈАЛИСТИЧКА ПАРТИЈА СРБИЈЕ

Figure 2.115. Logo of the Socialist Party of Serbia (SPS) when formed in 1990.

Figure 2.116. Logo of the Socialist Party at the end of decade. If one did not remember earlier designs, the logo's derivation from a rose might be missed.

apparatchiks, military pensioners, but also nationalists—in short, both Partisans and Chetniks.[132] The inexperienced and divided opposition, infested with secret service agents, felt pressured to adopt rhetoric even more nationalistic than the nationalists, exposing them to portrayal as *gibaničari*[133] and "butchers"[134] by those who dictated the level of discourse.

Still, the SPS felt very early on that the leader—whose cult they worked so hard to create[135]—was probably more popular than the party, so they distributed "double" posters whose function was to suggest that the parliamentary candidate whose face was next to the leader's was the leader's choice in the election.

Figure 2.117. Milošević's face on double posters implied that this parliamentary candidate in the 1990 elections had a recommendation from the very top. Photo credit: Draško Gagović.

All elections that followed were more or less according to the same plan. The ruling party gradually improved its visual identity while introducing cruder and more aggressive slogans: "That's the way it should be. Serbia won't bow her head." And finally in 1996, after so many social catastrophies, "Let's go on." It also perfected its methods for stealing elections.

Another tactic emerged during the first multi-party election, something which the party would use in nearly all later elections: one of Milošević's opponents would be

----

132 The Chetniks were guerilla fighters in small units from the Royal army of the pre-war Kingdom of Yugoslavia, reorganized by Dragoljub Draža Mihailović to fight in World War II. Their historical role is still widely disputed in Serbia, but one thing is certain: the Partisans were their political enemies. After the end of the war, the communists imprisoned Mihailović and sentenced him to death in July 1946. He was shot and buried in an unknown location. In 1948, American president Harry Truman posthumously awarded Mihailović the Legion of Honor medal for saving five hundred US pilots during the war.

133 *Gibaničar* is a Chetnik living the high life. The word derives from the Serbian national dish *gibanica*, a kind of salty cheese strudel.

134 Chetniks were notorious for butchering Partisans and their collaborators, as well as the non-Serbian population (Croats, Bosniaks, etc.).

135 With skillfully pushed rumors and panegyrics in the press, and especially in the most important medium—published "letters from readers"—the conviction was created in a well-orchestrated manner that Milošević was: a humble man living in a common, not-too-big apartment; of impeccable reputation; a good orator; decisive; completely sinless (although there might be people around him who are *a bit* suspect); the support he got was absolutely undivided and no one had any doubts about that.

conspicuously unqualified, but "promoted" to convince people that the election itself was a farce and that there was no serious alternative to the current leadership. In the first election, this foil was Nikola Šećeroski, a maker of brooms, brushes, and plastic toys with no party affiliation.[136] In the December 1992 elections, Milošević was met on the battlefield by Jezdimir Vasiljević (a.k.a. "Boss Jezda"), whose pseudo-private savings bank would soon be exposed as a Ponzi scheme. With the slogan on posters and in newspaper ads "Where can this hyperinflation get us?" he cynically used hyperinflation to take depositers' money and put it in the regime's pockets.[137] His campaign was a bad joke that got fewer votes than his bank had clients.

In most of the elections before 2000, the opposition participated with confusing campaign materials. Within the span of a few weeks, a party might represent itself using several different concepts and inconsistent slogans. This also occurred in the winter 1996 elections, which nonetheless differed from all previous elections by fulfilling the fantasy of a *united* opposition. What is more, this was also the first time irrefutable proof of large-scale ballot fraud and the falsification of election results led to persistent protest rallies.[138]

In the first elections held after the 1999 NATO military intervention, the ruling coalition was hoping to capitalize on its long-term campaign of "renewal and reconstruction" and the energy of "victory over the rest of the world" (as Serbian television described the punishing defeat in Kosovo). But that's not what happened. After the

ЧОВЕК ПРОМЕНА

Јездимир ВАСИЉЕВИЋ
независни кандидат
ЗА
председника Републике Србије

ЈА ТО МОГУ ДА ОСТВАРИМ

Figure 2.118. In the December 1992 elections, one of the presidential candidates was Jezdimir Vasiljević, who proclaimed himself the right person to set people free from hyperinflation. He was subsequently convicted for running a Ponzi scheme through his Jugoskandik bank in which some 80,000 depositers lost money.

---

136 According to *Wikipedia*, in this election Šećeroski received 3,168 votes.
137 Dinkić, *Ekonomija destrukcije*.
138 See Darka Radosavljević, *Šetnja u mestu–Građanski protest u Srbiji, 17.11.1996.–20.3.1997* [Walking in place–Civil protest in Serbia, 17.11.1996–20.3.1997] (Belgrade: Radio B92, 1997), a collection of texts (several of which cover visual aspects of the rallies), with a chronology and rich photo documentation.

euphoria fades from the long-awaited changes this election brought about, someone should carry out a detailed analysis. The opposition's success in 2000 may have been due in part to the fact that the parties participating in the campaign offered a program that was consistent in concept and integrated in implementation, while the ruling coalition's campaign this time was chaotic.

The opposition implemented a strategy of "gradual revelation" in the campaign for the presidency. On numerous billboards, eyes appeared with the slogan: "Who can always look you in the eye?" The answer was under the picture: "Koštunica."[139]

Sometime later, billboards appeared revealing the candidate's face, and the slogan changed to: "Who speaks for all of us today?"

Propaganda from the Democratic Opposition of Serbia (DOS) was coordinated with the leaders of all the DOS parties so any material that might confuse an average voter was pushed back. However, the ruling coalition organized an aggressive counter-campaign of vandalism and defacement against DOS posters.

----

139 At this stage of the campaign, in an SPS press conference that was broadcast on national television, someone speculated that those were Vojislav Koštunica's eyes. The Socialists' spokesperson replied with a hint of condemnation, "This is the kind of campaign they run in Western countries." Then he asserted that Al Pacino's eyes were actually used for the poster. But a zoom out to the whole face soon refuted that.

Figure 2.119. Initially, only presidential candidate Vojislav Koštunica's eyes appeared on billboards and posters in the general election campaign of 2000. The text says: "Who can always look you in the eye?"

Figure 2.120. Later, more of the candidate's face appeared on billboards and posters. The slogan changed to: "Who speaks for all of us today?"

Figure 2.121. The graffiti says: "A vote for death. Koštunica—NATO demon." Photo credit: Draško Gagović.

Figure 2.122. In the 2000 general election, the ruling coalition's rhetoric missed the mark and was a design disaster. One poster in this matrix says, "It's the people who choose, not NATO," while the other says "Freedom" (a word whose last syllable happens to be the word "Yes"). Photo credit: author.

Figure 2.123. JUL's campaign imagery in the 2000 election did not resonate with voters.

Presentations of the SPS and JUL, on the other hand, were confusing and generally ineffective, showing an utter lack of graphic skill. Posters from the series "It's the people who choose, not NATO" were based on the false assumption that everyone believed the message delivered by the state television every day—that all the opposition leaders were on NATO's payroll.

Another series of propaganda materials was a continuation of the JUL's earlier campaign featuring crowded pictures of happy families and girls holding bouquets of flowers.

A third series was intended to work on a local, family, and neighbor level. The problem was that that the person they chose to represent "the neighbor" was one of the most unpopular people the SPS had, and they chose him for Vračar, a municipality which the opposition regularly won. Consequently, his posters were often vandalized.

However, the main focus of the campaign was on the persona of the President, and his photos were often given special protection, under glass, on Illuminated billboards.

A separate poster, with a Partisan esthetic, followed a completely different logic. It addressed that segment of the electorate still fixated on the country's liberation at the end of World War II and the project of developing socialism. It was completely in the spirit of "remember the good old days." The President's face (when he was much younger) and an excerpt from one of his speeches were juxtaposed. Un-

Figure 2.124. The SPS campaign for the election in Vračar in 2000 had the theme "For the family." But the person they chose to represent that theme was quite unpopular, so the posters were often defaced.

fortunately, the team that published this poster lost sight of the fact that those old enough to find it inspiring had decreased significantly in number during the 1990s— and they did not need persuasion anyway, since most of them supported Milošević— whereas the number of those who were repelled by the message and its appeal to nostalgia had increased significantly.

Figure 2.125. Campaign posters for President Milošević were often placed on illuminated billboards, protected by glass to prevent vandalism. Photo credit: from the York-Zimmerman film 'Bringing Down a Dictator'

In the run-up to the September 2000 elections, there was a long and vicious "poster war." Of course, participants in this war would paste over and destroy their opponents' printed material from previous elections. But the regime's counter-propaganda campaign, combined with crude violence, exceeded anything that had been seen in earlier Serbian elections. The campaign was mainly directed against Otpor, the student-led organization that remained elusive and mysterious to the ruling coalition's political intelligence units. So they developed an irrational hatred toward the organization because they could not discover its structure and thus corrupt, control, and neutralize it.

The administration's "Madlen Jugend" poster recycled an illustration from a German magazine published during World War II, but did so in a "reprocessed" form so that the already well-known Otpor fist was incorporated onto the uniform of a Wehrmacht member and his flag. This was obviously an attempt to discredit the opposition and Otpor.

A range of similar posters preceded it onto Belgrade's streets. Some were aimed at satanizing Zoran Djindjić[140] (such as the parody of a

Figure 2.126. A Partisan-like graphic from the 2000 election. Photo credit: author.

Figure 2.127. A poster published by an unidentified government office charged with curbing change in society.

---

140 Zoran Djindjić (1952–2003) was a philosopher, the founder of the Democratic Party of Serbia (DOS), pro-European opposition leader, and the first prime minister of post-Milošević Yugoslavia. He was assassinated at the entrance of a government building in 2003 by Zvezdan Jovanović, a member of the Serbian Unit for Special Operations (JSO) which was dissolved after Djindjić's assassination.

well-known photo from the 1996–97 rallies in which the President of the Democratic Party carries his son on his shoulders: With sloppy editing, the son was replaced by the face of former US Secretary of State Madeleine Albright). Another poster featured Hashim Thaçi,[141] which was supposed to suggest a connection between the Serbian opposition and Otpor with the Kosovo Liberation Army. There were also smaller ones that imitated Otpor's graphics—with alterations, of course. One showed the Otpor fist holding a bundle of dollar bills, another had a text reading "p**OTPOR**a NATO agresiji" [Translator's note: "**Suppor**t NATO aggression"].

Everyone agrees that the outcome of the 2000 elections was to a large extent determined by the high voter turnout and by well-organized monitoring of the voting and

Figure 2.128. Billboard for the CeSID campaign whose motto was "I will monitor the elections." Someone added graffiti saying "Fuckin' snowball's chance in hell!"

ballot-counting. For the first time, there were several campaigns to animate younger voters and raise awareness of the importance of election process control. And so the nongovernmental organization CeSID (*Centar za Slobodne Izbore i Demokratiju* [Translator's note: the Center for Free Elections and Democracy]) had a campaign with the slogan: "I will be a poll watcher." Graffiti artists apparently were hired to attack almost all of their billboards, adding vulgar comments.

----

141 Hashim Thaçi was the first prime minister of Kosovo, then Kosovo's president from April 2016 until his resignation in November 2020 to face a war crimes tribunal.

2. Pathopolis

As during the 1996-97 rallies, the government was fixated on preventing the protesters from breaking through the police cordon, which was ridiculously placed on Kolarčeva Street.[142] "Counter-postering" was also led from a specific location: an intersection above Slavija square, where thugs and graffiti vandals hired from a local martial arts club worked out of a van provided by the Ministry of Science and Technology. Interestingly enough, the then-Minister of Science was a candidate in the local elections.

During the 2000 election campaign, defacement of the opposition's billboards and posters became an obsessive, well-organized, government-sponsored activity. Candidate Koštunica's face, which was the most widespread image, was a favorite target. The opposition responded by targetting the ruling coalition's billboards and posters.

Figure 2.129. Presidential candidate Vojislav Koštunica as a cat lover. Photo credit: Branimir Karanović.

Figure 2.130. Billboard defacement of Opposition leader Milan St. Protić (a candidate for mayor of Belgrade). Photo credit: author.

---

142 Kolarčeva is a street right in the center of Belgrade connecting Republic Square with Terazije.

Figure 2.131. The postcard version of a small intervention by Otpor: "He is finished"—took elements of the ruling party's propaganda to show who was finished. Photo credit: author.

Figure 2.132. "All of us are a bit socialist": an old SPS slogan takes on a new irony—one of many Otpor stickers. Photo credit: author.

Therefore, we can say with confidence that Serbia's recent revival of iconoclasm did not miss anyone whose face was found on campaign posters, not even a candidate for Belgrade mayor.

Nevertheless, the strategy of systematically damaging political opponents' portraits did not yield the expected results. So Otpor devised an alternative strategy of "small interventions." Despite not having a clear ideology, this organization understood quite well the impact of slogans and symbols. Their killer slogan, "He is finished," multiplied on stickers and postcards, appeared on nearly every building entrance, in nearly every elevator, and on nearly every traffic sign.

Other stickers joined this main motif, among them a paraphrase of an old SPS slogan: "All of us are a bit socialist"—which through context, became sharply ironic.

The strategy of small interventions included unsigned leaflets which mimicked those of the SPS. Among those distributed to citizens' mailboxes just before the election, the most successful was undoubtedly "Vote for my husband again!"

When the election was over and the continuity of the same circles governing Serbia was finally interrupted, with far less blood spilled than even optimists had predicted, there was a collective sigh of relief. Post-election billboards showing Vladan Batić, president of a minor party in the DOS coalition, appeared on the streets of Belgrade. Next to the image of the future Minister of Justice, there was a concise inscrip-

Figure 2.133. Irresistible subversion: pictured is Slobodan Milosević's much hated wife, Mirjana Marković, saying "Vote for my husband again!"

Figure 2.134. God must have been registered to vote in Serbia: a post-election poster of the Christian Democratic Party's president Vladan Batić says "Thank God!" Photo credit: author.

tion: "Thank God!" Since elections can only be won by those with citizenship and voting rights, this billboard might be taken as evidence of something the charlatans and amateur historians had claimed: God is Serbian.

Megalomaniacs

A modified kiosk or hand-painted ads are personal endeavors of minor intensity. But urban history is full of examples where not only impressive buildings but entire cities appeared as the result of an individual's will. A few late-Roman emperors, mostly with military backgrounds, built either cities or palaces as big as a city in obscure places where they were born. One of the most famous of these is Justiniana Prima near Lebane in southeastern Serbia. Since the hut where the future emperor was born was far from all roads (in the wilderness, just like today), the pompous episcopal seat with its basilicas and villas did not outlast Justinian's reign.[143]

---

143 Built by the Byzantine Emperor Justinian I to be the administrative center of the Balkan Archdiocese, Justiniana Prima was founded in 535 and abandoned in 615. Now it is an archaeological site known as Caričin Grad. See M. V. Zdravković, "Developing and Maintaining of the Long-term 3D Visualization Projects Caričin Grad–Justiniana Prima," in *Proceedings of the 23rd International al Conference on Cultural Heritage and New Technologies,* 2018, 1–11.

Figure 2.135. 3D computer reconstruction of the urban core of Justiniana Prima, based on the archeological remains. Integrating Rome and Byzantium's best urban design thinking, this was a planned city for the emperor's birthplace. It was intended to be the administrative center for the Eastern Church's Balkan archdiocese. Founded in 535, the city covered about 20 hectares, with "suburbs" for livestock and agriculture outside the protective walls. It had an integrated water distribution and sewage collection system, craft and trade shops, apartments and offices, but was abandoned in 615 when Justinian I's reign ended. Then it was demolished. All that remains are foundations, a few arches and some parts of brick and concrete walls. Photo credit: V. Zdravković, M. Urošević, M. Novčić, V. Ranđelović.

A city—and if not a city, then at least a building—is often a medium for developing utopian projects. Constructing a building creates a small world, and the construction of a city is more than that: It is the creation of an organized world. Because of this, at different times and in different places, there have been obsessed people who have wanted to play the role of a demiurge.

One of the most famous was certainly Ferdinand Cheval (1836–1924). Unlike numerous princes, popes, financial magnates, mobsters, or socialist leaders, this humble postman initiated his obsessive project alone, without stolen money. In 1879, at the age of 43, Cheval found a rock which attracted him on one of his walks around Hauterives in France. The situation repeated itself a few days later. That was the beginning of a mission that would last over thirty years and result in the "Ideal Palace"— a structure 26 by 14 meters at the foundation and up to 10 meters tall.[144]

From afar and in bad reproductions, the "Ideal Palace" resembles Angkor a little. It is a mega-mosaic sculpture, a structure surrounded by different colonnades, a kind of labyrinth decorated both inside and out. One could even say it has encyclopedic

---

144 Michel Thevoz, ed., *L'Art Brut* (Geneva: Skira, 1975), 31–36.

Figure 2.136. Ferdinand Cheval's "Ideal palace" (in French: Palais Idéal). Photo credit: Benoît Prieur (via Wikimedia Commons), CC-AS 3.0

aspirations: The dense collection of balconies, columns, caryatids, stone palms, and cactuses represent a touching personal reading of formal notions from the history of architecture, an attempt to gather them all in one place.

Somewhat different was King Christophe's project in Haiti. In 1812 the "first, last, and only"[145] black Christian king of this Caribbean country built the Sans-Souci Palace on a steep mountain above village Milot, some forty kilometers from the sea.[146] The king decided his palace was going to be more beautiful than the most beautiful European precedents, especially the French ones. The five-story building rose above a huge balcony decorated with balustrades. A double monumental staircase (a motif lifted from Versailles) brought you to the balcony. Below the whole construction, a stream flowed as some kind of rudimentary climatization; water flowed among the pools and numerous bathrooms, its babble giving a relaxing atmosphere reminiscent of the Alhambra.

The king, however, committed suicide in 1820 and the palace was pillaged. The earthquake which devastated Haiti in 1842 caused irreparable damage to the complex. Today there is no ceramic tiling in the interior, no tapestries, no library, no mirrors

---

145 See Marlene Daut, "Resurrecting a Lost Palace of Haiti," *Harper's Bazar*, 8 October 2021, https://www.harpersbazaar.com/culture/features/a37896377/resurrecting-a-lost-palace-of-haiti/.

146 Roloff Beny and Rose Macaulay, *The Pleasure of Ruins* (London: Thames and Hudson, 1964). Translated into Serbian as *Simfonije u kamenu* [Symphony in stone] (Belgrade: Izdavački zavod Jugoslavija, 1968). *Sans-Souci* is French for "carefree."

Figure 2.137. View of the Sans-Souci Palace in 1830. Engraving by J. Clark in Charles Mackenzie, *Notes on Haiti Made during a Residence in that Republic*, Volume 2 (London: H. Colburn and R. Bentley, 1830).

Figure 2.138. Recent photo of the Sans-Souci Palace, showing the symmetrical stairs. Photo credit: Rémi Kaupp (via WikiMedia Commons), CC BY-SA 3.0.

brought from Europe. Lush vegetation has broken through the mosaic and terrazzo floors and is taking away the last remnants of stucco. It has become a monumental ruin in which goats, scorpions, lizards, and snakes live on heaps of rubble.

Among similar projects but closer to our time is the construction of the majestic Basilique Notre-Dame de la Paix (Basilica of Our Lady of Peace) and the accompanying urban infrastructure in the miserable settlement of Yamoussoukro. Both are about a hundred kilometers north of Abidjan, in Côte d'Ivoire (Ivory Coast). Behind this obsessive project, there is the character of Félix Houphouët-Boigny, the country's first President, who in the late 1980s was somewhere between 84 and 93 years old, depending on the source you want to trust. Félix decided to celebrate his birthplace,

147

Figure 2.139. The Basilica of Our Lady of Peace (Basilique Notre-Dame de la Paix), some hundred kilometers north of Abidjan. Intended to be the largest Roman Catholic church in the world, the pope said he would not come to bless it if it was bigger than St. Peter's in Rome. Photo credit: Pierre Fakhoury - http://abidjan.city.ci/actualite/basilique-notre-dame-de-la-paix-yamoussoukro

where over 80% of the residents are still animists, by constructing the greatest church in the world, an enlarged replica of St. Peter's Basilica in Rome but with climatization and Bernini accessories. When the Holy Father said he would not come to consecrate the Basilica if the copy surpassed the original in its dimensions, the project was quickly scaled back, but the dome itself remained greater than Michelangelo's and is still considered the largest in the world. It is not clear whether, after the consecration, the population flocked to Roman Catholicism, attracted by the beauty of the building. But it is quite clear that the eight-lane highway connecting the sanctuary with the capital and the runway equipped for Concordes[147] are still empty.

Something that does not lag behind Félix Houphouët-Boigny's faith in ambition was constructed much closer to our country, on the most valuable land in the center of Bucharest, by a person that Mirjana Marković described in one of her inspired diary entries as Romania's "long-lasting, already old President."[148] The People's Palace was sixty percent completed when, in Dr. Professor Marković's words, the still unknown "mandator of his murder, whose cold-blooded brutality does not do justice to a European country at the very end of the twentieth century," had the Ceaușescus killed.

To prepare the area for the project in the early 1980s, many hectares of central Bucharest had to be cleared. Fourteen churches and monasteries, the whole Jewish quarter, and a range of buildings of both traditional and modern design were removed.[149]

---

147 The Concorde was Europe's supersonic passenger jet, in service from 1976 to 2003. It required very long runways for take-offs and landings.

148 Mirjana Marković, PhD., *Pretposledenje leto 20. veka* [The summer before the last in the twentieth century], women's magazine *Bazar,* 4 September (Belgrade: 1998), 8.

149 The reason so much land had to be cleared is because the project included not just the Pal-

Figure 2.140. Ceaușescu's People's Palace in Bucharest: the biggest building in Europe and second-biggest in the world. This is only the apex of the project which included the long Victory of Socialism Boulevard with large multifunction buildings, coordinated in design, lining both sides of the street. Photo credit: Vi Ko (CC BY-SA 4.0).

Figure 2.141. View from the balcony of the People's Palace, looking down Victory of Socialism Boulevard. Here we use the original names. But after the Ceaușescus were killed and the post-revolutionary government finished the construction, everything was renamed: the People's Palace became the Palace of Parliament and Victory of Socialism Boulevard became Unity Boulevard. Photo credit: Simon Laird (CC BY-SA 2.5) - https://commons.wikimedia.org/wiki/File:Palace_balcany_Unirii_view.jpg

Figure 2.142. The Palace of Parliament's International Conference Center, Bucharest. Photo credit: Frank Krueger-Boesing Fotodesign (CC BY-2.0)

This urban architectural monster is an agglomeration of styles—Renaissance, Rococo, Baroque, and Byzantine—with ideas from Transylvanian folklore. Everything is mixed and oversized. Hundreds of nuns from Moldovan monasteries spent years making lace curtains for windows up to seven meters tall. For security, the teams of architects working on the project were allowed to become familiar with only parts of it. Only the project's main architect, Anca Petrescu, who was trusted by the dictator (and, of course, by Ceaușescu's academician wife Elena), knew what the whole thing would look like. Hence, there was confusion behind the cold and formal facades, a confusion that made the Palace useless for anything. All details were carefully elaborated, but the totality slipped away.

Next to the Palace (which he proudly described as "the greatest building in Europe and the second-biggest in the world, after the Pentagon"), the former Romanian president began constructing a building for the Academy of Sciences. Like the People's Palace, it was unfinished when its inspirators departed from life.

In other words, Slobodan Milošević was not the only leader in southeastern Europe married to a scholar: Ceaușescu was too. However, we do not know if the Romanians supplied any ideas for building something worthy in Serbia to enhance the international reputation of Mirjana Marković PhD. Urbanistic undertakings during the Milošević era were reduced to proposals and pre-election news on state TV—including a major endeavor noisily promoted for sometime in the future called "The Third

---

ace, but the Victory of Socialism Boulevard, which is lined with large multifunction buildings of coordinated design on both sides of the street. The land also had to be re-graded so the Boulevard could rise up to the Palace, which sits on an artificial hill.

Figure 2.143. The "Chinese District" on Zemun quay. Photo credit: author.

Millennium"—something to do with the Sava Amphitheater on Belgrade's waterfront, an urban wasteland between the railroad tracks and the river.[150] A second project called the "Chinese District"—also noisily promoted—did not get realized as quickly as planned, although certain steps were taken on the level of demography, gastronomy, and trade.

Still, we cannot say that Serbia lacked megalomania. In the desolate facilities of a sugar refinery near Čukarica,[151] long-abandoned buildings were renovated for Ljubiša Ristić. Ristić was an unconventional theater director who became the president of the JUL,[152] one of the three governing parties during the 1990s. The public was fascinated by how quickly a shabby industrial facility became a shiny artistic/hospitality/IT center.

The main character in German director Werner Herzog's famous movie *Fitzcarraldo* (played by Klaus Kinski) was led by his obsession to build an opera house in the Amazon jungle. He didn't succeed. But Ristić did. As a journalist wrote in her text for the

---

150 A master plan for developing the Belgrade Waterfront (the area which had been called the Sava Amphitheater because of its topography) came from the United Arab Emirates, which also supplied funding. The project was embraced by Aleksander Vučić during his candidacy for President of Serbia in 2012. Vučić was elected and the plan was implemented, stimulating further renovations in the surrounding area. Milena Dragićević Šešić discusses this project in the foreword to this book.
151 Čukarica is a neighborhood in Belgrade.
152 Jugoslovenska Udružena Levica [JUL, the Yugoslav United Left] was founded in 1994 by merging nineteen small parties and movements. Its first president was Slobodan Milosević's wife, Mirjana Marković. Although it claimed to be a pro-peace Marxist-Leninist formation, its members included Serbia's richest businessmen and war profiteers. Ljubiša Ristić, who had at least appeared to be an anti-war activist, succeeded PhDr. Marković as JUL's leader. A sixteen-minute video interview with him is online at https://www.youtube.com/watch?v=nGkDFk5Y2iw as part of the "First Person History of Serbia."

Figure 2.144. An opera house in an (industrial) desert: this abandoned sugar refinery was transformed into the "International Art Center Šećerana." Note the new glass additions which contrast with the old broken windows above ground level. Photo credit: author.

national airline magazine, "For the time being, the opera house is just a ruin where an auditorium is going to be."[153] With this sentence the journalist touched the essence of the public's interest in the director/miracle-worker capable of turning a pumpkin into a fairytale palace.

In Yugoslav Left speeches, what really existed and what did not generally had the same status: Concepts like the sugar refinery's future opera house shimmered in a space between being and not-being *because it was about to be*. Such proposals were like a theatrical backdrop, which both is and is not a real construction. The rhetoric of pretentious illusion was in the very name—"The International Art Center." The use of the adjective "international" in a country under sanctions is a good joke. One could count on the fingers of one hand the number of countries that the director of this art center could enter freely. Besides, it was extremely hypocritical that "internationality" was being promoted by those who used party-state-television propaganda to turn the country into an oasis of xenophobia.

Such was the case with the "Yugoslav cultural space" exemplified by the KPGT[154] and the career of the man who, without any money—who specifically denied using JUL

---

153 Branka Krilović, "Medjunarodni art centar u Šećerani" [International art center in the Sugar Refinery], *New JAT Review,* no. 28, October (Belgrade, 1999), 96–99.
154 KPGT stands for "Kazalište, Pozorište, Gledališče, Teatar." These four words are synonyms for "theater" in the languages and dialects of the former Yugoslavia. That was also the name of

money—managed to build this technically perfect oasis of "the Yugoslav spirit."[155] He blamed unspecified "nationalists" as the destroyers of the former Yugoslavia, but did not mention the role of the League of Communists. He omitted to say that the tanks shooting at Zadar and Vukovar[156] carried the symbols of a party that evolved into the organization that Ristić himself headed, and that the bearded para-military crazies were organized by the caste gathered in JUL.

In an interview with *NIN,* Ristić claimed he was the victim of persecution by "ideological committees"—as if the people sitting in those committees were not part of the same apparatus which directed the money of those in charge of "self-management" toward Ristić's megalomaniacal and expensive "unconventional and non-institutional" projects. Of course, Ristić surely was not the only one punished in the system which preceded the "anti-bureaucratic revolution," for example, by being appointed as manager of a theater which he turned, as soon as he possibly could, into an "extra-institutional" subject by making it go bankrupt. Reality is usually no obstacle to a deep belief in one's own story or mission. This applies equally to political parties and those who lead them. The selective perception of one's self, the environment, and recent history was at the root of Ristić's decision to name certain halls in his "International Art Center" after former associates, despite the public protests of those who were still alive, and to stage Danilo Kiš's plays, despite his estate's refusal of permission.

Figure 2.145.
"Liveliness, cheerfulness, something dear to the soul"— provided by kitsch in the Še ćerana International Art Center. Photo credit: author.

Ristić's theater collective, born in the late-1970s, which claimed to be working toward keeping Yugoslavia unified through art.

155 The quoted phrases are from Jasmina Lekić's interview with Ristić, "Mermer i zvuci" [Marble and sounds], *NIN,* 20 January (Belgrade: 2000), 43.

156 Zadar and Vukovar are towns in Croatia that were seriously damaged during the 1990s war.

2. Pathopolis

Jasmina Lekić, the author of the interview with Ristić in *NIN*, admitted that there was some kitsch in the "International Art Center." But, she added, "that kitsch is present to a very small extent and it is there more to add liveliness, cheerfulness, something dear to the soul. Anyway, the idea is that a visitor should relax and forget about everything, from unrequited love to misery and humiliation, with which he has been living for a long time."[157]

Thus the "International Art Center" has the character of an anesthetic. It is nice to come across some kitsch that warms your soul in hard times—but it is much better to recognize where the hard times, misery, and humiliation came from.

Now that kitsch has been mentioned, what is it? A short definition might be a cultural product that is an insincere imitation of something artistic. From this perspective, the "International Art Center" is not just a place where there are kitschy elements here and there. Kitsch is in the very essence of this facility which embodies false authenticity. The basic motif on the front of the construction is a glass arcade that should make a visitor think he is entering the Pompidou Center in Paris instead of a provincial, decontextualized imitation—not unlike King Christophe's palace. This expanded cultural kiosk was set in the middle of nowhere, in the heart of an industrial desert, its purpose to entertain the unsophisticated—not unlike the writings of Professor Dr. Mirjana Marković. A close reading of Šećerana's architecture reminds one of her writings, in which the kitsch is also two-layered: on the surface (in her descriptions of climate change or bird songs), and deep down (in the perception of illusions as real and falsehoods as truth). Ristić's project can be said, in reality, to be a product of his manager and friend, Mirjana Marković—and not just because it was realized with money stolen from taxpayers. Although the "International Art Center" was built for audiences—that is, for the public—only party cadres visit it. It was designed for plays and concerts, but the most important performances are the sounds of mobile phones directing the movements of planes, trucks, and millions.[158] The *NIN* journalist, describing the accumulation of costly equipment, decorations, computers, furniture, canaries, and ornamental plants, admitted there was not a large audience, adding that although the shows had cheap tickets and free entry for certain categories of people, the program of events mostly generated advertising for a daily party newsletter.[159]

Just as in neighboring Romania, during the era of hunger and freezing, when residents could buy new toothpaste only if they returned the tube of the old one, yet they

---

157 Lekić, "Mermer i zvuci, "41.
158 The Serbian phrase *"avioni... kamioni"* (in English: *"planes... trucks"*) is a rhyming word-play referring ironically to people whose businesses thrive while others can hardly make ends meet.
159 Lekić, "Mermer i zvuci, "41.

would proudly say that more than seven hundred architects worked on the design of the "People's Palace," the Demiurge of the "International Art Center" said (with no less pride) that his construction approached the scale of the construction in Bucharest but without a single architect. Šećerana thus became a synthesis of Ceaușescu's pretentious self-sufficiency and Cheval's naiveté.

Like the People's Palace, King Christophe's castle, or let's say the 25 May Museum,[160] Šećerana could only function while some machinery pumped money into it. Therefore, the belief of a handful of theater employees (quickly conveyed to the press) that the ambitious facility was a gift to posterity was simply an illusion. The moment there would be no import quotas, smuggling, or party racketeering, the lights would go off and the waterfall would stop flowing—like the streams under the Haitian palace.

A superficial assessment might conclude that "Pink culture," the kiosk economy, and Šećerana have nothing in common because they belong to different spheres. But in fact they come from the same substrate. Created in the shadow of wars that were tragic for most people but immensely profitable for a few, nearly everything in this social ambience was compromised—that is, it could be described with prefixes such as "para-," "pseudo-" or "quasi-." Societies that put an equal sign between structures of government and criminal gangs are not rare in eastern and southeastern Europe. But it seems that in Yugoslavia, and especially in its capital Belgrade, this equation had clearer contours and a deeper imprint on the environment than in other places.

*   *   *

Changes in the urban landscape of Belgrade were only a projection of the devolution caused by Slobodan Milošević and his supporters. Imaginative attics that trampled on the architecture of the past, outrageous palaces, and a multitude of kiosks, all were concrete manifestations of the politics which, over ten years, wrought havoc on people's consciousness, moral principles, and the beliefs of whole generations. Jusuf Hadžifejzović once remarked that it is only one step from kitsch to blood.[161] A review of Belgrade at the turn of the third millennium must lead to the conclusion that such urban mutations could only be caused by a government whose arms were in blood up to their elbows.

----

160 Tito's birthday was celebrated on 25 May with the annual relay race for youth. The 25 May Museum houses birthday gifts given to Tito.
161 Hadžifejzović is an artist who lives in Sarajevo. "From Kitsch to Blood Is Only One Step" was the title of his performance at the Cetinje Biennale in Montenegro in 1991. More recently, this phrase (credited to Hadžifejzović) was carved in granite and shown at the 2013 Venice Bienale by Mladen Miljanović, Bosnia-Hercegovina's representative in the exhibition.

We Won (2): The Eternity Which Lasted a Few Months

On Monday, 12 June 2000, at 9:30 pm, as part of the celebration of the first anniversary of the end of NATO air raids, a monument called *Obelisk večne vatre* [Obelisk of the eternal flame] was inaugurated in New Belgrade.[162] In the presence of state, party, and military leaders, along with Professor Mirjana Marković (who could be considered the source of the idea to create this monument), Milutin Mrkonjić, the commissioner of "renewal and reconstruction," and people brought in by buses, the President of Serbia, Milan Milutinović, after a speech full of stirring slogans including the sentence "Now we will light it," pressed a button and lit the "eternal" flame—which would, it turned out, burn for only a few months.[163] Like everything created in the Milošević era, the headline was "nearly true"—that is to say, false—since obelisks do not have an element on the top, let alone a flame.

In analyzing this creation, we must start with the location. The area called Ušće [Confluence] is marked by the building that people know as "CK,"[164] which somehow ideologizes it. In addition, the Obelisk is situated within another ideological relic, the Non-Aligned Movement's Park of Friendship. Until recently, under the planted trees one could find bronze nameplates informing passers-by that a specific tree was planted by, let's say, Haile Selassie, Idi Amin Dada, or Jean-Bédel Bokassa. In happier times, there was even a guard service and pavilion where interested visitors could see the plan of the park, which made finding the right tree/person easy.

The Obelisk of the Eternal Flame is twenty-seven meters tall—a drastic reduction from the initially proposed height of seventy eight meters (to mark the seventy eight days of NATO's action against Serbia). It was erected as the joint effort of several public companies in just ten days—and it looks like it. The designers' names are written on a bronze plaque on the back of the monument: the Radović brothers (academic sculptors Svetozar and Svetomir), architecture graduates Marko Stevanović and Miodrag Cvijić, and the companies GOSI d.o.o. and Tripković-Djokić.

----

162 Apart from reports in the daily press, the weekly *Vreme* published a group of articles about this event in issue no. 493 (17 June 2000), including Biljana Vasić's "Noći i dani Mirjane Marković" [Nights and days of Mirjana Marković] and Slobodan Kostić's "Simbolika večne vatre" [Symbolism of the eternal flame]. *NIN* published a thorough analysis by its architecture critic Milorad H. Jevtić titled "Novi Socrealizam na Ušću" [New socialist realism on Ušće] in the issue dated 22 June 2000.

163 Right after the 5 October change of government, the new opposition (that is to say, the previous government) accused the new DOS government of "turning off the eternal flame." But this was a lie since gas from the tank barracks placed inappropriately close to the monument was cut off even before the SPS lost the 2000 elections.

164 As mentioned earlier, "CK" stands for the Central Committee of the League of Communists of Yugoslavia. The "business center" building in Ušće was their headquarters.

The designers collaborated on finding a solution for the obelisk as an assembled beam formwork. The material is visible even from far, despite the fact that it was painted white. There is obvious sloppiness in the way it was executed, giving the impression of being temporary or a stage prop. The pedestal with a cross foundation rises on a cubic base lifted by a step which here plays the role (unsuccessfully) of a visual transition. However, at the top we are greeted by the object's central misunderstanding: inside the bronze sculpture of a fire, there is a torch—that is, a real fire. Although you can put an equal sign between bronze as a sculptural alloy and the fire needed to melt metal, the whole concept is a bizarre overlapping of an entity with its representation.

An "eternal flame" is a special kind of monument, at least in cities like Paris, Warsaw, Leningrad/St. Petersburg, or Sarajevo, which have reliable gas supplies—unlike Belgrade. In other fire memorials, the flame is at ground level. You can approach it. A visitor can focus their thoughts and direct them toward the memorialized victims with a short meditation in front of the fire. With all its symbolic, subconscious, and other meanings, fire is enough for a monument on its own. But it is not enough here. Like a transvestite who must apply more makeup than a real woman, a monument for something that was a defeat but is portrayed as a victory must exaggerate its visual rhetoric.

Figure 2.146. After Milošević was removed from office, the "Obelisk of the Eternal Flame" started accumulating graffiti on its base and brass letters from the inscription were stolen, making the text unreadable. Because the Obelisk had been built without a legal permit, it was not protected by the Institute for the Protection of Cultural Monuments. This was sorted out years later and the monument was finally cleaned and repaired in 2019. Photo credit: Pinki (Serbian Wikipedia), released into the public domain.

The size and coloring of the Obelisk of the Eternal Flame have another aspect: there is a clear effort to evoke an association with Ivan Meštrović's *Pobednik* [The victor]. Erected between the two world wars on a high pedestal in Kalemegdan Park (after many heated discussions about the risk of putting a male nude sculpture in a pub-

157

lic place where it could corrupt the morals of women), The Victor is visible from Ušće on the other side of the river. Such an association with a well-known memorial of the Balkan Wars, made by one of Yugoslavia's most revered artists, shows a need to put the Obelisk (like other creations of the "ruling family") in a place it doesn't deserve, to connect it with genuine markers of history and tradition.

These features were enough for the Obelisk of the Eternal Flame to be recognized as a renewal of socialist realism.[165] Even the texts on the pedestal support that reading. On the front are words whose author we can recognize from the style, even if her name is not shown. Professor Marković, an academic thanks to one of the numerous Russian academies in which membership can be supplied by suitable sponsors, compiled her work by choosing verses from the most popular modern Serbian poet, Branko Miljković. On one side, there is an inscription carved in the marble slab:

> "All that lacks fire within itself burns out
> What burns out becomes night
> What burns not gives birth to day"

and on the other side:

> "TO OUR HOMELAND—Even if they kill me, I love you."

The main text on the pedestal tells us in letters glued to the marble (not engraved):

> "May this fire burn forever[166] in memory of the war that 19 NATO countries[167] fought against Serbia from 24 March to 10 June 1999. May it also burn forever in memory of the heroic defense of Serbia in which the whole nation took part. May it burn forever for the whole world.[168] To be free, the world must find courage and strength within itself, as we did in our fight and liberation in the spring and summer of 1999."

Only a few months after the opening ceremony (during which it was suggested that Slobodan Milošević should get the Order of National Hero medal), the pedestal proved that unfortunately there are thieves and destruction-prone individuals in the population: letters went missing, making the long inscription unreadable. This could be inter-

---

165 See Jevtić's article in *NIN*.
166 Forever, as we shall see, proved brief.
167 All the NATO countries are listed by name. The war itself had no name.
168 Note the megalomaniac, global, messianic pretensions.

preted as some kind of self-destructive, even suicidal impulse within such an important social formation as the nation. And this started before the 5 October "coup"—after which vandalizing the monument would not be seen as an attack on the state.[169]

The Obelisk of Eternal Flame materialized and made visible the hypocrisy and delusions of an era that spread from the epicenter of one family, one party, and one government to the farthest reaches of Serbia. Maybe we can say everything came full circle at this place, in Ušće: what started with rallies and dancing the waltz with the leader's picture ended as a spatial caricature. With its flame on top of a pole, the monument is more like a torch than an obelisk. Still, the nearby ruin of CK, left as a metal skeleton after NATO bombed it, was a reminder of the ruins all over the Western Balkans which were created before these local remains.[170] The inspiration for such an array of ruins, for "older and more beautiful" cities after the newer less beautiful ones were flattened, came from this epicenter. It seems that these "victories," whose real moral consequences would be felt by future generations, found answers not just in the flawed conception of a monument but in the ambiance of a city which—as they kept saying for a long time—"was not in a war."

---

169 Because the Obelisk of Eternal Flame was built without a legal permit, the Institute for the Protection of Cultural Monuments could not protect it. After the ouster of Slobodan Milosević, graffiti started to accumulate on the base and gradually all the letters from the long inscription were stolen. Serbia's current government finally repaired the monument in 2019. On 15 December 2020, there was a ceremony to relight the flame. Russian Foreign Minister Sergey Lavrov personally delivered the fire for the relighting. Serbia's President Vučić said in his speech that the flame was relit "to remind us eternally that Serbia and Russia, in their desire for the world to be a better place for future generations, won great victories through terrible ordeals, thus building strong ties between our fraternal countries… That is why our task today is to fight against the rewriting of history…" Minister Lavrov replied that "thanks to the consistent position of Serbia's leadership on preserving historical truth and the memory of our ancestors' heroic deeds, the eternal flame was lit in the heart of the Serbian capital. We consider this new monument in memory of the liberating soldiers a symbol of the spiritual and historical unity of the Russians and the Serbs." Quoted from "Eternal Flame—a symbol of Serbian and Russian traditions of freedom," Serbian Ministry of Defense website, 15 December 2020, https://www.mod.gov.rs/eng/16816/vecna-vatra-simbol-slobodarske-tradicije-srpskog-i-ruskog-naroda-16816.

170 The Serbian editions of this book were published before CK was reconstructed as the Ušće Business Center.

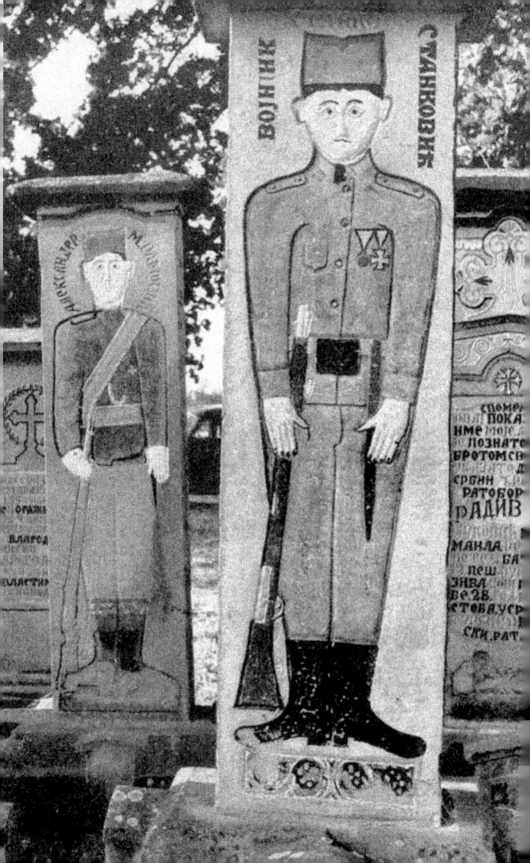

3

Necropolis

Princes, Living and Dead

In late November 1991, a letter from Madrid came to the office of Turgut Özal, who was then President of Turkey. As we know, all around the world people shower powerful individuals and institutions with letters, attempting to solve their private problems. We also know that a majority of such letters do not even end up in the archives. On their way to the recipient, the hardworking secretaries' hands redirect them to a wastebasket or to other officers in charge. But Özal's sender was not just an ordinary citizen suffering injustice. Next to his name—Alexei II—there was a whole range of surnames from history textbooks. This may have inspired the President's secretaries to at least read it.

Judging by what was at first briefly reported by the daily press,[1] the content of the letter was completely suitable for the surname and the titles: *Prince d'Anjou Alexei II Nemanjić Romanov Dolgorouki, etc., etc.*, requested that the President of Turkey return to Serbia the holy relics—and specifically, Prince Lazar's head[2]—which he claimed were in Sultan Murad's tomb in Bursa. The Serbian public quickly got acquainted with the contents of the letter. The magazine *On* [He] published it in January 1992:

----

1   *Borba* (Belgrade: 27 November 1991).
2   Prince-Czar Lazar Hrebeljanović (1329–1389) wanted to resurrect the Serbian Empire as the successor of the Nemanjić dynasty which had ruled Serbia for two centuries. He was killed in the Battle of Kosovo fighting against the Ottoman Empire led by Sultan Murad in June 1389. The Orthodox Christian Church venerates Lazar as a martyr and saint.

3. Necropolis

"SAR[3] PRINCE—THE GREAT MASTER
TO HIS EXCELLENCY
MR. PRESIDENT OF THE STATE
THE TURKISH REPUBLIC

Your Excellency,

It is my honor to address you as a double representative: the legal heir of the Sovereign and military order of St. John of Jerusalem, the Orthodox Order from Rhodes and Malta, Protector of the Orthodox people and Slavs, and as the only direct descendant of Serbian Tsar Lazar, who died in the Battle of Kosovo on that wretched day in 1389 which all Orthodox and Slavic peoples remember.

As the Orthodox Slavic peoples slowly exit from the deep and tragic dark of atheist and materialist communism, which had been oppressing and exploiting them for decades, my task is to contribute to the making of peace between Orthodox Slavs on one side and a Muslim nation on the other, while both nations are threatened now by dark black forces.

At this tragic moment, when the Serbian people, the people of my Nemanjić ancestors, are faced with one of the hardest temptations in their history, my heart and my blood are pushing me to fulfill my duties and to try to bring back to Serbia a symbol for her sons, no matter how belittled it is. Mr. President, I am talking about the head of my ancestor, Tsar Lazar, who was buried in Turkey, below the feet (remains) of Sultan Murad, who also died in the Battle of Kosovo in 1389. I am addressing you because the Serbs would accept this kind gesture from Turkey unanimously and with great joy, and at this painful moment it would be, for them and for all Orthodox Slavic people, a symbol of renewal and peacemaking for our peoples.

I do not doubt for a moment, Mr. President, that you and the authorities in Turkey will know how to estimate the real value of my request which I am sending to you today, as the Great Master of the only Order to support the rights of the Turkish Cypriots since a few years ago, given by our order's Great Supplicant to President Denktaş.

As an Orthodox Slavic prince, a direct descendant of the great Serbian dynasty Nemanjić, I am praying to almighty God that Turkey accepts my legitimate request to reconcile our peoples.

Mr. President, kindly trust my deepest feelings.

With much appreciation and respect,

Alexei

PRINCE D'ANJOU NEMANJIĆ ROMANOV DOLGORUKI
LAWFUL PRINCE
GREAT MASTER OF THE ORDER OF ST. JOHN OF JERUSALEM
In Madrid, in exile, 24 November 1991"

---

3   SAR is the French abbreviation for His/Her Royal Highness.

Unfortunately, we still do not know if Mr. Özal replied to the irresistible suggestions of this international crook, who was a pretender to several European thrones (including a nonexistent one—that of the Ukraine). However, the magazine *On* (which, following market trends, had previously offered a high-quality poster of Slobodan Milošević's face) worked hard to promote Prince d'Anjou Alexei II. The "Prince's" campaign was organized to neutralize the effect of the first visit to Serbia by Aleksandar Karadjordjević, Crown Prince of Yugoslavia, a man who also did not have a throne but, unlike the pretender residing in Spain, did not need to construct a lavish identity complete with pretentious writing. Nor was Prince d'Anjou Alexei II the only foreign fraud presented to the Serbian public in those years. Sometime earlier, but

Figure 3.1. Cover of On Magazine, 3 January 1992: Prince d'Anjou Alexei II Nemanitch Romanoff Dolgorouki (Order of Saint Jerusalem) wishes his future subjects a Happy New Year. Photo credit: On, in the author's collection.

with much less success than Alexei, the state television broadcast an interview with a certain *Oriental Emperor, the Tsar and King of Serbia, Bosnia, and Dušan the Mighty's Empire, the Great Moderator of Šumadija, Hadži-Marcijan II Lavarel Obrenović*. Another aspirant to the throne was Šćepan Mali, a Montenegrin falsely claiming to be Russian Tsar Peter III Romanov.

Prince d'Anjou Alexis II Nemanjić Romanov Dolgorouk sometimes added *de Bourbon-Conde, Volodar of Ruthenian Ukraine Kyiv* to his titles. At other times he added the *Duke of Durazzo and Bourbon*. At first his real identity was thought to be Michal Goleniewski, a Polish immigrant and CIA asset[4] who later claimed to be Tsar Alexei Romanov who had miraculously survived. But his real name turned out to be Victor Brimeyer. He did not reach perfection in the craft of misrepresentation: He was sentenced to eighteen months in prison in 1971 for using false names and titles. But he

---

4   For a recent biography see Kevin Coogan, *The Spy Who Would Be Tsar: The Mystery of Michal Goleniewski and the Far-Right Underground* (Oxfordshire, England: Routledge, 2021).

ran away in time to Spain, a country traditionally tolerant of pretenders. In Spain, he managed to get hold of a new ID with some of the well-known surnames listed in it.

Prince d' Anjou Alexei II was also discussed at the first multi-party Parliament of the Republic of Serbia in 1991. SPO deputy Mihajlo Marković stated: "the only living descendant from the Nemanjić family" was ready to help Serbia with 3.5 billion dollars and wanted nothing in return. He asked why the government remained silent about that offer.[5]

The public soon got an opportunity to see their future monarch: Alexei II became a necessary ingredient of the magazine *On* and frequent guest on the TV show "Zločesta deca" [Naughty Kids] on Radio-TV Serbia's national Channel 3. Along with many other pieces of evidence of Prince d'Anjou's high birth, the magazine *On* gave an irrefutable one—from Dragoljub Riović's mouth: a seer, prophet, psychic, and an expert in ichthyomancy (the nearly forgotten skill of reading the future in fish intestines).[6]

However, this "philanthropic opportunity" soon received a small cloud: the legal representative of Prince d'Anjou Alexei II (who did not need anything since he was "a highly esteemed and rich businessman, with an elaborate network of agencies") showed interest in the estate of Mrs. Vera Pahromenko-Mihajlović, who died in Belgrade without an heir. Newspapers wrote about the possibility that, stored in the safe boxes of JIK Banka, there was part of the Romanov treasure, perhaps including the golden cross with diamonds belonging to Tsar Peter the Great.[7]

Along with the publisher of the magazine *On,* the first promoter of Prince d' Anjou Alexei II in Serbia was Belgrade lawyer Borivoje Borović, who happened also to be Alexei II's consul. But the person with the most media exposure at that time was surely Vojislav Šešelj, who was lobbying for the pretender Nemanjić Dolgoruki.[8] Šešelj claimed to have been decorated by Alexei with the title of duke. This Doctor of National Defense and President of the Serbian Radical Party had a personal audience in Spain with the future sovereign and descendant not only of the Nemanjić dynasty but also that of Tsar Lazar (let's not even mention the Anjou and Romanov families). Dur-

---

5   *Politika* (Belgrade: 27 November 1991).

6   Magazine *On*, no. 54 (Belgrade: 1 March 1992), 57.

7   Milan Janković, "Afera Pahromenko ponovo uzbuđuje jugoslovensku javnost—Princ je živ?" [The Pahromenko affair upsets the Yugoslav public again—the Prince is alive?], *Politika ekspres* (Belgrade: 6 December 1991), and by the same author, "Carević ili obaveštajac?" [A Tsarevich or an intelligence officer?], *Politika ekspres* (Belgrade: 7 December 1991).

8   Šešelj was Serbia's deputy prime minister from 1998 to 2000. The subject of his doctoral dissertation was *The Political Essence of Militarism and Fascism*. But his magnum opus is a 1000-page compilation titled *The Ideology of Serbian Nationalism*, published in five volumes by the Radical Party between 2002 and 2011. An English translation is online at https://doczz.net/doc/1517755/the-ideology-of-serbian-nationalism.

ing that visit in February 1992, the false tsar decorated the false duke with a false Medal of Saint George and in return obtained his collected works.[9]

What's more, in the little town of Huesca (judging by a very detailed travelogue on the pages of *On*) they spoke about the possibility of renting the Great War Island in Belgrade for thirty or fifty years, about the Prince's investments in the free trade zone, as well as the fact that the Prince d'Anjou had already taken the first steps to bring special instruments from the USA to Bursa to X-ray "scan" the inside of Murad's tomb. According to the Spanish press, Vojislav Šešelj offered Alexei II the crown of his ancestors (at least the Serbian one), but after returning to his homeland this part of the visit was somehow covered up and relativized.[10]

In this now almost forgotten affair (whose main protagonist, the Anjou Prince, died in the meantime), it is not strange that an experienced international crook, with his team constructing false genealogies, wrote to presidents. It is also not strange that in Serbia some people were hoping to profit from the promotion of a new Šćepan Mali.[11] But it was

Figure 3.2. A faux-duke visits a faux-prince: Alexei II Nemanitch Romanoff Dolgorouki (left) and Vojislav Šešelj (right) in Spain. Photo credit: cover of On magazine, 1 March 1992 issue, in the author's archive.

---

9 Borislav Lalić, "'Princu' presto, 'vojvodi' titula–španska potraga Vojislava Šešelja za 'budućim kraljem Srbije'" [A throne for the 'Prince,' a title for the 'Duke'–Vojislav Šešelj's Spanish search for the 'future king of Serbia'], *Politika ekspres* (Belgrade, 13 February 1992).

10 The website of the Russian Imperial Family Historical Society says that "on the 11th of February 1992 in a private ceremony that took place in the Parador Nacional de Monte Perdido in Bielsa (Aragon), Alexis solemnly accepted the crown of Serbia. According to ABC [a Spanish newspaper]... Alexis in reality was accepting the crown of a huge nonexistent Serbia whose borders he claims were those of 1918. Evidently Alexis never traveled to Belgrade to sit on the Serbian throne! After this fiasco [the ceremony was not endorsed by the Serbian government or preceded by any referendum to restore the monarchy, so others saw it as simply an attempt to validate the Radical Party's goal of creating a "Greater Serbia" based on the 1918 borders], he had no chance whatsoever to be accepted into the 'Royal Club' as all its members rallied in support of His Royal Highness Prince Alexander Karageorgević" [a rival claimant to Serbia's throne who did not support territorial expansion]. Carlos Mundy, "The truth about Prince Alexis d'Anjou-Durassow, Duke of Durazzo," http://www.russianimperialfamily.com/en/the-truth-about-prince-alexis-danjou-durassow-duke-of-durazzo/.

11 Šćepan Mali ["Little Stefan"] (~1739–1773) arrived in Montenegro in 1766 and two years later replaced Prince-Bishop Sava as monarch after convincing people that he was actually the deposed

very strange that millions of Serbs, immersed in stories about their glorious past, did not know where Prince Lazar's head and relics were.

Two years before the "coronation" in Spain, Prince Lazar's relics were the center of the Serbian public's attention. On 28 June 1989, six centuries after he was killed on the battlefield, there was a grand jubilee in Kosovo Polje which abused elements of the Kosovo myth in the most brazen way, largely to benefit the cult of Slobodan Milošević. Lazar's relics were not part of the show, which gathered 2 million people (according to the Belgrade press) or 300,000 people (according to Reuters). This was above all a political manifestation: Discord with the mythological version of the battle in Slobodan Milošević's speech was transferred into the need to be in accord with his politics. But at that moment the relics were nearby, visiting the monastery of Gračanica,[12] an important stop on their way from Belgrade to the Ravanica monastery during a year-long procession whose route included many places where there would be fighting in the future Yugoslav war.

Starting in 1988, when the modern journey of Lazar's relics began, memories of the dead became more prominent in Serbia's contemporary life. The remains of people killed long ago were located and dug up in order to be properly buried. Re-burials for those killed in the fighting of 1941–1945 were broadcast on state television, with comments that fueled ethnic hatred. These "resurrections" compressed and cancelled linear time, so that long-past events became part of the present in a complex but tangible way.[13]

Relics are defined as the bodily remains (a whole body, its parts, or just a particle) of a person whose cult has been approved by the church. In other words, bodies can become relics only if the person was the subject of an existing, canonically approved, cult. In the Roman Catholic Church, strict and precise rules developed about how someone becomes designated as a saint. In the Eastern Orthodox Church, such strict rules were never formulated, although it is clear that some elements are necessary

---

Russian Tsar Peter III. According to Wikipedia, "A Russian delegation finally arrived in Montenegro in 1769, exposed Šćepan as a fraud and briefly imprisoned him, but released him and returned him to power upon realising that he was the most competent of Montenegro's potential rulers... In 1771, Šćepan was injured in an accident involving a land mine. From that point until the end of his life, he was carried around in a sedan chair... He ruled until he was murdered by one of his servants, bribed by the Ottomans, in September 1773." https://en.wikipedia.org/wiki/%C5%A0%C4%87epan_Mali

12 One of the most beautiful Serbian monasteries, Gračanica is on the World Heritage List. Ordered by Serbian King Milutin and built in 1321, it is in the village of Gračanica, 10 kilometers from Priština, in Kosovo.

13 Katherine Verdery, *The Political Lives of Dead Bodies: Reburial and Postsocialist Change* (New York: Columbia University Press, 1999). See in particular the paragraph "Reconfiguring time" in the section "Giving proper burial," 111–127.

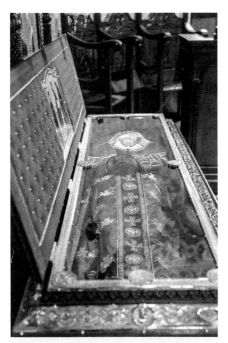

Figure 3.3. Prince Lazar's are the Serbian people's most venerated relics. Their whereabouts have been known for many centuries. Photo credit: Serbian Orthodox Monastery Ravanica.

Figure 3.4. In 1988, Prince Lazar's relics set off on their last travel (for now), back to the mausoleum in Ravanica. Photo credit: Imre Szabó.

for a cult to be officially recognized. In the case of Prince Lazar, there is enough historical material for us to believe that his cult was established soon after his death in the Battle of Kosovo. Among the elements needed for his remains to be recognized as relics was *translation,* the process of the relics being carried from the first grave into a reliquary, and placement of the reliquary into the prospective saint's legacy (in his case, the monastery of Ravanica, which Lazar founded). Translation is a key stage in canonization, carefully detailed in contemporary descriptions.

Prince Lazar's relics had the longest translation in Serbian history. In the First Great Serbian Migration (1690), the monks from Ravanica carried their most sacred object with them into exile. A church made of wood was initially erected in Szentendre.[14] Then the relics were translated to Vrdnik, a Fruška Gora monastery that would later take the name of Ravanica, in 1697. At the beginning of a new war between the

---

14 If we compare the Great Serbian Migration with the Jewish Exodus, we can clearly connect the translation of Lazar's reliquary with the Ark of the Covenant.

Austro-Hungarian and Ottoman Empires, they were moved to the town of Futog, and during the tumultuous year of 1848, to the Fenek monastery in Klenak village, then back to Vrdnik three months later. At the beginning of World War II, due to the proximity of a military facility with a gas storage tank, they were transferred to another monastery in Fruška Gora, Bešenovo, from where the Ustaše took them to Zagreb together with other monastery treasures. By the middle of 1942, they were allowed to be transferred to Belgrade[15] where they lay in St. Michael's Cathedral until Vidovdan in 1988, when they were finally returned to Ravanica after nearly three centuries.[16]

Leontije Pavlović, one of the few scholars given the opportunity to examine nearly all of the relics of local persons whose cults were recognized by the Orthodox Church, gives a precise description of Lazar's relics:

Lazar's head is separate from his body and wrapped up in a white embroidered cloth. Above it, there is a red canvas with a large embroidery and in the middle of it, a large crown with a pearl border. The head is with all the muscles on the face. There is no hair on the head and the earlobes are small. The skull is forcefully poked through at the back and a part of the bone has fallen into the now empty skull. The eyes are very well kept, the nose is flattened, and the upper part of the larynx and the tongue still exist. Some parts of the skin below the jaw hang loosely which leaves the impression of awfulness... Lazar's body, and especially the skull, are remarkably well-kept today, which is rare in the Serbian Medieval Age.[17]

Based on studies of the relics, and the fact that Lazar's original robe was kept together with the relics (the only item of clothing from the Serbian Middle Ages kept whole) we can say with absolute certainty that Prince Lazar's relics were already in Serbia,[18] so the tempting offer by Prince d' Anjou Alexei II Nemanjić Romanov Dolgorouki, etc., etc. and his local envoys was baseless.

----

15 Mihaljčić, 203, and Dr. Ljubomir Durković–Jakšić, "Spasavanje moštiju srpskih svetitelja kneza Lazara, cara Uroša i Stevana Štiljanovića prenosom iz fruškogorskih manastira 1942. godine u Beograd" [The rescue of the relics of Serbian Saints Prince Lazar, Tsar Uroš, and Stevan Štiljanović by translating them from the monasteries in Fruška Gora to Belgrade in 1942] in Branislav Živković, *Manastir Ravanic: Spomenica o šestoj stogodišnjici* [Monastery Ravanica: The six hundred-year memorial] (Belgrade: Episkop, 1981), 215–28.

16 There was an intention to make the translation earlier but some problem always intervened. If we accept the notion that Prince Lazar is some kind of metaphysical pillar of the nation and every location at which his relics reside differs from the one stipulated for it, this suggests a displacement or de-centering of the nation.

17 Leontije Pavlović, *Kultovi lica kod Srba i Makedonaca* [Personality cults among Serbs and Macedonians] (Smederevo, Serbia: Narodni muzej, 1965).

18 There is a complete record of the locations of the objects in Lazar's reliquary. In addition to the robe, there was also a covering for the face and an embroidery by nun Jefimija with its famous

The Battle of Kosovo, about which a complex myth was formed throughout the centuries, is still seen as the most important event in Serbian history.[19] In the legend of Kosovo, there are the leading (we could even say archetypal) characters of a ruler-martyr, heroes, and traitors. The central figure—Lazar—had some modulations in the way he was represented during different epochs. Initially, he was a martyr and picture-perfect ruler—or at least someone who maintained the idea of state continuity after the Migration. Suddenly today he is represented as a holy warrior. These modulations appear in artistic representations whose sequence starts with a *ktitor*[20] portrait in Ravanica, his only portrait painted while he was still

Figure 3.5. The authenticity of Prince Lazar's relics—even his cut-off head—was confirmed after research by Leontije Pavlović, the author of the most important study of the remains associated with veneration cults in Serbia. Photo credit: author.

alive. At the other end of the sequence, the annual exhibition "Soldiers as Artists" (*Vojnici—likovni umetnici*) has recently been revived in the Central Club of Yugoslav Soldiers. This is just one of many attempts to recontextualize military tradition for a new state (FR Yugoslavia), by defining a new lineage from the Battle of Kosovo to the First World War to a modern technologically equipped armada, while avoiding everything that happened in World War II, the post-war cult of the Yugoslav National Army, and the 1990s.

Saint Prince Lazar is obviously presented as a holy warrior on the invitation to the "Soldiers as Artists" exhibition.[21] Recently painted, but in the style of a late-Byzantine

---

text of praise. Lazar Mirković was the first who wrote about the robe: "Haljina Kneza Lazara" [Prince Lazar's robe], *Umetnički pregled*, 3/1937, 72–73, a detailed description and contemporary study in *Istorija primenjene umetnosti kod Srba* [The Serbian history of applied arts] by Dobrila Stojanović (Belgrade: Republička zajednica nauke Srbije, 1977), 296–297.

19 Olga Zirojević, "Kosovo u kolektivnom pamćenju" [Kosovo in the collective memory], in Nebojša Popov (ed.), *Srpska strana rata—Trauma i katarza u istorijskom pamćenju* [The Serbian side of the war—Trauma and catharsis in historical memory] ((Belgrade: Republika, 1996, 201–231) is not only a perfectly concise synthesis reaching to our time but also a very reliable guide through the most relevant literature on this subject.

20 *Ktitor* was the person who donated the construction cost to found a church or monastery in the Middle Ages.

21 Miodrag Marković, "O ikonografiji svetih ratnika u istočnohrišćanskoj umetnosti i o predstavama ovih svetitelja u Dečanima" [On the iconography of holy warriors in East Christian art and representations of these saints in Dečani], in *Zidno slikarstvo manastira Dečana* [Wall painting of Monastery Dečani], Book DCXXXII (Belgrade: SANU Special Editions, 1995).

fresco, the image shows Lazar in the full combat gear of a medieval knight. As far as we know, this is the first representation of that type, since Lazar is conventionally shown in his ruler's robe. With this newly minted, pseudo-antique portrait, Lazar takes over the role of the archetypal hero-warrior, which in the Kosovo legend had belonged to Miloš Obilić. (Miloš, who killed Sultan Murat during the battle, had earlier been cast in the role of the saint, even though his cult was non-canonical—that is to say, unofficial. But then, starting in the nineteenth century, he was represented as a holy warrior.) Thus, the way the main figures in the Kosovo legend were depicted changed as the centuries passed, although the roles they filled were limited in number.

Every history is a story that the living tell about the dead and their legacy. It can say a lot about people from the old days, but it says at least as much (although involuntarily) about the living.

Figure 3.6. Invitation to the exhibition "Pripadnici Vojske Jugoslavije likovni stvaraoci" [Members of the Yugoslav Army as Artists] which used medieval iconography and military photographs to re-present Prince Lazar as a holy warrior.

Rulers' Graves

Tombstones—modest ones and as well as large mausoleums—are important elements in the legacy of former generations. Whole epochs can be read from them, or at least some important aspects of the societies that created them. From tombstones, we can learn a lot about relationships with ancestors and attitudes toward death, but also about the aesthetic preferences of those who erected those memorials. The concept of beauty, when analyzed, reveals a whole set of ideals almost constituting an inventory of a social moment. Many societies give more generously to the dead than to the living.

The end of the twentieth century in Serbia brought the renewal of many old local sepulchral traditions. Sometimes it came down to just copying. Sometimes the search for ideas was more imaginative and subtle—whether the role model was an older mausoleum or in the modernist national idiom. United with new fashions and outside influences (the mass media, what expats saw while working abroad, etc.), but also supported by the expansion of technical possibilities (easier import of stone, improvements in image transfers), tombstones in Serbia from the 1960s onward display fascinating fusions of influences which correlate with changes to the social horizon. But to get to the story told to the living by the grave markers of twentieth century Serbia, we need to get back to the double tradition: the high one belonging to the monuments of rulers and nobles, and the lower one connected to common people.

In the process of Stefan Nemanja's canonization, artistic models were defined that established spatial and symbolic norms for rulers' graves. As a rule, the graves are in the western tray of the mausoleum (the funerary part) and shaped like a sarcophagus. Some twenty examples have survived to the present, in temples created on the lands of the medieval Serbian state. At the place reasonably considered the very center of Serbian medieval culture and an important exterritorial place in the national history, the brother of the greatest Albanian national hero, Gjergj Kastrioti Skenderbeu, is buried. That his grave is in the most important Serbian sanctuary clearly testifies to how different the relations between Balkan peoples in the past were than in the twentieth century, and even different from what modern accounts depict.

After the medieval state collapsed, Serbia was ruled by foreigners in distant capitals, which interrupted the local tradition of ruler's mausoleums. But the tradition continued without interruption in nearby countries. Austrian tsars from the Habsburg dynasty were buried, as a rule, in Vienna. The burial was preceded by dismemberment, with some parts of the body separately embalmed and placed in separate locations. In that custom, we can discern a faint echo of the myth of Osiris, whose body parts were distributed all over ancient Egypt (Misíra). This territorialization of death, spreading the remains around a wide area to "claim" the land symbolically, can be recognized as one of the elements in a cry that turned into a bellow during the 1990s Western Balkan wars: the claim that "Serbian territory is where there are Serbian graves."

Even the traditions for burying Roman Catholic popes preserve some of the ancient rituals. The procedure consists of light embalming, display of the body, and before this, a ritual in which the Cardinal Carmelengo lightly knocks the deceased Pope on the forehead with a special silver hammer and calls him by his Christian (not papal) name. When he does not reply, the Cardinal informs him: "You are dead." The papal ring is taken off his hand and broken. This ritual stimulated the imagination of many writers, among them Miloš Crnjanski,[22] whose *Kod Hiperborejaca* [Among the Hyperboreans] begins with a description of Pope Pius XI's slow death.

----

22 Miloš Crnjanski (1893–1977) was one of the most important creators of Serbian literature in the twentieth century. His most famous works are *Lament nad Beogradom* [Lament over Belgrade], *Seobe* [Migrations], and *Roman o Londonu* [A novel of London].

3. Necropolis

The twentieth century brought the first atheist state. In an earlier chapter it was noted how ancient practices moved into the official new tradition, exemplified by the embalming of Lenin and his mausoleum in Moscow. To maintain his body, a whole institute with many employees was created in Moscow. For a long time it was the best-equipped biochemical laboratory in the Soviet Union. When, after the breakup of the USSR and during the presidency of Boris Yeltsin, it was decided not to continue financing the institute charged with maintaining a corpse, which was also embalming the leaders of friendly countries, the Institute started to work on the market principle. So its clients became the only people in Russia who could afford the costly embalming procedure: the new rich and criminals.[23]

After 1948, Josip Broz Tito's leadership deviated from the paths taken by other Eastern bloc countries. So when he died after a long illness in the Clinical Center in Ljubljana, Slovenia, at the end of April or the beginning of May 1980, the planning of his burial and mausoleum also deviated from "Iron Curtain" norms: there was no talk of mummification or cloning.

It is interesting to note that Tito's funeral partly followed the pattern established when King Aleksandar Karadjordjević (aka Alexander the Unifier) was killed in Marseille in 1934, and his body was transferred by train via an "integrative" Yugoslav

Figure 3.7. Tito's tomb in the House of Flowers. Photo credit: Draško Gagović.

----

23 Ilya Zbarsky and Samuel Hutchinson, *Lenin's Embalmers* (London: Harvill Press, 1998).

route, which the body of the founder of "the second Yugoslavia" would partly repeat in 1980.

One of the forms of de-Tito-ization (which started in the late 1980s) consisted of endless unveilings and discoveries of "the real ultimate truth" about the charismatic Marshal's life and adventures. In these texts, published mostly in the yellow press but also in hardcover books, the long-time Yugoslav president appeared as an exponent of a Comintern-Vatican-Masonic conspiracy—which would seem to make him the only point where these conflicting ideologies met and thus a far more important personality than he was thought to be. In such texts, his *bon vivant* dimension materializes in the fathering of whole squadrons of children spread around Central Europe and Russia. Another important thread was speculation regarding Tito's "real" identity. Until now the askers of this question had not used the information on a family tomb in the Zemun graveyard.

Next to other family members, a man was buried whose name is not common in this region: Josip Broz. For conspiracy theorists (who were not lacking in the 1990s), this rare but familiar name and the year his death (1941) were interesting starting points for research to prove Tito's "double identity." In any case, it is a fact that there are two graves in the Belgrade area containing the remains of individuals named Josip Broz. We have yet to discover who is who in this story.

Figure 3.8. Josip Broz's tombstone in the Zemun graveyard: confirmation of the thesis that Tito was not really Broz? Photo credit: author.

Figure 3.9. Tito's official grave in The House of Flowers. Photo credit: Ferran Cornellà (via WikiMedia).

Subjects' Graves

As we have seen, a ruler's burial and grave convey significant information about a society's ideological horizon and principles. But many people other than rulers are born and die. So we have to consider that tombstones which have modest ambitions and do not cost much can also tell us a lot about the time and society in which they were created.

Serbian tombstones during the Turkish occupation varied greatly. Since the population was mainly rural and not very mobile, regional norms developed.[24] Almost all tombstones and memorials created in the sixteenth or seventeenth century retained medieval burial traditions to some extent. In some regions the monuments were influenced by *stećci*,[25] a tradition that originated in Hum and Podrinje.[26] These are mostly in the form of a slab of partly processed stone, laid down. Sometimes there is an anthropomorphic scene on the slab—strongly stylized as a rule, to the extent that they may appear to be just geometric designs. Upright tombstones are another large group. These can be of diverse shapes and include many differently designed crosses.[27] In the nineteenth century, many grave markers were made of wood, especially in those areas where wood was the main construction material.

There is a special group of tombstones created in the areas of Kopaonik and Ras called the "Studenica monuments"—upright tombstones [*usadnici*] made of marble

Figure 3.10. "Studenica" monuments—upright tombstones—were made of marble from Mount Radočelo. They rarely had any inscriptions. The human figure is stylized and older examples (15th to 16th century) were fully 3-dimensional. Photo credit: Republic Institute for the Protection of Cultural Monuments, Belgrade, Serbia / Nikola Dudic.

---

24 For a complete overview with many graphics see Nikola Dudić, *Stara groblja i nadgrobni belezi u Srbiji* [Old graveyards and tombstones in Serbia] (Belgrade: Republički zavod za zaštitu spomenika kulture, 1995).

25 "Stećak" (plural: stećci) is a medieval type of tombstone mainly found in Bosnia, Serbia, Croatia, and neighboring countries.

26 Hum was a medieval principality in what is now Bosnia-Herzegovina and Croatia. Podrinje is the Slavic name of the Drina river valley in Bosnia-Herzegovina.

27 Jelen Erdeljan, "Srednjevekovni nadgrobni spomenici u oblasti Rasa" [Medieval tombstones in the Ras region] (Belgrade: Arheološki institute and Novi Pazar: Museum Ras, 1996). See also Dudić, *Stara groblja i nadgrobni belezi u Srbiji*.

from Mount Radočelo in Central Serbia, which was also used for formwork and architectural ornaments in the Church of the Virgin in Studenica.[28]

Studenica monuments rarely had inscriptions, and the human figure is stylized. Older examples come close to being sculptures "in the round," while newer ones are in low relief or even flat with linear-geometric stylization.

We know these monuments were transported by horse from the center near Studenica, where they were created. The oldest ones date back to the fifteenth century, but they stopped being created when roadside stone monuments became dominant. Therefore, we can say this artistic phenomenon was part of the recovery from centuries of Ottoman occupation.

Roadside monuments,[29] mainly made of soft sandstone, show the characteristics found in the sepulchral art of many times and places. Apart from the figure of the deceased in low relief (usually frontal and colored) and an epitaph (which often has high literary or documentary value), these monuments contain general symbolic figures (plants or flowers), illustrations identifying the deceased's profession (through his tools), as well as indications of his social status and wealth (such as an image of a cow or a pocket watch). Such items were markers of affluence, like owning a luxury car today.

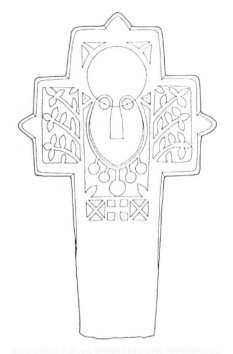

Figure 3.11. A newer type of Studenica monument: almost flat with linear-geometric stylization. Drawing by Nikola Dudiño, from his book *Old Cemeteries and Tombstones in Serbia*. Photo credit: Republic Institute for the Protection of Cultural Monuments, Belgrade, Serbia / Nikola Dudic.

---

28 Mirjana Ljubinković: "Studenički majstori kamenoresci i njihovi nadgrobni spomenici oko Petrove crkve kod Novog Pazara" [Master stonemasons from Studenica and their tombstone monuments around Peter's Church near Novi Pazar], *Zbornik Narodnog muzeja* V (Belgrade, 1967).

29 These are called *krajputaš* ["the stone near the road"]. The poet Branko V. Radičević introduced the term, which is now applied to all monuments of this type. However, it was originally meant in a narrower sense, as monuments for warriors buried on the battlefield, far from home (therefore, cenotaphs).

The appearance of the Singer sewing machine on roadside monuments shows the beginnings of globalization as American technology reached even the Balkan hinterlands.

Many iconographic elements on monuments of this type originated in older times but show a high degree of vitality because, as we shall see, they survive on completely different modern monuments.

Figure 3.12. A representation of a cow on a 19th century roadside monument demonstrated the deceased's wealth. Photo from Branko Radičević, Seoski nadgrobni spomenici i krajputaši [Village Tombstones and Wayfarers], (Belgrade: Publishing House "Jugoslavija", 1965), 33.

Another (European) tradition is carried by urban tombstones. They appeared with the nineteenth century revival of Serbia as a state, especially after Mihailo Obrenović took over the administration of Serbian cities from the Turks. The first Serbian graveyard of modern times—that is, from the time of the Austrian occupation—was located next to Varoš kapija, near St. Michael's Cathedral and the Building of the Patriarchate in Belgrade. From there, the graveyard was transferred to Tašmajdan in 1826. Novo groblje was founded in 1886. They transferred some monuments from Tašmajdan there, so nowadays it has grave markers older than the graveyard itself.[30]

Today, more than one hundred years after it was founded, the crowded Novo groblje cemetary represents the most prestigious part of Belgrade's "necropolis." In it you can read the history of a thin layer of Serbian society in different ways.

Figure 3.13. On this grave marker, scissors and the Singer sewing machine (as well as tools of care and healing on the narrow side) identify the deceased's interests. Photo from B. Radičević, 1965, page 38.

---

30 Bratislava Kostić, *Novo groblje u Beogradu* [The new graveyard in Belgrade] (Belgrade: JKP Pogrebne usluge, 1999). This book gives an historical timeline, a catalogue of works of art, and a list of notable persons buried in this, the largest necropolis in the capital city.

Figure 3.14. It is widely believed that the great comediographer himself (Branislav Nušić) was responsible for his tomb's pyramidal shape. Photo credit: author.

Figure 3.15. The monumental tomb of Milorad Drašković, a minister who was assassinated, made by sculptor Toma Rosandić. Photo credit: author.

You can note its dark side, its rises and falls, and even find proof in stone of the specifically Belgradian wit, where black humor is prominent. An example is Branislav Nušić's[31] family tomb. Its pyramidal shape comes not from freemason symbolism, as some might suppose. On the contrary, there is a widespread belief that Nušić himself was responsible for the unusual design. By creating a memorial without any horizontal surfaces he thwarted in advance the threats of revenge by desecration that had been announced by those hurt by his satirical texts.

Novo groblje can also be considered Serbia's national park of nineteenth and twentieth century sculpture because it contains works by many famous and nearly-famous sculptors. The monumental tomb of Milorad Drašković (a minister who was assassinated), is one of the masterpieces of its era, made by sculptor Toma Rosandić.

Apart from the monuments that could be listed in the national artistic heritage, there are those of not so high value, but which nevertheless bear witness to the prin-

---

31 Branislav Nušić (born Alkibijad Nuša, 1864–1938) was a playwright, satirist, theater director, journalist, and controversial social critic.

ciples of the time in other ways. The architecture of family tombs and their sculptures demonstrate the taste of those who ordered them, and record the language of visual symbols and metaphors, among which, for example, there is a broken column with fluting whose ionic capital has fallen to its base. The symbolism of the broken column is clear: "a pillar of the community" has been lost. This image occurs as a metaphor in many places, even in verbal form, as part of an epitaph or lament carved into the tombstone's surface.

Changes in what can be called "epitaph communication" have been thoroughly described by Ivan Čolović.[32] He notes a great revival of the tradition in the 1960s and 1970s. (We might add that this boom was concurrent with the rise of

Figure 3.16. The broken column's symbolism is clear. Photo credit: author.

"debtors' socialism" in Yugoslavia—the time of "borrowed prosperity"). It especially penetrated Novo groblje as the elite necropolis, and Čolović concluded that "symbolic communication on [grave markers] still relies exclusively on artistic language as if it were the only form that could be both expressive enough and aesthetically adequate." In practice, the renewal of epitaphs as an artform was accompanied by advances in sepulchral sculpture.

Due to the huge number of monuments in Novo groblje, we can follow precisely the changes of style in the artwork—or, more correctly, changes in the taste of those who paid for these creations. "Soft" abstraction, in which a strongly stylized yet recognizable human figure is still dominant, is represented by a monument which uses the vocabulary of Cubism. Aside from the simplification and geometrization of the figure, the fact that he is shown wearing bell-bottom trousers confirms that this sculpture dates from the late 1970s.

----

32 Ivan Čolović, *Književnost na groblju* [Art in a graveyard] (Belgrade: Narodna knjiga, 1983). A second version of the same text, including analyses of other types of neo-folklore, appears in Čolović's *Divlja književnost* [Wild literature] (Belgrade: Nolit, 1986).

Figure 3.17. Belgrade's Novo groblje cemetary reveals the changing styles of sepulchral artwork—or more precisely, changes in the taste of those who ordered the tombstones. This Cubism-influenced figure has bell-bottom trousers which were popular in the 1970s. Photo credit: author.

Figure 3.18. Radical abstraction in sepulchral sculpture for the graves of private persons mirrored the trend in public memorials during the time of "enlightened socialism." Photo credit: author.

Abstract forms are used in a group of private monuments. These are similar to public monuments erected during the same period, when the language of socialist realism was rejected in favor of the equally implausible "socialist aestheticism."

A monument created in the language of "associative abstraction" is a similar solution. Its stacked layers can be read as waves, open books, or simple smooth forms, with a cross on top as a discrete sign.

Čolović also noted a trend that is the opposite of abstraction, which he called "new epitaphs." These seem to occur

Figure 3.19. Monument in the style of "associative abstraction." Photo credit: author.

mainly on the monuments of those who died too young or by accident. Often the grave marker has a description of the circumstances of the tragedy. New techniques like photoceramics and photoengraving on stone enable memorialists to present visual details about the events that cost someone their life, such as a traffic accident.

Monuments are sometimes decorated with the attributes of the deceased's business or profession—for example, an image of a boat, an airplane, or a helicopter. Books are represented on many monuments. They can function symbolically as "the book of life," but they may also represent a beloved object or the hobby of reading.

Figure 3.20. New photo printing techniques enable the presentation on gravestones of images suggesting how someone died. Photo credit: author.

The ancient tombs of Egyptian pharaohs often showed the deceased surrounded by an inventory of objects from his daily life. This tradition continues today, whether the beloved object is a pet, a cigarette, or a coffee cup—it can be an integral part of the monument. Some families create special rituals to keep the deceased within the active "flow of time." This is the case when, for example, a real cigarette is regularly put between the fingers of the deceased's statue or fresh newspapers are put under his arm.

Figure 3.21. This boat on a grave marker suggests the deceased had been a seaman. Photo credit: author.

Figure 3.22. A sculpture of a bi-plane on a pre-World War 2 monument in the Zemun cemetary suggests the deceased had been a pilot. Photo credit: author.

Figure 3.25. Is this a monument for an author or does the deceased hold his favorite book? Sculptors can also use a handheld document as a place to put a life motto. Photo credit: author.

Figure 3.23. Not all professions are represented in sculpture and not all identities have been reduced to names: photography is increasingly used on monuments, even when the images will degrade in a few years. Photo credit: author.

Figure 3.26. A stone poodle and urn decorate this black marble funerary slab. Photo credit: author.

Figure 3.24. A sculpture of an open book is often used on monuments to symbolize "the book of life." Photo credit: author.

Figure 3.27. "A passion that surpasses life": real cigarettes are periodically put between the fingers of this grave sculpture by family members to keep the deceased in the flow of active time. Photo credit: author.

Figure 3.28. The family puts fresh newspapers under this statue's arm. Photo credit: author.

Figure 3.29. Simplicity can make a grave marker more elegant, but also more ambiguous when we try to interpret a symbol like a motorcycle helmet. Photo credit: author.

Figure 3.30. A bicyclist in his moment of triumph. Does such a sculpture on a grave represent the idea of triumphing over death? Photo credit: author.

Figure 3.31. Playing a musical instrument is among the most common themes on grave markers, for both amateur and professional musicians. Photo credit: author.

A motorcycle helmet as part of the grave marker could represent the deceased's passion, or profession, or the way they died (in a crash).

Besides symbols of professions, the vocabulary of new monuments tends toward literalness and naturalism. Thus, a profession or passion might be represented not simply by showing a relevant tool, but by showing the deceased performing a certain action, such as this ambitious sculpture in Centralno groblje[33] for a group of cyclists, or statues of people playing a musical instrument.

A tombstone in the Zemun cemetary displays an officer of the guard that was made using a technique which became especially popular in the late 1960s and 1970s. The image was created on a polished granite slab with shallow scratches or indentations made with a tool much like a dental drill. This method exploits the tonal difference between the polished surface and the incised marks to produce an image with shading,

Figure 3.32. Frontality, thoroughly elaborated details on the uniform, and the fact that all the fingers can be seen, connect this grave marker of an officer of the guard with roadside stone monuments. Photo credit: author.

Figure 3.33. Roadside stone monuments (and sometimes cenotaphs) are created in some kind of sandstone. This type of monument originated in the 19th century and blossomed in the first decades of the 20th century, as Serbia fought a series of wars for liberation. They are characterized by the frontal presentation of a soldier in low relief, as well as a range of attributes connected to the person's profession or personality. Photo credit: author.

----

33 Centralno groblje [the Central graveyard] opened in 1939 in Voždovac, 7 kilometers from the center of Belgrade.

which could be—but does not have to be—photo-realistic. A certain rigidity and naiveté of the officer's half-figure (especially his uniform) suggests that the stone mason was simply referring to a photo, rather than using it as a template.

This composition reminds us of roadside stone monuments, despite the missing lower part of the figure.

A charming detail of the officer's monument is that some of his medals and badges were obviously left out during the design phase so they were added later, below his hand.

Figure 3.34. Some of the officer's medals and badges apparently were forgotten while the monument was being designed, so they were added later, without being positioned on his chest. Photo credit: author.

The same engraving technique was used to create a composite monument for a married couple of World War II fighters in Novo bežanijsko groblje.[34] The monument bears three representations of the wife and as many as five representations of the husband. Bronze busts show the couple in middle age and the same couple appears much older across the bottom in two dimensions. There are also two other pictures of the husband from during the war when he gained prominence: The first is a youthful representative portrait, and the second presents him from the waist up. He is in uniform in both. On the face of the monument, he is presented as a gunner, and on the back, she is a Partisan nurse and he is her patient. There is no unused part on the granite stele, just *horror vacui* as is found in some primitive art. It turns the visual rhetoric into cacophony.

Two political symbols compete for attention on the front top-center. The first is the hammer and sickle, a symbol with an even stronger ideological charge than the five-pointed star, and the second is an object in the shape of a star: the Commemorative Medal of the Partisans. It is impossible to determine which of these two symbols is more important here. The Commemorative Medal is not the only medal the deceased received—there are six others but they are presented on a smaller scale: all of them together occupy as much surface as the two dominant ones.

The appearance of later changes on relatively new tombstones says a lot about Serbian principles at the end of the twentieth century. After the "national awakening" at the end of the 1980s, which included a strong and quick return to religion

---

34 Novo bežanijsko groblje (the new graveyard in Bežanija) is located in New Belgrade.

Figure 3.35. A composite monument of a married couple of WW2 fighters. Photo credit: author.

Figure 3.36. The back side of the same monument. A touching lack of drawing skill gives it a folk-art character—the fossilized memories of a layer of society that was slowly becoming extinct. Photo credit: author.

Figure 3.37. On this gravestone, the place where a 5-pointed star had been was carved away and a brass cross put there instead. Photo credit: author.

and those traditions of Orthodox Christianity identified with ethnicity, the five-pointed stars carved into monuments became unwanted. But attempts to modify tombstones toward more favorable ideological signs were impeded by the permanence of materials like granite. A practical solution was to carve a shallow indentation where the star had been and put a brass cross there. But the speed of the religious revival often exceeded the normally slow rate at which traditions change, leaving gaps in legitimation.

Therefore, clashes between traditions can occur. For example, the "Miroslav" alphabet on one grave (an eminently national Orthodox signal) finds itself next to Our Lady of Lourdes and Cupid playing

Figure 3.38. In this picture, the "Miroslav" alphabet clashes with sculptures of Our Lady of Lourdes and Cupid playing a lute. Figurative religious sculpture has been censured by Orthodox churches for more than a thousand years—since the Iconoclastic Controversy. Photo credit: author.

the lute, both sculptures being far outside the traditions of Orthodoxy.

The graveyard in Mali Mokri Lug[35] is special among Belgrade necropoly. It can be considered a village graveyard which became a suburban graveyard and then an urban graveyard as Belgrade grew.[36] Although even the "civil" sepulchral tradition recognizes the form of a chapel over a tomb (there are many examples), "houses over a hole" are a special feature of the Mali Mokri Lug graveyard which have little in common with that tradition. Only the initial impulse might be the same: to show wealth.

As already noted, epitaph writing on tombs blossomed in the 1960s and 1970s. Lavish tombs shaped as chapels—or even better, as vacation homes in a graveyard—are another phenomenon of that time. More were built in the fertile areas of Serbia as well as in places from where large numbers of expat workers went abroad.

The appearance of one such a tomb would usually precipitate a competition, so newer examples were more lavish or ambitiously designed than older ones. As noted earlier, "vacation" homes in a socialist economy were considered a form of savings independent from banks. The architectural styles of "weekend" houses migrated to graveyards, so balconies on tombs were not rare. It would be fruitless to make some kind of stylistic survey of these creations because the most diverse influences intertwine in this wild-growing architecture.

Still, most of these structures are shaped like chapels in the "Neo-Byzantine" style, more or less. However, many look like little weekend houses, kiosks, and even pago-

---

35 Mali Mokri Lug is a part of the Belgrade neighborhood of Zvezdara. Once a small nineteenth-century village at the outskirts of Belgrade, Zvezdara is still less urbanized (favorable for a peaceful life) even though it is just fifteen minutes from the city center.

36 This is not the only graveyard of this type in the wider zone of Belgrade. Far from it. But it has been the subject of news stories more often than other graveyards because it is close to the city center and right next to the busy "Tsarigrad road" [an Ottoman-built road connecting Belgrade with Istanbul, and more locally, connecting Belgrade and Niš].

Figure 3.39. The graveyard in Mali Mokri Lug has, not just chapels, but little houses over some graves. Photo credit: author.

Figure 3.40. A tomb with a balcony in the graveyard of Mali Mokri Lug. Photo credit: author.

Figure 3.41. Small house in the Mali Mokri Lug grave-yard, next to an automobile repair shop. Photo credit: author.

Figure 3.42. Mali Mokri Lug symbolizes Serbia's disorientation in the 1990s. Photo credit: author.

das. Most of the constructions are designed to be seen only from the outside. But there are also those furnished inside as residential homes. In them you can find tables (set for a meal), sofas, refrigerators, or TV sets. The family gathers there in a custom called *daća*.[37]

The tradition of spatially connecting the home of the living with the home of the dead is older than civilization itself. But it is still not clear that building a house-like structure in an isolated necropolis is a good way to restore memories of the deceased. Questions are also raised about how such cities of the dead connect with newer local traditions. Just as suburban architecture can promote false authenticity, recent Serbian customs regarding the dead appear confused. Summer houses in a graveyard certainly seem like a malformed idea, perhaps reflecting a rural or small-town misunderstanding of urban customs. Another characteristic of the Mali Mokri Lug graveyard confirms this: the lack of traditional orientation for the graves. With Orthodox believers, the deceased are supposed to be buried with their heads to the east. But that was abandoned in this graveyard long ago as families fought for space. Now, everyone buries their bodies wherever and however they can. If Kaludjerica, the biggest "informal settlement" in the Balkans, is paradigmatic of a suburban mentality, then Mokri Lug, as a paradigmatic necropolis, reveals the mentality, values, role models, and ideals of Serbia in the 1990s.

----

37 In *daća*, or *parastos* in Greek (παννυχίς), a family brings food to the grave to have a meal with the deceased.

"Hush Thou Night... "[38]

Pleasant metaphors are often applied to graveyards ("garden of eternal peace," for example). But it is questionable if such metaphors apply to the graveyard in Zemun, which is adjacent to New Belgrade. This "kingdom of silence" has been raked and desecrated by bullets. Next to one of the entrances, there is a map of the graveyard showing where many of the leading perpetrators of "tough times in Belgrade" are buried. It has served as some visitor's target. Maybe it was someone who was already or soon to become part of a fight among clans, gangs, or "crews" which marked life in Belgrade in the 1990s, in the shadow of wars, and defined its only authentic subculture.

Epitaphs on roadside stone monuments would sometimes use euphemisms like: "He suddenly died in the presence of authorities"—meaning that he was sentenced to death, then hanged or shot. Nowadays such evasive descriptions would be difficult to explain—not because the status of a death sentence is unclear, but because the distinction between the authorities and perpetrators of crime was lost in the 1990s. A great number of those who were part of the political elite during the Milošević couple's rule were also involved in profitable business arrangements delicately described in the press as being "on the other side of the law." Both the police and secret services were regularly implicated in criminal activity. After the 5 October 2000 re-

Figure 3.43. Map of the Zemun cemetary, where many important protagonists of the capital's "tough time" were buried, was a target of an unknown gunman. Photo credit: author.

----

38 Often sung at funerals, "Hush, thou night" is the title of a lullaby written by Jovan Jovanović Zmaj (1833–1904). Here is the first stanza, translated by Dragana Stojanović-Beširević:

Hush, thou night, my darling's sleeping
pearly branches over her head leaping,
and the bustling branches of the tree
let tiny nightingales fall down with glee.

gime change, the extremely large stash of narcotics found in the safe of a Belgrade bank used by the police demonstrated the potential profitability of police work and showed just one way the ruling elite accumulated wealth. Even senior politicians were among those who died in shoot-outs, although such murders were rarely described as political assassinations. More often (and more precisely) they were described as "business deals gone sour."

In that same circle, but at the other pole, were the Belgrade underworld's "heroes from the base." During the 1990s the media made them celebrities and role models: In a whole range of TV talk shows, those smiling and often charming guests had opportunities to present their crimes as daring mischiefs, armed robberies in Western Europe as "adventures," and their prison sentences (served for their mentors in the communist nomenclature who often hired them to discipline troublesome expat Serbs) as "universities in crime." They considered themselves true representatives of Serbia, guerrilla fighters against the brutal and unfair sanctions imposed by capitalist countries. Popularized by the press, the underworld exposed itself as an important but under-appreciated subculture. They shot movies whose heroes were criminals. They set styles of behavior, clothing, and speech for the younger generation. They were profiled in an encyclopedia of Yugoslav crime.[39] The importance and representativeness of this subculture was confirmed by Janko Baljak's[40] documentary *Vidimo se u čitulji*

Figure 3.44. Frame from *Vidimo se u čitulji* [See you in the Obituary], a documentary film directed by Janko Baljak. Photo credit: RTV B92, 1995.

With honest job, you can't make any money.

---

39 Marko Lopušina, *Ko je ko u Yu podzemlju* [Who's who in the YU underworlds] (Niš: Zograf, 2000). Some of the data used in the final part of this text is from that source.

40 Janko Baljak (b. 1965) is a Serbian film director and tenured professor. He was also one of the founders of Radio B92, which struggled to keep independent journalism alive during the Milošević regime. Baljak's 35-minute documentary film "See You in the Obituary" (subtitled in English) is free online at https://www.youtube.com/watch?v=IEDMbvZnqSE.

[See you in the obituary]. Thanks to the director's talent and the well-chosen subject, this film became one of the most compelling portraits of Serbia in the 1990s.[41]

Ivan Čolović looked at this circle from a different angle. Without discussing what the underworld heroes *actually* were, he dealt with them as if they were para-literary characters, and in the public media imprint of their careers he found characteristics of mythic heroes and protectors, brutal yet just.[42] He also noted that "the life of gangsters comes to us only as a composed story. And usually, that story starts from the end: from the death of the main character. Therefore, as a rule, the story is epitaph-like, necrological, and retrospective."

Of course, this "retrospective" view has one more chapter, one *post scriptum,* which usually remains outside the field of analysis: the tombstones commissioned by families or surviving colleagues. If journalists or city gossip spread verbal legends about these tough guys, there are verbal expressions of a very different sort on their tombstones: graphic, three-dimensional, and often originating from the protagonist himself—or from those nearest him, since in this circle, there was no case of a tombstone being erected while the protagonist was still alive (although that is actually common in Serbia, as discussed below). A tombstone is a message directed to posterity and that is why it condenses the life of the deceased in the language of metaphor, or in the more direct message of an epitaph. As in all previous times, attention and money are given to create the grave marker and inform future generations about the deceased's social status, as well as the taste and principles of those who ordered the tombstone.

Tombstones of members of the Belgrade underworld were created by unknown as well as by widely recognized artists. The case of a sculptor who in his youth was a state artist creating monuments about revolutionary socialism using abstract forms, and in his old age, with a similar social status, making figurative memorials for criminals or neo-Chetnik warriors, says a lot not only about the society that accepts such shifts as unremarkable, but also about the artist whose mutable beliefs reveal their weak and floating morality.

A granite stele of Miroslav Bižić (known as "Biža") in the Zemun graveyard, with its stability, its portrait in high relief carved into a rustically processed boulder, is intended to show a personality as stable as stone. Bižić was first a police officer, from the time when there was an intimate connection between the police, the Communist

---

41 The book which served as a template for the movie *Vidimo se u čitulji* was by Aleksandar Knežević and Vojislav Tufegdžić, *Kriminal koji je izmenio Srbiju* [The crime that changed Serbia] (Belgrade: Radio B92, 1995). It contains a range of interesting data and documentary photos.

42 Ivan Čolović, *Bordel ratnika* [A brothel of warriors] (Belgrade: Biblioteka XX vek, 1993) and *Pucanje zdravlja* [Health shot] (Belgrade: Beogradski krug, 1994).

Party and "our naughty boys outside." Then he was the owner of a private detective agency. He was killed by gunshots from behind by an unknown assailant in New Belgrade in 1996.

A quote from the deceased is engraved as his epitaph on a horizontal slab at the foot of the stele. He whose life disappeared in the magnetic field between police and criminals obviously knew the reality of the Belgrade underworld. His quote brings us a distillation of that experience:

> [Translation:] "Not one of us is invulnerable and no one can run away from what's in store for them. If someone decides to kill someone else, that person can't adequately protect himself."

In the same way that Ljuba Zemunac's[43] biography in *Bordel ratnika*[44] was cited in numerous newspaper articles, feuilletons, and even books, as defining the prototype of Belgrade's "tough guy," his tombstone in Zemun became a model for the memorials of many others in the same circle. Magaš (aka Zemunac) was killed long before the series of brutal street murders in Belgrade which many saw as acts of revenge, as well as those which were undoubtedly politically moti-

Figure 3.45. Granite stele of Miroslav Bižić ("Biža"). Photo credit: author.

ć

Figure 3.46. Distilled advice that the leading connoisseur of the Belgrade underworld leaves on his grave for those yet to come. Photo credit: author.

---

43 Ljubomir Magaš aka Ljuba Zemunac (1948–1986) was a Serbian criminal, boxer, and one of the best-known personalities of the Yugoslav underworld. He was convicted three times for rape and was the target of an Interpol warrant for car theft. He specialized in robberies and extortions, and was a suspect in a murder case. In the end, Magaš was killed in Frankfurt by another Serbian criminal.

44 Ivan Čolović: "Smrt Ljube Zemunca ili paradoks o zaštitniku" [The death of Ljuba Zemunac or paradox of a protector] in Čolović, *Bordel ratnika*.

vated assassinations. On his tombstone, erected by his friends, there are no religious or ideological symbols. The strongest (and almost the only) element is on top of the tomb: a life-size bronze statue of Magaš as a boxer. The proportions of the head and body suggest a short-statured man but since he is known to have boxed in the light-heavyweight division, these proportions may just be a flawed representation.

An integral part of Magaš' tombstone is an epitaph which Čolović analyzed in detail.[45] In this example of "new epitaph literature," the "knight from the asphalt" is profiled in a couple of verses. Magaš is compared to Robin Hood (*Robinu Hudu vodili ga puti* [His journeys took him to Robin Hood]). There is a focus on his leading position (*Sve je kod njega postalo viteško / Rodjen za vodju ostao je prvi* ["Everything of his became knight-like

Figure 3.47. The cemetary monument of Ljubomir Magaš (Ljuba Zemunac) became a model for the monuments of many others from the same circle. Photo credit: author.

/ A born leader, he remained Number One]). And finally his death abroad is mentioned (*Nemačkom zamkom izrešetan pao / U svoju zemlju dostojanstven leže* [In a German trap, he fell riddled with bullets / In his native country, he lay down with dignity]). The verbal epitaph makes this tombstone unusual in the circle from which it comes, as if it were a remnant of some older, more literate time. Tombstones erected when death in the streets accelerated to a previously inconceivable extent were mainly limited to descriptions of a scene.

The concept of a grave marker with a life-size bronze figure in a characteristic pose wearing his favorite clothes is repeated by Branislav Matić Beli's tomb in Centralno groblje. According to the authors of the book *Kriminal koji je izmenio Srbiju* [The crime that changed Serbia], Matić Beli's murder in August 1991 was "the first public execution of a notable Belgrade 'whiz for biz outside the law'." It was also memora-

---

45 Čolović, Smrt Ljube Zemunca ili paradoks o zaštitniku," 5–6.

ble for its brutality, which would, unfortunately, become normal. It seems this murder had something to do with a change of political allegiance. As the king of Belgrade car dumps and a well-to-do man (according to press reports and the authors of the above book), Matić was politically indecisive: he switched his enchantment with Milošević for enchantment with the opposition. He was also one of the founders and benefactors of the future paramilitary formation called the Serbian Guard,[46] created under the patronage of the Serbian Renewal Movement.[47]

Another death was connected with the Serbian Guard in a more active way. Matić's closest friend, whose tomb is also at Centralno groblje—Djordje Božović ("Giška")—was killed on 15 September 1991, just

Figure 3.48. The grave marker of Branislav Matić Beli also features a life-size bronze statue of the deceased. Photo credit: author.

days after his paramilitary unit was fielded to Croatia. Some believe he was attacked from behind to show that the governing parties and their services believed only they should be directing paramilitary units, not opposition parties like SPO.[48] The bronze memorial of a person whose prematurely-ended paramilitary career was comparable only to Arkan's (see below) is designed as a figure standing in front of a gate-like construction. He is dressed in a uniform characteristic only of the brief final stage of his life. This uniform, however, indicates how he wanted to be remembered—not as an underworld hero, a prisoner in several European countries, an executor of brutal Udba[49] orders, but as a soldier, even if just a para-soldier. On the lintel, there is

----

46 The Serbian Guard was a paramilitary unit that participated in the 1990s wars in Croatia and Bosnia. It was formed by SPO leader Vuk Drašković and his wife Danica, along with Serbian gangsters Djordje Božović ("Giška") and Branislav Matić Beli.

47 The Serbian Renewal Movement's name in Serbian is Srpski Pokret Obnove (SPO).

48 Vuk Draskovic's Serbian Renewal Movement was considered oppositional because he challenged the ruling parties in elections.

49 Udba (full name: Uprava državne bezbednosti [Directorate of State Security]) was a secret police organization and information agency during the second Yugoslavia. It was created in 1946 but

Figure 3.49. One might think the creator of Djordje Božović's grave marker was inspired by the funerary art of ancient Egypt. The deceased stands in front of a gate—connecting the world of the living with the world of the dead? Photo credit: author.

an inscription flanked by two elegant isosceles crosses. The inscription tells us that "he fell heroically in 1991 leading his *Obilićes* in the battle for the liberation of Gospić and the defense of *srpstvo*."[50] The gate at Djordje Božović's grave marker is covered with handwriting. The writing starts in the Latin alphabet (which is logical, since like all Belgrade "tough guys" of the second generation, he spent much of his life in the Latin-alphabet-using West). But when the word "God" appears, the handwriting switches to Cyrillic.

Aleksandar Knežević ("Knele") was only 21 when he was killed in room 331 of the Belgrade Hyatt Hotel at the end of October 1992. His short life was marked by speed and tumultuous events, verbalized and transformed into themes like those which Ljuba Zemunac described. Knele's tombstone at Topčidersko groblje[51] does not boast or try to fascinate with cheap effects. On the contrary, this is a serious, almost normal (but not inexpensive) monument of black granite with a stylized gable and two side columns.

On the front and back sides, there is the same photograph in color. In one, a somewhat wider shot of the figure; in the other, a specific portrait detail: Knežević dressed in a multi-colored tracksuit, unzipped just enough to show a range of heavy gold chains with medallions—essential status symbols. His photo from the monument was repro-

----

stopped working under that name when the SFRY fell apart in the 1990s. It mostly dealt with surveillance, emigrants, external enemies, and other countries' secret services.

50 *Srpstvo* is the abstract notion of the Serbian nation, including all Serbs regardless of where they live. Nowadays, *srpstvo* is usually connected to the Kosovo myth. This reading is reinforced by use of the word *Obilićes*, a reference to the soldiers of Miloš Obilić, who is believed to have killed Sultan Murad during the battle of Kosovo.

51 Topčidersko groblje is one of the oldest graveyards in Belgrade, and undoubtedly the most prestigious necropolis of the modern mafia subculture.

duced on the cover of the book *The Crime That Changed Serbia;* on the cover of the weekly *Vreme;* and in nearly all the newspaper articles where Knele is mentioned. Repetition of the same photo suggests a certain iconization, reminiscent of popular movie stars who died too young. Nearly ten years after Knele's death, fresh flowers are still being put on his grave every day, and as a special sign of affection, there are bows on the surrounding trees and fence. This shows the persistent high regard for him in certain Belgrade circles, perhaps similar to James Dean.

In Serbia, a simple rule has been valid for a century: He who does not get an obituary in the daily newspaper *Politika* cannot be considered dead. Only in the last few decades has a populist daily—*Večernje Novosti*—come close to *Politika* in the number of obituaries and death notices. With the start of wars in the West

Figure 3.50. Aleksandar Knežević's monument on Topčidersko groblje. Photo credit: author.

Balkans, and as the nation's "oldest daily newspaper" turned into an overtly party-controlled platform, the way funerals and memorial services are announced changed significantly. But before these changes, Ivan Čolović analyzed this type of public communication in numerous examples from the former "large" Yugoslavia.[52] A similar deep analysis in the 1990s would give, one suspects, very interesting results and clarify more recent changes.

By the end of the 1980s and at the beginning of the 1990s, there was a sudden increase in the number of death notices published in newspapers. Previously only family and perhaps best friends and padrinos bought expensive newspaper space.[53] But then, neighbors, schoolmates, wedding guests, and many others started to buy

---

[52] Ivan Čolović, *Divlja književnost: etnolingvističko proučavanje paraliterature* [Wild literature: An ethnolinguistic study of paraliterature] (Belgrade: Nolit, 1984).

[53] In the 1990s, when *Politika* turned into a party-controlled gazette of the regime's wartime propaganda, its circulation fell drastically. But the obituary pages continued to attract the few remaining readers of this once reputable daily. Therefore, one might say that death notices financially supported the promotion of war—death for death.

in, so that the number (and in certain periods, the size) of the death notices became a measure of the deceased's social status. This measure gradually inflated. In the second half of the 1980s, the death of Ljubomir Magaš (Ljuba Zemunac) was followed by about one hundred notices. Knele's death at the start of the 1990s drew 360 notices. As for Arkan in the late 1990s (as in the case of those killed in the state assassination attempt on Ibarska magistrala[54]), his death notices almost equaled the size of the rest of the newspaper.

At one moment, the custom of openly stating names and sending "last good-byes" in death notices was recognized as helping the police compile their dossiers. This led to a shift toward the minimization of details and at times a coding of communications by those who had something to hide. The most drastic example was surely a notice that took an entire newspaper page, with a small photo of the deceased in the middle, signed "From your dearest." In this way the outer world was excluded from the notice, since neither the deceased nor the "dearest" were named—and thus the announcement lost its original *raison d'etre*. But clearly, it got another one when nicknames were used: only the smallest circle of acquaintances would know who "Jaguar" and "Panther" are shown in Figure 3.51.

Figure 3.51. To "Jaguar" from "Panther": a death notice published in Politika's obituary section. When it was realized that the custom of including comments or biographic notes in death notices helped the police fill out their dossiers, notices became less informative, or even coded so only the deceased's inner circle could understand the communication. Photo credit: author.

The tomb of Zeljko Raznatovic is located at Novo groblje. He is better known as "Arkan," a criminal with a high position in the police/state security service—in addition to being a pastry shop owner, a "business man," art collector, football club owner, war crimes suspect, Member of Parliament, and national hero. He was murdered on 15 January 2000 in the lobby of the Hotel Intercontinental. His tomb can be seen as the final piece of identity or "image" construction for this important protagonist of polit-

----

54 The target of the Ibar Highway assassination attempt on 3 October 1999 was the politician Vuk Drašković. Members of the Special Operations Unit (JSO) of state security slammed a truck full of sand into Drašković's motorcade to make it look like a traffic accident. Drašković survived, but four of his associates were killed.

Figure 3.52. Arkan's tomb can be seen as the final element in construction of his image. Photo credit: Draško Gagović.

ical-police-wartime-criminal-entertainment-sports life. Earlier elements of his image construction included a wedding and a wall calendar.

On twelve monthly posters forming a wall calendar printed in the early 1990s, Ražnatović dressed in Serbian military uniforms from different times. In this sequence of photos, the particularly interesting one was the "wounded" Ražnatović. In this picture, his head and hand are wrapped in bandages and "blood" appears to seep through the bandage on his hand.

A somewhat different fashion show with historical costumes was Ražnatović's wedding to the folk-singer/entertainment-star Svetlana Veličković ("Ceca") as his bride. This was the event of the year in showbiz. Parts of it were broadcast on television, and video cassettes of the wedding sold quickly.

Both during the wedding and on the calendar, the groom changed outfits frequently, But a special place belonged to the Serbian Army's World War I parade uniform. This uniform of a duke-general, with a tall šapka[55] (similar to šajkača[56]) never went historically in combination with a pectoral cross, but never mind such details. In this event his cross was too big even for a metropolitan bishop (unless it was part of a medal). But his need to absorb all desirable aspects of something recognized as tradition gave an obvious theatrical effect to the uniform.

At the root of every theatrical effort is the proposition that something which is *not* can be represented as something that *is*. By costuming himself as a "commander," Ražnatović attempts to cloak his paramilitary formation (famous for its war crimes

---

55 A tall hat worn by officers, usually in ceremonies.
56 The Serbian national costume hat.

in Bosnia and Slavonija[57]) in the identity of a military formation objectively coded as a liberation army.

A bust of Ražnatović, shown wearing the same uniform, but without the pectoral cross, and with the Order of the Star of Karadjordje 3rd Class (which we know he did not receive during his lifetime) is the central feature of his grave monument. Made somewhat larger than life-size, the bust stands underneath a deep granite arch which is another reference to the distant past: an arcosolium.[58] If it is true that rulers' tombs (including those from the Nemanjić dynasty) presented some kind of ideological testament, there is no doubt that this is the case with his monument too.

First of all, we can see that the "military" version of a person with many faces and professions was chosen for eternity. Thanks to the uniform, this aspect was probably the easiest to process artistically. If, for example, they had chosen to represent Arkan the casino owner, his bust would not be any different from Arkan the football fan or Arkan the MP. On the other hand, the uniform clearly conveys the attribute of power, which is extremely important to all members of the criminal subculture. Power is also expressed by the simple monumental forms of the tombstone, which do not distract from the primary narrative or hide the fact that the monument itself must have been expensive. Finally, the presence of the arcosolium reference confirms that this is the tomb of a prominent person, even though the masses might not catch the reference.

It also distracts from the attempt to get something symbolically that *does not belong to him*. In the case of this "hero of our time" it is *salvation*, thanks to his belated turn to religion, which outweighs all his actions and work with the communist secret police. From the perspective of his belatedly discovered spirituality, all those activities can be ignored as youthful mischief.

Figure 3.53. Skole's and Ćanda's grave markers adopted ideas from Željko Ražnatović's tomb. Photo credit: author.

---

57 A geographical part of today's Croatia. Its name originates from the Latin word for "the land of Slavs".

58 An "arcosolium" was an arched recess used for entombment in Roman catacombs.

The tombstones in Centralno groblje of "Skole" and "Ćanda" (Zoran Uskoković and Zoran Davidović, killed in spring 2000) show that the structure and concept of Željko Ražnatović's tomb quickly— within a few months—redefined the model the criminal subculture sought to emulate. Busts of the deceased are in a rudimentary transparent arcosolium topped by a cross. Of course, everything is in a somewhat more modest scale, since the underworld respects hierarchy.

It seems that the police were also interested in eliminating inconvenient witnesses. So instead of testifying in the Hague, Radovan Stojičić ("Badža") ended up in the Alley of Meritorious Citizens at Novo groblje in Belgrade. [59] The Alley of

Figure 3.54. Radovan Stojičić ("Badža"), buried in the "Alley of Meritorious Citizens." Photo credit: author.

Meritorious Citizens was built in 1965 according to Svetislav Ličina's design. It was planned as a separate mound with twelve concrete semi-domes in which graves and urns were to be arranged radially.

In every era, societies must answer the question: Who among them is considered "great." The fact that the remains of Ivo Andrić,[60] Miloš Crnjanski,[61] and numerous scientists and artists were joined in the late 1990s by the remains of those who turned the police into Milošević's pretorian guard speaks of the system and the time.

An unusually complex monument marks the grave of Zoran Šijan, a former kickboxer and a man considered the leader of the Surčin clan[62] (according to *Ko je ko u*

----

59 Stojičić was Serbia's acting minister of the interior. His previous activities in Kosovo and Croatia attracted the International War Crimes Tribunal's interest. According to investigator John Cencich, Stojičić "reported to Milošević and used his position to further his criminal activities and ties to organized crime throughout the region. During the early morning hours of April 11, 1997, an armed, masked man entered Mamma Mia's restaurant in downtown Belgrade. He ordered everyone to lie face down on the floor. Several shots were fired at close range and Stojičić, 46, was killed… Undoubtedly, many people wanted Stojičić dead. At the top of the list was Slobodan Milošević, who knew that the war crimes tribunal was closing in." John R. Cencich, *The Devil's Garden: A War Crimes Investigator's Story* (Washington, DC: Potomac Books, 2013).
60 Andrić won the Nobel Prize for Literature in 1961.
61 Crnjanski was a diplomat, essayist, and poet who wrote the lullaby headlining this section: "Hush Thou Night."
62 The Surčin clan was among the most influential mafia groups in the 1990s and most likely connected to government officials. They specialized in car theft, extortion, debt collection, the illegal ciga-

YU podzemlju [Who's Who in the Yu Underground]). His grave marker has a multiplicity of signs and elements, but in a way that is quite different from those previously described. The face of the deceased (killed in late November 1999) appears twice: once as a photo in a medallion held by an angel on one of the granite slabs, and once as a life-size bronze figure in full 3D. In front of the bronze figure there is a round, hyper-realist coffee table in polychrome marble. On it is a replica in stone of a one-liter Coca-Cola bottle, a packet of cigarettes (there are no letters on it but the relation of the red and white stone in this perfectly-made sculptural collage clearly indicates the brand: Marlboro), and finally, a stone ashtray.

This arrangement provides a pop-art experience even Edward Kienholz[63] would not be ashamed of and its iconography clearly represents the everyday life values of the subculture whose most prominent figure was the deceased. These values are contained in the hit song that the turbofolk singer Viki used to sing back in the day titled "Coca-Cola, Marlboro, Suzuki"[64]:

----

rette trade, and drug smuggling. The clan's leader was Zoran Šijan who was killed in his Mercedes in November 1999.

63 Kienholz (1927–1994) was an American sculptor known for his large and complex tableaux using found objects.

64 "Suzuki" is clearly missing from the monument's table, for the simple reason that it was too difficult to represent. But it was an object of affection for Šijan as well, in the form of a Jeep rather than a motorcycle. The well-known turbofolk song by Violeta "Viki" Miljković is about young people's crazy, superficial life.

Figure 3.55. The unusually complex monument for Zoran Šijan. Photo credit: author.

Figure 3.56. Detail of the table in Zoran Šijan's monument, showing the stone Coke bottle, Marlboros and ash tray. Photo credit: author.

201

"Koka-kola, Marlboro, Suzuki,
Diskoteke, gitare, buzuki.
To je život. to nije reklama.
Nikom nije lepše nego nama..."

[Coca-Cola, Marlboro, Suzuki,
Discos, guitars, bouzouki.
That's life. It isn't a commercial.
No one has a better time than us...]

Marko Lopušina's just-mentioned book *Ko je ko u YU podzemlju* also provides a list of the people who attended Šijan's burial. Apart from people in the music business and the crowned queen of the prophets (Cleopatra), city officials from the Serbian Renewal Party also paid their last respects to the deceased, who was the husband of a famous folk singer for many years. The coffin was put into the ground with the sound of the song *Tiho noći, moje zlato spava*.[65]

All the grave markers described—despite differences in approach, ideas, and messages—are characterized by hard forms and black granite. These are clearly "male" monuments, many of them military-like, even in cases where the deceased had not served in the military. Maja Pavić's tombstone was completely different.

She was a twenty-five-year-old woman unfortunate enough to be next to the wrong person in the wrong place at the wrong time. A TV host by profession (she worked for Studio B and TV Pink), she died in a burst of stray bullets that killed her friend, Rade Ćaldović ("Ćenta"), a doyen of the Belgrade underworld. Her monument in Centralno groblje is made

Figure 3.57. Maja Pavić's monument was made from a highly polished coarse-grained aggregate whose dominant tone is the color of white coffee. Photo credit: author.

---

65 "Hush thou night, sleep my darling." The reader might also recall that the author's portrait appeared on the 500 billion dinar banknote issued in 1993 during hyperinflation.

of highly polished coarse-grained aggregate whose dominant tone is the color of a coffee latte. The impression made by the brass letters (reduced to her name and years of birth and death), a gilded cross with a climbing plant, and a small photograph in a medallion, is ascetic, almost bashful. It has the feeling of modern boutiques or fashion magazines. A subtle "feminine" character is stressed by the roundness of angles and edges. In the color photo in the medallion surrounded by rudimentary arms of the cross, we can see Maja Pavić with a mobile phone in her hand.

Figure 3.58. Maja Pavić's photo shows her "in touch" with others, "on call" as the business world requires. Photo credit: author.

She was killed just when mobile phones stopped being a status symbol and became important tools for an active life. If we accept the thesis that a grave aims to show the essence of what the deceased was while alive, such a designed portrait proves that those who created it saw the young host as a modern, stylish, dynamic person, constantly "in touch" with others, always "on call" as the business world requires. Of course, it also shows Serbia as a country in which new communications technology unstoppably flooded in, despite sanctions.

At the beginning of 2001, there was an odd story in the newspapers about a family that put a mobile phone in the coffin of their deceased. When they dialed the number after a while, someone answered. And so, with the help of the police, they found the grave had been robbed.

All religions create a connection between the world of the living and the world of the dead. Communication with the dead—in sleep, in visions—belongs to the domain of God's special mercy. But it also demands deep faith and focused prayers. As in many other areas, Serbs are here somehow "off balance"—always late and in search of shortcuts. Therefore, the motive to put a mobile phone in a tomb indirectly testifies to the re-paganization of Serbia which, at the transition to the third millennium, happened in the shadow of a publicly proclaimed return to religion and tradition.

Millennium Bug in the Graveyard

For a long time in our country it has been a custom to erect a tombstone while the person is still alive. This syntagm can sometimes be read on the tombstone itself, and this tradition is not unusual among Christian nations. In the Middle Ages, life was considered to be a preparation for death—as the lobby to the entrance of another and better world, as they believed. Almost every ruler and grandee would start their reign with the construction of a mausoleum, or at least a tomb within some existing structure. Therefore, a great number of those able to pay could influence the conception of their future tomb and supervise the quality of the work done.

From time to time, newspapers report particularly bizarre cases of mausoleum construction. One example was a person living near the town of Požega who, in a local graveyard, constructed for himself some kind of mausoleum/museum and equipped it with the most modern gadgets. The future mausoleum user gladly described to journalists every aspect of his undertaking and proudly posed for photos on the roof of his creation. Our morbid "Cheval" was by no means an isolated example. Similar news stories have come from all continents.

The cult of trust in great ideological and national projects for the broad Serbian masses has its own negative in terms of small things. Someone who would believe every crazy claim—for example, that Serbs *are the oldest of all peoples,* that everything that happens to them is the result of a planetary conspiracy specifically targeting them—and having learned from experience (being robbed multiple times by various banks and para-banks) such a person will leave nothing to chance in his everyday life. When small things happen, a Serb does not trust anyone. So, for example, he will not even believe his successors will write the year of death on his already prepared tombstone. In an attempt to reduce the *unpredictability* to a bare minimum and make the work easier, the Serb will have the year of his birth, a hyphen, and the first two figures of his death "19" carved underneath his name on his monument.

However, the range of misfortunes that befell our little man was joined by the passage of time. The years starting with "19..." leaked away, yet he has not left this world. And so this temporal shortcut—widely seen in Serbian graveyards—proved a bad investment and undoing it meant re-carving the surface to insert either new stone plates or brass letters and numbers.

Figure 3.59. Millenium Delta Clock, Republic Square, Belgrade. Picture credit: Studio Cubex (founded by Ksenija Bulatović), https://cubex.rs/portfolio-item/millenium-delta-clock/

Millennium Bug in Republic Square[66]

The area around today's Republic Square was until the mid-nineteenth century a border area between the settlement surrounded by walls and the settlements outside the walls. Paving the square covered the remains of Stambol Gate, Belgrade's most important and best fortified entrance. We can reliably describe the appearance of the gate. It was made of dressed stone and bricks, with a thick layer of earth above the arches. Similar to the smaller gate kept at Petrovaradin Fortress, it had three entry points, with the central one for carts larger than the side ones for pedestrians. The gate was pulled down in 1868 when construction of the National Theater started.

During the period of Ottoman administration, it was a favorite location to show mutineers' severed heads on spikes. Something of that mutinous tradition persists (but without the severed heads) in the area turned into a central square and decorated with an equestrian statue of Prince Mihailo Obrenović, because almost all mass rallies (1941, 1991, etc.) took place or at least began there.

Wishing to give Belgrade a public clock—an object uncommon and hard to maintain in the Balkans, where the number of Ottoman clock towers[67] exceeds the number of public clocks—the Delta Holding company, in cooperation with the city administration, announced a design competition. Explaining their noble intention, they stated, among other things, that they were taking this step "because we are on the threshold of a new millennium whose coming should be marked by a modern and aesthetically valuable construction."

Co-sponsored by Delta Holding and the Association of Belgrade Architects, the competition was announced on 24 March 1999. Someone may notice that in the history of Belgrade that date is not remembered as the day a competition was announced but as the day Serbia was bombed for the fourth and final time in the twentieth century. Due to the NATO intervention, the deadline for the anonymous submission of architectural designs was postponed until 24 June. Out of fourteen designs submitted, the jury of experts chose the design of graduate architectural engineer, Ksenija Bulatović. And it was implemented.

----

66 Republic Square, in the center of Belgrade, is surrounded by the city's most prominent buildings
    such as the National Theater and National Museum.
67 Clock towers were common in towns under Ottoman rule.

The construction, a high-tech clock tower eleven meters tall, weighing four tons and created in stainless steel and glass, offered a radical contrast to the existing environment. The half-transparent form, with platforms inaccessible to mere passers-by, summarizes the experience of historical avant-garde works of the twentieth century and interprets them in terms of the most modern architectural technology.

The clocks (digital and radial), whose precision was monitored by the infallible atomic timer in Frankfurt, were made by the Swiss company Girard-Perregaux, founded in 1791. When it was inaugurated in mid-1999, the clock counted the seconds until the arrival of the year 2000. A huge contribution to the discussion of whether the third millennium started on 1 January that year or the following year was given in favor of 2000 by the chirping diary inscriptions of the then-first lady of Yugoslavia, Prof. Mirjana Marković PhD. In a society that cherished with high regard the Director of the Directorate of the Yugoslav Left, this calendrical gaffe was silently ignored. Anyway, isn't it better to wait for the new millennium twice instead of once?

With the beginning of what was still the final year of the second millennium, the clock stopped "counting down" and turned into a simple timer. According to the tradition established during the 1996-97 rallies, the New Year was greeted in Belgrade at Republic Square. The "revolutionary" gathering of people on 5 October 2000 could hardly be surpassed. The energy of the tired population was on the decline, so it was not clear if there would even be an organized New Year's Eve party at the turn of the new millennium.

Nevertheless, the city authorities set the stage and organized a modest concert. On Delta's high-tech clock with a link to the outside world, at one second after midnight, the clock read: 01. 01. 1901.

In this way, the infallible device confirmed something we had suspected for a long time—that Serbia finished the twentieth century with an *unsatisfactory* mark (F) and would have to do it over again.

Figure 3.60. At midnight, the Millenium Delta Clock in Republic Square jumped back to 1901. Photo credit: author.

Biographies

Mileta Prodanović

Mileta Prodanović was born in Belgrade. He studied architecture and painting at the University of Arts in Belgrade, where he received his undergraduate and masters degrees, followed by post-graduate study at the Royal College of Art in London. He subsequently earned a PhD at the University of Arts, and is now retired from his positions there as Rector and full professor.

Prof. Prodanović represented Yugoslavia at the Venice Biennale in 1986. He has exhibited his paintings in solo and group exhibitions in Rome, Venice, Vienna, Prague, Paris, Graz, Budapest, Dusseldorf, Regensburg, Toulouse, and elsewhere.

Prodanović has published many works of fiction and essays in the field of visual arts and journalism. During the 1990s he published essays on war, culture, and poli-

Photo credit: Aleksandar Gazibara.

tics in Yugoslav newspapers and magazines. He was a founding member of the Writers Forum and a member of the editorial boards of the *Belgrade Circle* and *New Moment*. He has won many awards in the field of literature and art, including the Serbian Academy of Sciences and Arts Ivan Tabaković Award, the Lazar Trifunivić Award for art criticism, the Borislav Pekić Award for literature, and the Sava Sumavonić Award for visual arts.

In addition to *An Older and More Beautiful Belgrade* (2001), his books in Serbian include: *Dinner at St. Apollonia* (1984), *New Clinical* (1989), *Travel Between Images and Labels* (1993), *The Dog With The Broken Spine* (1993), *Celestial Opera* (1995), *Dance, Monster, to my Soft Music* (1995), *Red Scarves All Silk* (1999), *This Could Be Your Lucky Day* (2000, which he also adapted and directed for the theater), *Garden in Venice* (2002), *Elisha in the Land of Saintly Carp* (2003), *Agnes* (which won the best book award of 2007), *Ermine* (2009), *Ultramarine* (2010), and a collection of poetry (*Miasma*, 1994).

Milena Dragićević Šešić

PhDr. Dragićević-Šešić is former Rector of the University of Arts (Belgrade). She is now the UNESCO chairperson for Interculturalism, Art Management, and Mediation. She has published twenty books and more than 250 papers translated into seventeen languages, many of them concerning subjects addressed in *An Older and More Beautiful Belgrade*.

Maria Milojković

Maria Milojković lives in Belgrade and works as an English/Serbian translator. Her translation experience is diverse, from financial documents to legal contracts, publicity for rock concerts, foreign trade, and art. She has a master's degree in postmodern English literature and is an online content creator for *Medium.com*.

Robert Horvitz

A US citizen living in Prague since 1991, Horvitz began visiting Serbia and the other Yugoslav republics in 1993 as the Open Society Institute's regional consultant for electronic media and journalism. More recently he has been producing policy studies for the European Commission, the World Bank, the International Telecommunication Union, and national governments on the regulation and use of radio frequencies. He currently teaches at Anglo-American University in Prague.

Index

Note: "f" following a number indicates that the reference is in a footnote on that page.

Index

Index